DICTATORS, DRUGS & REVOLUTION

Dictators, Drugs & Revolution

Cold War Campaigning in Latin America
1965 - 1989

by

Sewall Menzel

Bloomington, IN   authorHOUSE   Milton Keynes, UK

To order additional copies, please contact:

AuthorHouse™
1663 Liberty Drive, Suite 200
Bloomington, IN 47403
www.authorhouse.com
Phone: 1-800-839-8640

AuthorHouse™ UK Ltd.
500 Avebury Boulevard
Central Milton Keynes, MK9 2BE
www.authorhouse.co.uk
Phone: 08001974150

First published by AuthorHouse 10/5/2006

ISBN: 1-4259-3553-2 (soft cover)
ISBN: 1-4259-3554-0 (hard cover)

Printed in the United States of America
Bloomington, Indiana

This book is printed on acid-free paper.

To Michelle

CONTENTS

PREFACE

My first introduction into Latin America came with my assignment to the U.S. Army's 82nd Airborne Division at Fort Bragg, North Carolina, and its deployment into the Dominican Republic in 1965. As fate would have it, this would not be my last assignment into the region and many more with the U.S. Southern Command, the Defense Intelligence Agency, and the U.S. Department of State would follow throughout the 1970s and 1980s, as Washington directly confronted a number of tyrannical dictators, international drug traffickers, and Communist revolutionaries. By the late 1970s I had been designated by the Army's Military Personnel Center in Alexandria, Virginia, as a foreign area officer specialist, what some called a "soldier-diplomat" for Latin America. This designation would cause me to work in, travel around, and study virtually every Spanish-speaking country in the Americas. In conjunction with my studies in Spanish at the U.S. Army's School of the Americas (USARSA) Command and General Staff Course, I was able to interface with students from around the region; a number of whom who went on to the highest levels of military command in their own respective countries. More importantly my contact with these various military colleagues from the region over a period of some fifteen years gave me an insight into their thinking and value systems in play. All this contributed to a better understanding of the Latino culture and why things happened the way they did during America's Cold War experience in the Americas.

This memoir has a number of purposes. First and formost is to correct some misperceptions held by the general public concerning some of the operations undertaken by the U.S. military throughout the region. Another is to provide some insight into the historical backdrop which impacted on each one of the campaigns which I either participated in directly or was associated with due to my assignment of the day. And finally to provide a critical analysis as to why some campaigns were more successful than others, given the countervailing culture and values in play. Latin America has always been a complicated milieu to work in and America's Cold War experience in the region demonstrated this truth over and over again. To this end, it is hoped that some lessons can be gleaned from this experience which might help future generations in their own endeavors to deal with Latin America and its related problems and politics.

INTRODUCTION

The United States has always maintained a special relationship with Latin America. In 1801 Thomas Jefferson summed it up quite succinctly stating: "Peace, commerce, and honest friendship with all nations - entangling alliances with none!" Nonetheless, there developed over the years a dichotomy between the "mind your own business" or international political isolationism advocated from the time of George Washington and the reformist moral imperative to "do good works" in the American image. Beginning with the protective intent of the 1822 Monroe Doctrine in response to the collapse of Spain's empire throughout the Americas, a full generation later found the government in Washington still very much tending to view the region through a national security prism. This was primarily because of the advent of the Spanish-American War in 1898 and the ten-years (1904-1914) construction of the Panama Canal; two events which initially propelled the U.S. willy-nilly into the milieu of Caribbean politics and eventually the rest of the Americas.

The framework for future U.S. interventions into the region was provided shortly after the turn of the century by the strategic consideration of creating a Caribbean bulwark, shielding the Atlantic approaches to America's economic jugular vein - the trans-isthmian Panama Canal. This national security imperative stemmed in large part from the fact that Europe's navies of the day, those of the Germans, French, and British, could readily project their power into the Carribbean to threaten the Canal, provided they had forward positioned naval bases and more importantly coaling stations with which to supply the then coal-fired marine engines of their battleships. Any disorder or fiscal mismanagement involving foreign debts on the part of Caribbean nations, in the main relatively defenseless island countries, might thus give the European great powers a pretext to intervene in the region and thereby threaten America's Canal, or so the reasoning went.

To prevent this from happening and to assert Washington's interest in protecting its "American Lake" or Caribbean interests, in 1904 President Theodore (Teddy) Roosevelt proclaimed his famous Corollary to the Monroe Doctrine which had been originally designed to keep the European powers at bay in the Americas. Teddy now stated that "cronic wrong doing or impotence leading to the loosening of the ties of civilized society may require the United States to exercise police power." And so Washington's "big stick" or intervention policy came into play. The basic idea was to bring political and financial order to the region, if not hemisphere. To insure that this was accomplished over the next several decades, numerous invasions, if not outright occupations took place with U.S. Army soldiers and Marines intervening in Nicaragua (1912-1933), Haiti (1915-1934) and the Dominican Republic (1907-1924) among others. Interventions also took place to guarantee the capital and markets of the United States ("dollar diplomacy"), which often involved the signing of loan contracts by local authorities and the turning over to American Wall Street banking concerns the control of the local customs houses, currency systems and even the national railways. Those local authorities in compliance with this policy were maintained in office by the armed forces of the United States.

Washington considered it inevitable that the United States should exert a decisive influence in the internal affairs of the Caribbean republics, so long as disorder and insolvency might expose them to aggression by European powers. Woodrow Wilson proclaimed during the interventions undertaken during his presidency that: "I am going to teach the South American Republics to elect good men." Democracy was now promoted at the point of a bayonet *for* the people around the Caribbean, forgetting the Thirteen Colonies own experience, which indicated that in order to be successful a democratic process must come *from* the people. In short, authoritarian action was being undertaken to achieve liberal goals.

Indeed, the countries of the Caribbean did have significant problems. All, virtually without exception, remained locked in a medieval and semi-feudal colonial experience which weighed heavily on their customs, traditions, value systems, and attitudes in play. This situation did contribute to problems of chronic instability, rigid class structures, lack of viable political institutions, and economic underdevelopment. Political elites maneuvered and battled each other in order to gain power. Gaining power meant strong government which, in turn, meant exploiting the spoils of victory, including patronage and government favors and positions for cronies and friends; all at the expense of the public at large. Capitalism was often *monopoly* capitalism, involving the sale of primary resources such as bananas, coffee etc. benefiting the few. It mattered little to these elites whether their country fell into debt or not and local treasuries were plundered accordingly from one administration to the next. To rectify the situation Washington took action and by the 1930s most of the Caribbean/Central American governments were virtual satellites of the United States. "Progress" was denoted by financial and political stability, roads constructed, number of cities and towns with potable water, quantities of public works and schools, and improved sanitation, e.g. the stamping out of malaria. But other reforms were underway.

The advent of the Good Neighbor Policy of President Franklin D. Roosevelt in 1934 abrogated the Roosevelt Corolary and the other inteventionist policies promulgated over the first several decades of the century. Now Washington advocated the prohibition of intervention of any state in the affairs of another. Into this virtual political vacuum of weak and relatively unprotected U.S.-sponsored democratic structures stepped a series of vicious dictatorships, most of which were military, and without exception spawned from the U.S. Army- and Marine-trained constabulary forces found in each country. Some of the dictatorships (Fulgencio Batista - Cuba, Rafael Trujillo - Dominican Republic, and Anastasio Somoza - Nicaragua) even turned their rules into family dynasties, lasting in some cases for periods of over forty years. Basic human rights, justice, democracy, transparent government and equal political participation by all the people of the Caribbean countries was merely a façade, if not charade, as local tyrants rigged elections at will and ruled with an iron hand.

As the storm clouds of war in Europe and Asia raised their ugly heads in the late 1930s, stability and loyalty to the United States now became paramount in Washington's agenda for the region. An American diplomat commented about Anastasio Somoza, the *caudillo*-style "strong man" of Nicaragua: "He may be a son-of-a-bitch, but he's *our* son-of-a-bitch!" Nonetheless, during World War II Allied propaganda promoted extensively democracy and human rights as legitimate ideals which all nations in the world should be striving to attain. And this dynamic in particular gave hope to many reformist groups, struggling against the tyrannical dictatorships that had evolved throughout much of the Americas.

When the Cold War began in 1946 and the United States and the Soviet Union faced off in their great power confrontation which would last some forty-five years, various reform movements clashed with the ideology of anti-Communism professed by many of the entrenched dictatorships. Since Washington needed the latter's political support against the Kremlin in both the United Nations and the Organization of American States (OAS), Latin American dictatorships were initially tolerated as long as they supported U.S. policies; reform suffered accordingly. Nevertheless, the advent of the late-1950s Communist revolution of Cuba's Fidel Castro, overthrowing the tyrannical Batista regime, came as an unpleasant surprise to Washington. Castro's effort also produced a shockwave which reverberated throughout the region, giving hope to nationalists and would-be revolutionaries seeking to redress the tyranny of an entrenched elite few over the disenfranchised many. Very quickly the Cuban leader's militant advocacy of Communist revolution throughout the Americas as a way of overthrowing dictatorship and bringing about political and socioeconomic change was seen as not only a serious threat to Washington's influence in Latin America but also considered a threat to the national security of the United States.

To deal with the crisis during the late-1950s and early 1960s policy changed and Washington began to experiment with a variety of solutions to the challenge of Communism inside the hemisphere. The Eisenhower, Johnson, Kennedy, Nixon, Carter, Reagan and Bush administrations all promulgated their own particular prescriptions for dealing with not only Castro-inspired revolution, but also the entrenched dictators and, as time went on, a new phenomenon involving international drug trafficking in the region. Military operations in the form of "campaigns" became part and parcel of the political and socioeconomic solutions advocated by Washington for this portion of the Cold War battlefield.

It was into this emerging if not fluctuating political situation that I found myself drawn through my initial assignment as an airborne artillery officer to the U.S. Army's 82nd Airborne Division. This was an initial engagement, if not love affair, with Latin America which would last most of my twenty-five years Army career and, indeed, well beyond.

C H A P T E R   I

PEACEKEEPING IN THE DOMINICAN REPUBLIC
1965-66

The 82nd Airborne Division, based at Fort Bragg, North Carolina was grandly touted during my cadet days at The Citadel as *the* elite division in the U.S. Army. It was also considered a plum assignment for any new lieutenant who wanted to do something exciting and be associated with the "devils in baggy pants." Since I was destined to begin my career as an artillery officer, the thought of someday parachuting into Cuba to throttle the likes of Fidel Castro and Communism had captured my imagination. I therefore opted for the 82nd's airborne artillery component. Unexpectedly however, while the assignment to the division would send me into the Caribbean, it would be in a wholly unusual manner, for a different purpose, and to a place that I virtually had never heard of - the Dominican Republic.

The summer of 1964 found me reporting to the 1st Battalion, 320th Airborne Artillery (1/320 Arty), one of several artillery battalions which made up the 82nd Division's field artillery force. Each battalion had eighteen 105mm howitzers, divided evenly among three firing batteries, which were identified alphabetically: A, B and C. Each of these batteries, the battalion headquarters (called headquarters battery) and the division artillery (Divarty) headquarters had the capability to coordinate and otherwise focus each cannon's high explosive projectiles on any target within the howitzer's maximum range of 11,000 meters or roughly six miles. This "massing" of fires meant that Divarty's some 54 guns could potentially be quickly trained in a matter of a minute or so on a single enemy target. One did not envy the enemy soldier who was on the receiving end of this massed firepower. Each battery directly supported one of the nine airborne infantry battalions which formed the fighting corps of the division. In addition one of several forward observers (FO) from the battalion's supporting battery was attached to each of the infantry company commanders to coordinate and direct artillery fires as needed. This gave the infantry commanders on the ground an extra firepower asset in combat which only required that they point out a target in order to get explosive results.

Being part of the artillery brought me into contact with soldiers, in the main senior ranking sergeants, who had actually jumped into Sicily and Normandy during World War II, some twenty years earlier. The bronze stars on their jump wings attested to their combat jumps and courage on the battlefield, and the fact that they had "been there, done that!" In the 1/320 Arty, Master Sergeant Alfonso Del Priori and other stalwart veterans of those 1943-45 years were interesting, hard-drinking characters and virtual legends who had started out as privates, survived the numerous parachute landings, battles and fire-fights of the war and were now finishing their careers as master sergeants and sergeant majors in their beloved airborne division. They may have been "old duffers," but they did serve as an inspiration for the hundreds of young paratroopers, such as myself, now following in their footsteps. Although often outnumbered, they had fought German tanks and panzer grenadier infantry... and won! For this reason the German enemy had called the paratroopers "the devils in baggy pants." To this end, they were the constant reminder and living proof that the 82nd Airborne had a combat tradition to live up to and might one day be called again into battle.

By the mid-1960s, these combat veterans were backed by a new corps of highly experienced and professional noncommissioned officers (NCOs) or sergeants who made up the next generation of paratroopers. Hispanics, blacks and whites formed this highly integrated group of all-star soldiers. For the airborne artillery they were the key ingredient to any future success in combat, training the soldiers in the employment and functioning of the howitzers, the fire direction centers, the rigging of the cannons for parachute drops and even conducting their own battery's parachute jumps as part of their standard role as leaders and jump masters. This was known as "sergeant's business" and they did it extremely well.

Parachuting or "airborne operations" as they were called were the bread and butter of the division. Soldiers snapped off salutes hollering: "All the way Sir!" and the officers would respond: "Airborne!" This excitement of military parachute jumping was what the 82nd Airborne was all about and understandable as anyone who has experienced that surge of adrenalin during a jump can attest.

As the plane approached the drop zone, usually about a half mile or more long, the jump master and his assistant would holler out "get ready!" Then the command to "stand up and check equipment," would take place with all four rows (called "sticks") of up to 15 to 20 paratroopers each standing in a semi-crouched position facing to the rear of the plane with their parachute static line device in one hand and the other hand extended towards the nearest wall or support. With the parachute on his back, a smaller parachute reserve buckled across the stomach and carrying bags of equipment, weapons, ammunition and other items tied to the body, sometimes dangling down to below one's knees, the average paratrooper inside the plane was a bulky, gangling bundle of energy just itching to exit the plane.

At the command of "hook up" the static line devices were snapped into place and secured on hanging cables running the length of the plane. Upon hearing "check static lines" each soldier checked the equipment and static line of the man in front of him to ensure that it ran directly from the parachute backpack directly to the arm nearest the cable (A nylon/canvas static line inadvertently wrapped around the neck of a jumper usually meant instant death and possible decapitation to boot!). From the rear to the front of the stick, each soldier hollered that all was "OK" and that he and the man in front of him was fully checked and ready to jump. The side doors of the C-130 aircraft would then slide open and the jump master would holler and signal with his hand over the throbbing roar of the engines: "Stand in the door!"

The first trooper in the stick was the lead man and would deliberately shuffle into a position facing outwards with both hands griping the sides of the door opening and one foot partly extended out over the exit ramp. Looking down and to the front of the plane out of the corners of his eyes he could usually see the drop zone rapidly approaching. In an actual combat jump this was a perilous moment and any number of paratroopers standing in doors have been hit and even killed by enemy bullets before they could actually jump. At this point stomachs tightened as each trooper poised for the inevitable. The plane's pilot would then signal the beginning of the jump by switching a signal light on the side of the door entrance from red to green. At the instant the green light came on the jump master would holler "Go!" The lead man, who was already reacting to the green signal light, would hurtle from the aircraft, being buffeted by the wind for a few seconds until his chute was pulled out by the static line from his back pack and then opened. The rest of the descent was pure joy and the thrill of floating around in the air much like a slow motion bird until you landed was an exhilarating minute or so in one's life.

The division's soldiers saw themselves as part of a macho outfit. Aggressive and hard charging, wearing spit-shined, black jump boots with trousers bloused into them, along with red, white, and blue parachute patches on their overseas hats, and silver airborne wings on their chests, these were the paratroopers of the 82nd Airborne. They ran their one mile run each morning to maintain their physical fitness, using what was known as the "airborne shuffle," chanting and hollering as they went along. Songs such as "Blood on the Risers" and "We Are All-Americans" were sung out or hollered along with the various chants. The elan and esprit de corps of these men was second to none! Indeed, paratroopers were a different breed of cat from the rest of the Army. The 82nd was part of the XVIIIth Airborne Corps, which included the 101st Airborne Division at Fort Campbell, Kentucky, and the entire force was part of the U.S. Strike Command, which, with the support of the Air Force, could marshal some hundreds of C-130 transports to move the paratroopers almost anywhere in the world to conduct an airborne assault. Easier said than done of course.

During the mid-1960s, the Strike Command required that a full company of about 180 paratroopers always be on alert, standing by in their barracks with weapons at the ready, for immediate emergency deployment by aircraft and parachute. Shortly thereafter, the remainder of the battalion, some 500 strong, was supposed to follow. All the 27 principal infantry companies from their nine parent battalions in the division were rotated twice a year through these usually week-long, alert standbys. To demonstrate that it was ready to deploy at a moment's notice, the 82nd conducted a series of parachute assault demonstrations called "Red" and "Blue Chips," involving parachute drops and frequently live firing of the soldiers' weapons. Sometimes even howitzers and their tow trucks were air dropped, but, after a couple of these slammed into the ground from 1200 feet when their parachutes malfunctioned, the cannons were merely positioned on the drop zone to await the arrival of their parachuting gun crews. Nonetheless, these were impressive shows to watch for an outsider, and the public, as well as government and military officials, were always invited.

This begot an unintended situation brought about by the fact that the repetitive demonstrations became time consuming distractions of less and less training value. They also tended to cover up a serious problem that the division had with maintaining its units in a fully manned condition and ensuring that they were also adequately trained for combat. Personnel turbulence, caused by soldiers frequently transferring in and out of their units, going off to schools of one sort or another and being detailed to administrative, post support duties, undermined the ability of the combat units, particularly the artillery, to maintain a high level of combat readiness month in and month out.

Another factor seriously undermining combat readiness was the overriding emphasis which the Department of the Army was then placing on vehicle and equipment maintenance and its related management, all to the detriment of training. In part, the Army had brought this situation on itself during the Cuban missile crisis of 1962 when it found that one of its armored divisions at Fort Hood, Texas, was unprepared to deploy a major portion of its tanks and vehicles to Florida in support of a possible invasion of Cuba. For want of spare parts, complemented by a lackadaisical attitude towards ensuring that all vehicles could shoot, move and communicate, a second armored division had to be striped of the necessary tanks and equipment to flesh out the first. As a result, and to ensure that this would never happen again, Secretary of Defense Robert McNamara directed that intensive vehicle and equipment maintenance would now be the order of the day. The command material maintenance inspection (CMMI) was the result.

Woe to the artillery battery or infantry company commander who flunked an unannounced, surprise CMMI of their motor pool and arms room. Even driving down a road or going to and from a training area was hazardous, as dozens of inspectors armed with clipboards and checklists conducted roadside spot checks, scrutinizing every inch of one's vehicles and weapons. With their careers on the line, commanders at all levels took the inevitable course of action of keeping all their vehicles in the garrison motor pools for maintenance, taking no chances on getting bad marks or even failing an inspection. The net result of this setting was that there was little or no time for real field training. I found this out first hand as an acting C battery commander when Captain Guffey, the battalion operations officer, verbally blasted me out of his office for even "thinking" (a 2nd lieutenant was supposed to follow orders and nothing more!) that I was going to take the battery out to the nearby training area on maneuvers in the face of the CMMI threat.

In only two instances were there any reprieves from the merciless CMMI inspectors. The first was when a large scale maneuver exercise pitted the 82nd Airborne against another division and the other was when each artillery battalion would undergo its annual operational readiness test (ORT). During the fall of 1964, the 82nd tested the 11th Air Assault Division in a division versus division exercise covering parts of both North and South Carolina. At one point in time the 1/320 Arty took on portions of a brigade of the 11th Air Assault, backed by some 200 helicopters, in the unofficial "Battle of Bisco" (South Carolina). Despite being trained into what I thought was a hot-shot artillery forward observer at the Fort Sill, Oklahoma "School of Fire" in the summer of 1964, I found that the air mobility of the Air Assault troops and their ability to outmaneuver (helicopters are ten times faster and more agile than vehicles on the ground) and take under fire my jeep and the battery I was assigned to was simply astounding. I was witnessing another dynamic in play in the evolution of modern warfare. The 11th Air Assault "proved" itself during this exercise, changed its name to that of the 1st Air Cavalry Division, and then deployed into the Vietnam War about six months later.

It was, however, during the ORT that an artillery battalion was actually tested in terms of its combat capabilities in the field. First and foremost, each battalion was brought up to strength in terms of its personnel. This was done by freezing all the assignments of the soldiers already in the battalion and by bringing in replacements from other like units (stripping away key personnel to fill gaps, but at the same time furthering weakening the lending units) throughout the division. In addition, a few weeks of intensive training and live fire practice were permitted as a pre-ORT preparation and train-up. During the ORT, artillery batteries fired from the field during the day and at night using high angle and normal firing techniques, made "hip shoots" or sudden, unexpected deployments off of roads to get their initial adjustment rounds on the way in support of the forward observer's requests for fire, and sometimes even made impromptu maneuvers such as ambushing imaginary tank columns. There was no doubt about it, this was the best training you could get - *but it only came once a year.* Apart from doing well on CMMIs, an artillery unit's performance during the ORT would make or break an officer.

Nonetheless, after the ORT the 1/320 Arty, much like its sister battalions, found itself back to where it had been in a relatively short period of some months, again shorn of key personnel. This situation, when coupled with the CMMI syndrome, made many units less than fully combat ready for the better part of the year. All this changed for the better in April 1965 when the 82nd was suddenly placed on alert for possible deployment to a Caribbean island country known as the Dominican Republic. The alert came as a complete surprise, as few people in the division knew anything about the crisis then taking place in the "Dom Rep," let alone its background. U.S. interests in the country were actually fairly deep and went back to the early part of the century.

In terms of its national politics prior to the turn of the century, the Dominican Republic had not enjoyed the best of reputations. Ironically, U.S. President Ulysses S. Grant had tried to purchase the Republic in 1870 for $1.5 million in order to establish a naval base at Samana Bay on the northern coast. Only a suspicious Senate, by a ten vote decision, managed to defeat the treaty of annexation and the formation of another American territory. By the turn of the century, of some forty-three serving Dominican presidents, only three were said to have completed their terms of office. This political turbulence flew in the face of President Teddy Roosevelt's famed 1903 "Corollary" to the Monroe Doctrine which stated that, if the United States wished to prevent European penetration into the region, it must help the Caribbean republics eliminate chronic disorder and fiscal mismanagement. There was considerable concern that the European powers of the day (England, France, Germany and Italy among others) would use their respective navies to force the financially bankrupt and generally chaotic Dominican government to pay its international debts via military occupations and the establishment of naval bases, potentially threatening US sovereignty

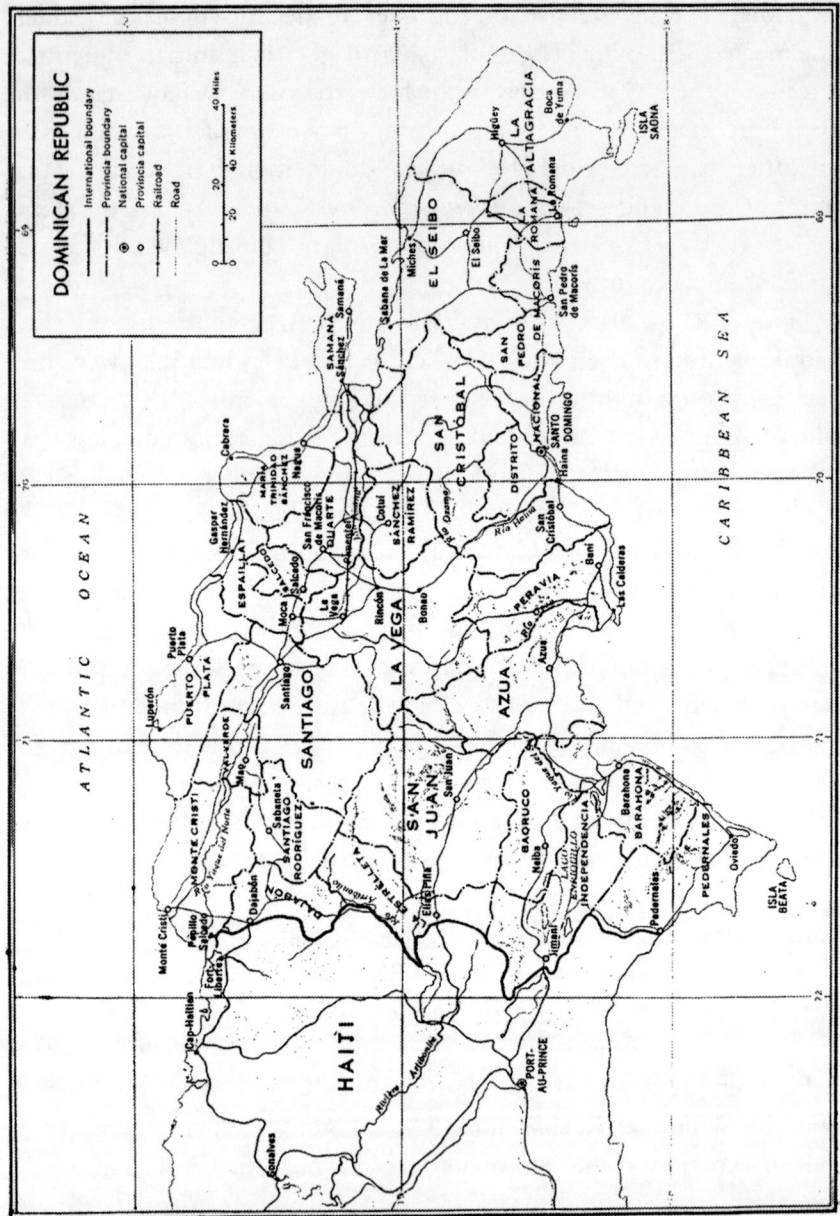

and national security interests throughout the Caribbean, especially the Caribbean approaches to the Panama Canal.

To avoid this possibility, the U.S. government applied the Corollary by taking over the collection of Dominican customs duties in 1905, which it continued to manage until 1941. This eventually included a

U.S. Marine occupation of the Republic from 1916 to 1924 (adjacent Haiti was occupied by the Marines from 1915 until 1934) "to protect American interests and to support present constituted authority" and to forestall possible German intrusion and otherwise protect American investments. The custom house revenues, the only specie by which foreign debts could be serviced, had perennially disappeared into the pockets or private accounts of whatever Dominican political faction was then holding office. Woodrow Wilson, president of the United States in 1916, promised that he would teach Latin Americans to "elect good men." As such, the promotion of democracy at the point of the bayonet became overnight a moral duty by the United States in its application of U.S.-style constitutional government.

As armed Marines and sailors supervised elections, debts to foreign creditors were paid off and the country eventually became solvent, as well as "honest." During the occupation, the U.S. Navy administration passed a land registration law that broke up numerous peasant communal landholdings and helped American sugar companies consolidate their control over much of the economy, largely in the rich southern coastal plains. For some five years U.S. Marine garrisons tried to enforce law and order in the face of an ever growing popular resistance made up of mostly peasant insurgents. The resistance only really ended when the Marines eventually left the country in 1924, leaving in their wake a Marine-trained constabulary force known as the National Guard. Nonetheless, infrastructure in the form of railroads and port facilities was improved and Dominican workers' salaries were paid on time. In addition, public works projects involving the building of roads, health clinics and some 500 schools were undertaken (Of the roughly one million population, 80 percent were illiterate). The Marines could be proud of what they accomplished, but was it enough? After their departure, Dominican politics went on much as before the occupation in its traditionally authoritarian and endemically corrupt manner.

Exploiting the social unrest fueled by the hard times triggered by the Great Depression, Rafael Leonardo Trujillo, a former sugar plantation guard, worked his way up through the National Guard's ranks and then, as its commander, overthrew the government in 1930. Only 36 years old he then had himself, as the only candidate, "elected" president with more votes counted than there were eligible voters. Thus began one of the most corrupt, vile, ruthless, depraved and degrading caudillo-style dictatorships in the history of the Americas, lasting some 31 years. Coincidentally helping him along was Franklin D. Roosevelt's "Good Neighbor" policy of the mid-1930s, which changed the U.S. policy towards Latin America and the Caribbean from one of intervention and repression to one of non-intervention and respect for whomever came to power. While utterly ruthless in dealing with his political opponents, Trujillo did promise a form of total support for U.S. government interests in the Dominican Republic, causing one Washington official to quip: "He may be a son of a bitch, but he's *our* son of a bitch!" (a quip also applied to Somoza of Nicaragua)

Now operating the country as a virtual corporate fiefdom of gigantic proportions, Trujillo gained considerable political support from Washington by meeting the heightened demands for Dominican sugar and ferro-nickel exports in support of the U.S. war efforts during World War II and in Korea. In turn, Trujillo lavished economic concessions upon U.S. investors and made generous campaign contributions to U.S. congressmen. Over the years he eventually came to own more than half the country's assets. Self-deification and the gratification of an insatiable vanity was part and parcel of Trujillo's style, even changing the name of the capital from Santo Domingo to "Ciudad Trujillo" and building monuments to himself throughout the country. The effects would not have been so damaging if Trujillo had plowed his fortune back into the development of the nation, which by and large he did not. By 1960 the Trujillo family fortune was estimated at upwards of $800 million, an amazing amount by any standard at that time, which was ensconced in numerous unnamed foreign bank accounts. This was in contrast to the annual per capita income per person of about $200 and an unemployment rate running between 30 and 50 percent inside the country.

Using fraudulent elections as a democratic façade, he exploited, manipulated, abused and ran roughshod over the Dominican people for several decades, debauching a generation of young women along the way. If you were part of the Trujillo's coterie of insiders, family circle and bootlicking cronies, demonstrating your loyalty to "El Jefe," you could become rich and "well connected." But, if you disagreed with the dictatorship and refused to tolerate its excesses, you only had one real option - to migrate. All Dominicans either served him in a servile manner or were imprisoned, persecuted, murdered or deported. There was no in between.

During the early years of the Cold War period or late 1940s, Trujillo further ingratiated himself to Washington by declaring himself an anti-Communist. He brought stability to the Dominican Republic and that was a major priority in the U.S. national security policy for keeping the Caribbean free of Communist encroachment. Stability in the Dominican Republic was accomplished through an impressive police apparatus, systems of spies, and an overwhelming domination of the economy by the Trujillo family. Despite his brutal methods, vulgarity, and abusive, tormenting coercion of the mass of the population, he remained in good stead with the administrations of Harry Truman and Dwight Eisenhower throughout most of the 1950s. The cynicism and tyranny of the regime was largely ignored as Trujillo avidly supported fellow dictators Fulgencio Batista in Cuba and Anastasio Somoza in Nicaragua, even trying to assassinate the Socialist-oriented, liberal president of Venezuela, Romulo Betancourt. Nonetheless, with the advent of Fidel Castro's successful Communist revolution in Cuba in 1958 and a corresponding critical reappraisal by the Eisenhower administration of its policies for the Caribbean, Trujillo's days in power were numbered.

The administration of John F. Kennedy concurred with its predecessor Eisenhower administration that the internal excesses of the abusive and corrupt Batista dictatorship had lead to Castro's own successes and that similar conditions then existed in Trujillo's Dominican Republic. While Eisenhower was unsuccessful in convincing Trujillo to step down as part of a political and socio-economic reform process, Kennedy continued a newly contrived policy of encouraging Dominican dissidents to overthrow the dictator when reform was not forthcoming. It worked, and on 30 May 1961 Trujillo was shot and killed in an ambush. Yet this was but a portion of a milieu of events taking place during those early months of 1961, which saw the decisive defeat in April by Castro of a U.S.-sponsored invasion force at the Bay of Pigs on Cuba's southern coast. Another and more important event in terms of the Dominican Republic's future was the unveiling of the Alliance for Progress, just two months after the new American president's inauguration that January. The Alliance was in response to and reflected Kennedy's personal perception that: "Those who make peaceful revolution impossible will make violent revolution inevitable."

Combining political, economic and social reform, as well as internal security measures, the Alliance for Progress was the most ambitious U.S. approach to Latin America ever designed. It was a creative attempt to reassert a positive American influence in the region and most especially in the Caribbean. The architects of the $20 billion program undertook to inoculate over a ten-year period of time all the countries potentially vulnerable to a Castro-style revolution. This was to be accomplished through the antidote of applying democratic politics, economic development, the elimination of illiteracy, the expansion of the middle classes, and U.S. military aid and training programs, nominally called "counterinsurgency." In essence, the program caused Washington to become directly involved in the internal affairs of many of the countries in the region. As such, the Dominican Republic became a primary target country slated for reform.

Immediately after Trujillo's death, the problem for Washington was how to maintain order, facilitate a transition to democracy and keep Trujillo's two sons from gaining power. At this time Joaquin Balaguer, the former vice-president, was sharing power with one of the sons, Lieutenant General Rafael (Ramfis) Trujillo, Jr., who was the head of the armed forces. A naval task force sent by Kennedy and anchored off the coast nearby Santo Domingo reinforced the point and the dynasty was ended, with Trujillo's wife, sons and top ranking henchmen being forced into exile. With the assistance of the Organization of American States (OAS), a Council of State, which went through several iterations, was formed in January 1962 as a caretaker government to prepare the country for its first free election since 1924. The surviving Trujillo political elite, lead initially by Joaquin Balaguer, quickly filled the interim government's positions, jockeying for power while trying to expropriate El Jefe's assets. Balaguer had been the dictator's presidential secretary and toady during much of the dynasty and as vice-president had actually run the country in accordance with his boss' instructions during the last four years of Trujillo's rule.

With a caretaker government in power and a political void in existence, numerous political, labor, and student organizations mushroomed in a country where freedom of speech and of organization had not existed for decades. Political exiles returned, parties and independent unions began to form and demonstrations of political interest became commonplace.

Juan Bosch, a long-time Trujillo opponent, returned from exile in Cuba and Puerto Rico to become the reform candidate. A charismatic speaker, Bosch articulated the idealistic democratic reforms he intended to invoke when elected. Freedom of speech, assembly, political thought, and justice for all, the basic rights so often taken for granted in the United States, resonated favorably with the Dominican population. Now wildly popular throughout the country, he had previously gone into exile in the later part of the 1930s to escape Trujillo's retribution for his astute criticism of the dictatorship. Influenced in part by Roosevelt's "Four Freedoms" speech about peace, freedom and prosperity, he then wrote a book critical of the Trujillo regime and cast his lot with Jose Figueres of Costa Rica and other Latin American social democrats of the 1940s, attempting to confront dictatorship around the Caribbean.

The elections of December 1962 found Juan Bosch's populist, reform-minded Dominican Revolutionary Party (Partido Revolutionario Dominicano - PRD) winning by more than 60 percent of the vote not only the presidency but also control of the legislature. Many of those who had previously linked their fortunes to the now ousted Trujillo family, including some of the middle class, now found their National Civic Union party decisively defeated. This had come as a bitter and most unpleasant surprise to a minority elite accustomed to a servile population, which had previously always supported their interests. But the people had voted, and voted freely for the first time in 38 years.

Assuming the presidency in late February 1963, Bosch and his newly elected national assembly drafted a new constitution with numerous liberal reforms. These included laws for maintaining an open political environment, legalizing any and all parties, including the Communist party as was the case in the United States, a land reform program to get land into the hands of poor peasants who wanted to become farmers, an open economy, nationalization of some of Trujillo's former properties to support the land reform effort, educational and judicial reform, religious freedom and divorce, and an assertion of civilian control over the military. It was in education that Bosch started to make his mark, creating the beginnings of a mammoth adult-education program to reduce illiteracy and train Dominicans in the many technical skills needed to eventually develop the country. Even the United States Peace Corps was recruited to help out in the countryside.

He was also very serious about civil liberties, stating that no one of any political persuasion would be prosecuted unless they broke the law. Indeed, his championing of social reform, caused the Kennedy administration to enthusiastically view the newly elected government as a "showcase of democracy" in contrast to Castro's openly Communist dictatorship in Cuba. In fact, Bosch was the target of numerous verbal attacks by Fidel Castro himself. With the Dominican Republic now a bastion of liberal reform, Alliance for Progress monies and programs were duly apportioned by Washington to assist in reforming the country. Unfortunately for Bosch, while he was an adept political analyst and critic, he was not a very competent public administrator.

Despite a seemingly promising beginning, Bosch's inability to efficiently manage his government's reform program and his penchant for adhering to the advice of incompetent cronies, as well as entering into bizarre business and financial arrangements and his obvious and open threat to the previously well-entrenched Trujillo elites, undermined his political fortunes. The threat to the old Trujillo power base now caused the military and related business and industrial interests to work to overthrow Bosch to protect their still considerable powers and influence. The U.S. embassy in Santo Domingo was not impressed with the apparent mismanagement of the new government and the ever increasing tensions between Bosch and the military and other elite economic groups. It also did not like Bosch's independently minded decisions, often taken without consulting the American ambassador (and thus considered an "insult" by Washington). In effect, these attitudes eventually spelled out his doom and contributed to the quashing of his infant constitutional democracy.

The showdown came when Bosch tried to relieve Colonel Elias Wessin y Wessin, commander of the San Isidro air base and armed forces training center. The effort to impose civilian control over the military failed and Wessin, along with elements of the police, led a revolt that overthrew the government and again sent Bosch into exile to Puerto Rico, after only seven months into his presidency. Armed, trained and enriched by the U.S.-sponsored counterinsurgency aid programs, the

Dominican military, although no longer completely unified, now had effectively replaced Trujillo as the nation's power center. Kennedy furiously protested the ouster of Bosch in September of 1963 and promptly withdrew his own U.S. ambassador, refusing at once to recognize the new military-appointed civilian junta or governing triumvirate. Less than two months later however, Kennedy was assassinated and the U.S. policy changed again. The "showcase for democracy" would now live a very short life.

After Kennedy's assassination in November 1963, President Lyndon Johnson recognized the anti-Bosch junta and replaced the former U.S. ambassador with Tapley Bennett. All economic and military assistance programs continued much as before and the junta promised that formal elections would be held sometime in 1965. With Bosch gone, the old guard Trujillo elites, who saw themselves as conservatives, sought to regain control over Dominican politics. For a time, led by junta leader Donald Reid Cabral, who was also a wealthy businessman with roots in the old Trujillo oligarchy, they succeeded. During this period roughly $100 million worth of aid was sent by the United States to demonstrate its commitment to the new regime. Nonetheless, the apparent stability that had returned to the Dominican republic during this period masked the anger and frustration of those Dominicans who felt that their democracy and constitutional government had been betrayed. The Republic now became a seedbed of groups of conspirators plotting ways in which to reestablish constitutional rule and return Juan Bosch to the presidency.

Ironically, Reid's own austerity programs, which froze wages at a time of rising prices for such basic foodstuffs as rice and beans (the staples of the poor), and attempts to bring the military more firmly under his personal control over the next year and a half backfired, angering the senior military commanders who were enjoying their own relative independence and power. Some of the relatively junior officers sympathetic to Bosch, recognizing the split between Cabral and their military seniors, seized the moment to launch a countercoup on 24 April 1965 to take power. The pro-Bosch junior officers and about a thousand of their soldiers, led by U.S.-trained Colonel Francisco Caamano Deno, called themselves "Constitutionalists," but were quickly termed "rebels" by the

Santo Domingo-based U.S. Embassy. The supporters of the conservative Wessin and former Trujillo factions were known as "loyalists."

What had been intended as a military coup and uprising by a handful of officers had now turned into a popular revolution, which quickly became a civil war. Tens of thousands of Dominicans rose up in Santo Domingo and outlying towns to denounce the loyalists and Reid, whom they saw as uncaring and illegitimate. They took to the streets very much in the form of a disorganized mob, occupied the presidential palace and went on the radio to urge the people to support the revolution. PRD supporters, now in an informal alliance with Christian Democrats, students and a host of other political factions, including some smaller Communist groups who had actually been taken by surprise at the turn of events, all joined the revolution. "Return to Bosch and the 1963 Constitution" became the battle cry of the Constitutionalists. The loyalist military saw this as a direct threat to their own interests and even survival as a powerful influence inside the country and they rallied their forces at the San Isidro air base to the northeast of Santo Domingo, the naval base at Haina to the west, and at the town of Santiago further to the north. On the next day or Sunday the 25th air attacks were unleashed by Wessin y Wessin to randomly strafe the city and its 100,000 population with U.S.-supplied P-51 propeller-driven fighter planes in the hopes of coercing the rebels into surrendering.

As a reaction against the strafing and in anticipation of a ground counterattack by the loyalists, thousands of weapons were looted from local armories by the rebels and handed out to the civil populace at large. Assisted by naval commandos and led by Caamano Deno, the rebel forces were able to win control of the center of the downtown section of Santo Domingo in a matter of hours. Nonetheless, the celebration of this victory by scores of thousands of the city's inhabitants was premature. The city was in a state of virtual chaos as Donald Reid resigned and the U.S. embassy notified the Department of State (DOS) that evening that there were problems within America's showcase for democracy.

Unfamiliar with the anti-Wessin and anti-Reid Cabral leaders who made up the revolution and convinced that the rebels were controlled from the onset by Communist elements, if not Fidel Castro himself, the embassy staff alerted DOS that things were now out of hand and getting worse, placing in jeopardy the lives of Americans living within the Republic. While worried that Communist elements could seize the Dominican Republic, the other major concern for Washington was that American lives would be in danger. It was imperative to organize an evacuation and the JCS directed the U.S. Atlantic Command (CINCLANT) on Monday the 26th to conduct the operation. As this was happening, a directive reached the 82nd Airborne Division to place two of its battalions on full alert for possible combat operations in support of CINCLANT. Things were beginning to happen.

The anticipated ground attack against the rebels from the direction of San Isidro did take place and heavy, bloody fighting broke out in the eastern part of Santo Domingo along the Ozama River. In the vicinity of the Duarte Bridge (named after the 1844 independence hero Juan Pablo Duarte and also referred to as the "Bridge of the Americas"), the rebels were reasonably well entrenched in an area known as Ciudad Nueva, which also encompassed the southeastern quadrant of Santo Domingo and the colonial zone formed by the Ozama River on the east and the Caribbean Sea to the south. The narrow streets and old buildings made for a natural defense of the zone. The Ozama Fortress, a primary police weapons depot for Santo Domingo, bordered the river to the south of the Duarte Bridge and was held as a loyalist stronghold of several hundred policemen who were supportive of Wessin's military. The fortress, as well as the bridge, became the focus of heavy fighting. Molotov cocktails, consisting of whisky bottles with a gasoline and oil mixture and a cloth wick, which was lighted just before the bottle was thrown, rained down from rooftops and windows on Wessin's tanks, soldiers and policemen. Despite numerous attacks across the bridge, the loyalist forces were forced back each time. The losses were heavy on both sides and casualties numbered in the hundreds.

While a stalemate of sorts ensued, it was announced that most of the Dominican navy had opted to remain on the side of the loyalists. In addition, the rebels received information that a former Trujillo general, Augusto Montas Guerrero, in command of the San Cristobal infantry regiment to the west of Santo Domingo had not only decided to support Wessin but had also moved his regiment to the International Fair Grounds in the vicinity of the Hotel Embajador on the western outskirts of the city. In short, the rebels were now hemmed in and virtually sur-

The Bridge of the Americas (aka Durate Bridge) over the Ozama River in Santo Domingo was a major focal point for the initial operations of the 82nd Airborne Division during its peacekeeping mission in the Dominican Republic (1965-1966). (82nd Abn. Div. photo)

rounded. At this time or throughout Tuesday the 27th, a number of the rebel commanders began to have doubts about the outcome of the uprising and a few requested asylum at some of the foreign embassies within the city. Things appeared to be favoring Wessin's loyalists more and more, as most Dominicans in accordance with their experience from the Trujillo years cautiously awaited the outcome of the initial fighting before choosing sides. Since no one wanted to be on the side of the loser, it was better to be a "fence-sitter" and wait and see what would happen.

Colonel Caamano, in the absence of Juan Bosch who unexpectedly remained in Puerto Rico, assumed full command of the movement and began to rally his forces Tuesday afternoon and evening. By the next morning of Wednesday the 28th, the rebels were obviously still in the fight and still held most of the city, including all the utilities such as the telephone exchange, the power plant and banking institutions. Barricades had been crudely constructed across most of the streets and avenues leading into downtown Santo Domingo and these were fiercely defended with machine guns and an assortment of Spanish 7mm Mauser rifles and submachine guns taken from the captured arsenals. In fact the rebels had been so successful that they had captured from Wessin's forces a number of cannons and a handful of Czechoslovakian, pre-World War II tanks. Despite some two thousand people having been killed, the tide now appeared to be turning in favor of the rebels.

A loyalist junta and provisional government under Colonel Pedro Benoit at Wessin's San Isidro base reacted to this change of events by radioing Tapley Bennet at the U.S. Embassy to request United States intervention, declaring all the while that they could not protect the lives of American citizens or any other foreigners in the country, unless U.S. military forces intervened. Considering that the Benoit junta now represented the "legal" government in the Dominican Republic, Bennet threw his weight behind the junta's request for intervention. He was at this time in contact with a sympathetic Thomas Mann in Washington, who was the State Department's resident expert on Latin America. Mann was holdover from the Eisenhower administration and was well remembered for his terse comment: "I know my Latins. They understand only two things - a buck in the pocket and a kick in the ass!" The 82nd Airborne Division, now on alert, was about to give the Constitutionalist-supporting rebels a "kick in the ass."

While the 82nd Airborne had received the alert message from the JCS on Monday the 26th of April, it happened that that very week there had been scheduled a Blue Chip V, joint Army-Air Force exercise under STRICOM auspices. This involved a full infantry brigade, its supporting artillery, as well as the division headquarters staff, Air Force C-130s, parachute rigger teams, loading equipment, airfield control teams, and parking space and billeting for participating support units at Pope Air Force Base (A.F.B.) adjacent to Fort Bragg. Because the JCS did not order the cancellation of the Blue Chip exercise in order to fully support the deployment to the Dominican Republic, STRICOM insisted on continuing to carry out the Blue Chip exercise as the division's top priority. As a result, the division was not well focused to deal with the JCS directive of 28 April which ordered that the entire 3d Brigade would now form the lead assault echelon and that the Air Force would now marshal some dozens of additional aircraft at Pope A.F.B. to airlift the brigade to the Dominican Republic. The initial alert was followed by more directives from the JCS a day or so later for an additional four battalions (an entire brigade plus part of another) to also prepare to participate in the air assault. Now the division was involved in not only conducting a complicated training exercise but *also* attempting to make preparations to go into formal combat for the first time since World War II. None of this of course made any sense, as Pope rapidly became overcrowded and STRICOM competed with the JCS for use of the 82nd Airborne Division's assets, involving some 11,000 men.

The situation was confusing and Major General Robert York, the division commander, found himself in the unenviable position of trying to determine what his mission would actually be, what the combat situation was on the ground, and how one could identify who were the friendly and enemy forces. It was expected that the lead elements would have to airdrop on or in the vicinity of the San Isidro airfield, secure that base as an airhead for the follow-on echelons (two more infantry brigades, supporting artillery, headquarters and medical support) of the division, advance to the Duarte Bridge and even assist in the evacuation of Americans as the situation required. As York's staff was ferreting out the possible missions, the launch order arrived late in the day of the 29th.

President Johnson had ordered CINCLANT to land Marines to link up with the US Embassy in Santo Domingo and protect the evacuation of some 1400 Americans who had been assembled at the Embajador Hotel closer to the coast on the western fringe of the city. The aircraft carrier USS Boxer was positioned off shore to accomplish this. In addition, the entire 82nd Airborne was now to be airlifted to the Dominican Republic as part of JCS "Operation Power Pack I."

There now took place a mad scramble to disengage from STRI-COM'S Blue Chip exercise and to reconfigure the division's equipment for a combat parachute assault. The previous diversion of assets to support the Blue Chip airborne demonstration now cost the division valuable time as it was found that Pope could not simultaneously handle the quantity of aircraft required for the combat deployment (over 140 C-130s) and the Blue Chip requirements. Load masters and riggers now worked round the clock in a frenzy to get 3rd Brigade loaded out and airborne. This also meant the issuing of rifle and machinegun ammunition, grenades, as well as mounting artillery and anti-tank ammunition, and vehicles on special cargo platforms for airdrop. As such, it was very much the hard work of the veteran NCOs that saved the day and enabled the operation to get off the ground. The initial assault echelon went airborne the evening of Thursday the 29th of April. The invasion was on!

At 2:15 AM of Friday 30 April the two lead infantry battalions (1/508 and 1/505) from 3rd Brigade and Troop A of the 1st Squadron, 17th Cavalry (the division's reconnaissance battalion) air landed at Wessin's San Isidro airfield. York had received instructions *while in the air* that it would not be necessary to airdrop his forces and they would air land instead. This meant that the first increment of some 30 aircraft would make a night landing, while the remaining 110 aircraft would go to Ramey AFB in Puerto Rico and await their turn to be routed into San Isidro.

Air landing meant that, while the force would be able to land intact in a secure manner, all the equipment loads which had been so carefully rigged for parachute drop would now have to be completely de-rigged. This laborious process meant using bayonets and axes to cut through the tough nylon tie-downs and lines that anchored the heavy equipment to the cargo platforms. At dawn, with the 1/505 Infantry securing the airfield, the 1/508 Infantry and A Troop 1/17 Cavalry, following the main road out of San Isidro and assisted by their compasses and Texaco roadmaps, headed to the southwest towards the eastern bank of the Ozama River and its Duarte Bridge. It was expected that after crossing the river they would establish a bridgehead on the west bank and eventually link up with the Marines out to the west in the vicinity of the U.S. Embassy, forming what would be a neutral international security zone (ISZ) and further isolating the rebels in their urban enclave. York, now the overall ground force commander, had been able to meet with Vice Admiral Kleber Masterson of the Naval joint task force (JTF 122) and Ambassador Bennet to confirm the basic plan which envisioned that once the ISZ or corridor had been secured, Washington would then order operations to defeat the Constitutionalists. The problem at hand, however, was securing the corridor.

As the morning went on and the paratroopers made their approach to the Duarte Bridge, Colonel Caamano's forces finally succeeded in overwhelming the police defending the Ozama fortress, capturing its arsenal intact. This having been done, they now began to confront the paratroopers rapidly spreading out along the river's eastern bank. The 17th Cavalry's jeep-mounted 106mm recoilless rifles slammed one round after another into the rebel-held buildings on the west side of the river. The 106mm was designed in the 1950s as the Army's answer for defeating the heavily armored Joseph Stalin III Soviet tanks. It now served the paratroopers as the equivalent of light artillery in a direct fire role and its high explosive anti-tank fire was focused on the buildings overlooking the western end of the Duarte bridge.

The paratroopers realized that, if the rebels could force their way across the bridge, there was always the chance they might try to destroy or damage it enough so it would not be usable. Supported by their own bazookas (3.5 inch anti-tank rocket launchers) and machineguns, and fortified by some El Presidente beer passed out by the local populace, the airborne infantry worked its way across the bridge and, in some hard fighting, seized several blocks of buildings and houses which would constitute the 82nd's bridgehead over the river. Instead of hills and ridgelines, the "key terrain" for Santo Domingo now involved buildings,

The 106mm recoilless rifle mounted on a 1/4 ton jeep, as in this 1965 photo above, wrote havoc with rebel snipers inside Santo Domingo. (82nd Airborne Division Museum photo)

streets and alleyways, providing the necessary observation and fields of fire that infantrymen liked to have in their favor.

Mortars and artillery were at first restricted and then not employed at all. In one case, 105mm artillery, firing from locations several miles to the northeast of the Duarte Bridge, placed a series of parachute-flare, magnesium illumination rounds over the city that night to provide enough light to reveal the rooftop locations of some of Caamano's sharpshooters. As the parachute illumination flares floated down in the tropical breezes, they tended to land squarely on the city's rooftops, igniting several fires. A hot telephone call from the city's mayor to the U.S. Embassy caused Ambassador Bennett to direct that all future artillery fire within the city be terminated.

In itself, the bridge crossing did not end the fighting by any means, as Caamano's rebels began a hot fire fight using snipers armed with Mauser rifles and a Dominican manufactured submachine gun with a 32-round magazine. While not particularly accurate, the weapon was still deadly at shorter ranges of fifty to one-hundred yards. While contending with these threats, the paratroopers also took control of a narrow peninsula of land known as San Souci which jutted out from the east side of the river's mouth into the Santo Domingo harbor. This site had a series of eight-story high flour silos from which one could not only see across the river and along George Washington Avenue, which paralleled the sea coast, but could also gain a commanding view of the rooftops of the rebel positions within the eastern part of the city. It was from the rooftops and upper story windows that the snipers were attempting to harass and otherwise pickoff the paratroopers. The colorful Christmas tree-styling of the Army fatigue uniform of the day with its shinny brass buckle, yellow chevrons on the sleeves, white name tapes, and often gold and silver collar insignia made particularly inviting targets.

One sniper in particular became very bothersome for the 17th Cavalry's troopers. Shooting from his window and then ducking to one side out of sight behind the building's wall to avoid being hit by counter fire, this rebel was causing a lot of anxiety among the paratroopers from his near misses. Using their 106mm recoilless gun's spotting rifle, which fired a .50 caliber tracer round to assist in sighting in on a target, a cavalry gunner fired a tracer through the lower part of the window or about waist high. After the sniper fired his next shot and ducked out of sight, the gunner then shifted his now oriented sight to a spot along the wall where he estimated the sniper was hiding. A second later the recoilless rifle fired, sending its missile of death towards the sniper's location. A loud explosive flash obscured the target. Once the smoke and dust had settled, one noted that there was now a large one meter-diameter hole in the wall and the sniper was not heard from again, virtually obliterated by the blast. The 106s were also used in their primary anti-tank role, destroying a number of Caamano's captured tanks over the nest several weeks.

To the west of the rebels' position within the city, the 6th Marine Expeditionary Unit of some 1,500 men had landed tanks and amphibious armored infantry carriers which enabled them to work their way along the coast to the Hotel Jaragua and then north about two miles to secure the U.S. Embassy. Harassed by random snipers, which were operating independently and were therefore not under Caamano's control, the Marines secured their corridor which in time became the ISZ.

At this time it became readily apparent that the rebel command did not control the thousands of people allegedly fighting in its cause, many

Santo Domingo: International Security Zone/Corridor

of whom were still armed and roaming the streets, seeking out Army and Marine targets of opportunity. A number of leftist groups, such as the 14th of June Movement, which had been left out of the planning for the uprising and were taken by surprise by the early events, now began to try and fight their own irregular, guerrilla war against the Americans. This was the unfortunate political price that was now being paid for by the Constitutionalists for arming bands of uncontrollable civilians during the first few days of the revolution. The Communist factions now hoped to increase their political fortunes by exacerbating the situation between the American and rebel forces by creating as much bloodshed and confrontation as possible, radicalizing the uprising into a full-blown revolution. Sniping was the tactic and its indiscriminate nature, killing many innocent people throughout the city, undermined the position of the Constitutionalists who were now blamed by the Embassy for each and every hostile action or sniping incident that took place. Add to this situation the numerous thrill-seeking hoodlums who enjoyed a sense of power and adventure that came from shooting a "Yankee" and one can sense the chaos that actually reigned throughout the city. When the Constitutionalists tried to make their case that they were not responsible for the sniping and that they were not Communists, they were met with a great deal of skepticism from not only the American Embassy but also elements of the international press.

By Saturday the 1st of May, Ambassador Bennett had been able to get the Papal Nuncio, Msgr. Clarizio, to work out a temporary cease-fire agreement between Wessin and Caamano. This appeared to reinforce President Johnson's interest in getting the Organization of American States (OAS) involved in working out a political solution to the situation in the Dominican Republic. Over the next several days the rest of the 82nd Airborne flowed into San Isidro, which when combined with the Marines, totaled some 14,000 troops on the ground. Lieutenant-General Bruce Palmer, designated by the JCS as the U.S. ground commander assumed control of all these forces. Palmer recognized that he needed to improve his line of communications and directed General York to take action accordingly.

Taking advantage of the cease fire on the 1st of May, Troop A of the 1/17th Cav conducted a reconnaissance through rebel controlled territory to determine the best route for a corridor to the west. While it succeeded in linking up with the Marines, the way had been contested and the paratroopers had to fight their way through into the ISZ, losing two men killed and some five wounded in the process. The cease fire was obviously of a very tenuous nature. That next Monday, the 3rd of May, three battalions of airborne infantry (2/325, 1/505 and 2/505) from the newly arrived 2nd Brigade broke out of their bridgehead shortly after midnight, moving straight west for about three miles in a surprise move to link up with the Marine controlled ISZ. As the first battalion secured its portion of the new corridor, the next passed through the lead battalion, moving in a leapfrog-style maneuver until reaching the ISZ. This now secured the east-west corridor which had been part of the plan to establish a ground line of communication (LOC) between the 82nd Airborne headquarters and the loyalist junta government at San Isidro and the American Embassy in the western part of the city. It also served to isolate Caamano's main rebel forces from some of his irregular factions operating in the industrial area of the city to the north and, most importantly, to negate any chances he would have of bringing about a military victory for the Constitutionalists.

The rebels found themselves, in the main, sealed off in one square mile of the city bounded by the Army and Marines to the north and west, the Ozama River to the east and the Caribbean sea to the south. York assigned at least two battalions of infantry or about 1500 men at any given time to patrol the corridor and keep it open to traffic. All combat infantry and cavalry rotated "tours" of duty in the corridor or LOC as it was better known and along the Ozama River, facing Caamano's rebel forces. Except for seven check points which served to regulate traffic in and out of the zone, the paratroopers and Marines controlled access to the rebels by sealing off all roads and alleyways. People could generally come and go as they wished, but they could not carry weapons and ammunition in and out of the zone. Some attempted to use ambulances, hiding weapons underneath wounded civilians and rebels, but were found out.

As a result of the days of fighting between the two factions and the imposition of the corridor, the population inside the rebel zone now found itself on the verge of starvation. To ease the situation somewhat paratroopers shared their C-ration meals and provided emergency medical treatment to the populace. Later on, Army civil affairs units undertook civic action missions to ensure that food, in the form of rice, powdered milk, beans, cooking oil, cornmeal and water, and medical supplies from the Agency for International Development (AID) reached the needy. In addition, there was a major sanitation problem in that garbage and other refuse was being thrown out into the streets but not retrieved. In turn, as many of the streets as possible had to be cleaned and electricity and water restored to the city to bring it back to some sense of normalcy. This was not an easy task to accomplish, especially when under harassment from sniper fire. Fortunately most of the rebels involved in the sniping had never been trained in the use of firearms and were very poor shots, lessening the chances of a paratrooper actually being hit. Nonetheless, it was tense, nerve wracking work that the paratroopers and their civilian Dominican counterparts did not enjoy.

At this point in time the Constitutionalists had fully established themselves in their part of the city. While they were now isolated, their enclave was the political center and bastion of the uprising. What was now needed was for the original leaders of 1963, such as Juan Bosch in particular, to assert themselves by assuming their constitutionally elected positions and formally proclaiming a new government for the Dominican republic. Had Bosch come forth at this moment, this would have provided the revolution with a just and accepted leader, which from a legal and moral stand point would have been an unassailable political position - the illegally deposed president of the country reassuming once again his rightful, elected position as the nation's president! But where was Juan Bosch?

Remaining in Puerto Rico, Bosch had opted to allow events to run their course and, when the revolution was in dire need of a leader to rally the people behind its cause, there was now no one of any real stature known throughout the Dominican Republic, let alone the world to serve this purpose. A political void existed. Into this void stepped Colonel Caamano, the highly successful and acknowledged military leader of the uprising. With Bosch opting to remain in Puerto Rico and with the support of former members of the old 1963 Congress, Caamano was now chosen to serve as a provisional "Constitutional President" of the country until February, 1967 (when Bosch's original presidential term would have run out). Many of the lawyers, doctors and merchants, who had joined the rebels' cause in the hopes that Bosch would once again assume the presidency, now became despondent as they saw the civilian political leadership of their uprising become militarized. Albeit Caamano was sworn in as the new president with great fanfare by the rebels inside Santo Domingo, the Dominican people throughout the remainder of the cities and towns of the countryside remained neutral, if not skeptical of the proceedings. In their eyes Bosch was the president; Caamano was not. And now Bosch had abdicated his position! Nevertheless, Caamano would remain as the de facto Constitutionalist leader until the end of August.

The tactical problem for the paratroopers trying to keep the LOC open and secure was how to deal with the constant sniping which was openly promoted by members of the Communist 14th of June Movement. Rundown and half-constructed buildings and houses, and tangled underbrush and trees provided excellent cover to the innumerable snipers whose sporadic firing was kept up day and night. Sometimes they would shoot from the rooftops and other times they would stand well back inside an upper story room where they could not be seen and fire from their shadowy protection. Often only the direction of the sound of the weapon would be the tip-off as to where the sniper was hidden. The enemy or the "bad guys," as the snipers became known, could only be identified when they shot at you. Otherwise they hid their weapons and blended into the population as ordinary civilians protected by the Geneva Convention and the rules of war which prohibited soldiers from firing on innocents.

Sometimes terrible situations occurred, such as when a rebel youth engaged some Marines with a submachine gun while hiding behind an old man riding a bicycle. The Marines, in self-defense, had no choice but to shoot down both the old man and their actual assailant. The standing rule of engagement was do not shoot unless you are shot at and return fire only if you can identify a real target. Over time the use of anti-tank weapons, such as bazookas and recoilless rifles now required special permission in order to shoot back at snipers.

By the end of the second week of the revolution, there were some 14,000 paratroopers and supporting forces of the XVIIIth Airborne Corps, which included the 82nd Airborne Division, and some 7,000 Marines of the 4th Marine Expeditionary Brigade inside the Dominican Republic, all under the command of Lieutenant-General Bruce Palmer. In short, Palmer was now a theater commander and at the beck and call of Washington. In Washington, the OAS at U.S. urging was working to form an inter-American peace force for the Dominican Republic and countries such as Brazil, Costa Rica, Honduras and others were being invited to participate. It was hoped that world opinion would no longer see the U.S. efforts as being only militaristic and unilateral, but as a united Latin American mission designed to bring about peace. In line with this, some hundreds of tons of food and medicines had been distributed to the population on both sides of the civil war. This was in response to the fact that food shortages were a chronic problem and that the hospitals continued to have difficulty handling the masses of injured and wounded. In addition, the outbreak of an epidemic was always a lingering possibility and needed to be avoided at all cost.

Inside the Dominican Republic, the San Isidro junta had been replaced, again at Washington's urging, with a new "Government of

National Reconstruction" led by General Antonio ("Tony") Imbert. Imbert was infamous as one of Trujillo's thugs who had carried out gangster-style political executions on behalf of "El Jefe" during the latter part of the dictatorship. Now he was a provisional president for the loyalist side and fully supported by the United States!

Once installed as the new loyalist leader and sensing his invulnerability to any rebel reprisals, Imbert immediately began attacking the Constitutionalist enclave inside Santo Domingo with P-51 Mustang fighters armed with rockets and machineguns. After successfully destroying the rebel-controlled radio station, the fighters proceeded to continue their firing runs at random, strafing both the downtown area and the ISZ at will. It was an embarrassing time for the United States, as its official protégé had become a "lose cannon on deck." It was bad enough that the rebel snipers were shooting up the foreign embassies nearby the American Embassy; now the loyalists were doing the same thing from the air. Ironically, out of this situation Caamano's rebels now found themselves being protected from Imbert on the ground by the very paratroopers and Marines that had initially encircled them inside the city. This held true only for the downtown part of Santo Domingo, as Imbert's forces in a series of counterattacks gradually forced the rebels out of the northern part of the city. This brought about a virtual deadlock between Caamano and Imbert as the defended ISZ/LOC kept each one from getting at the other's throat.

Inter-American politics were now in full play during the middle of May as President Johnson announced that he was withdrawing some 1,700 U.S. troops. As the Marines reduced the size of their forces as the first of a number of major increments to depart, these were replaced with over a thousand Brazilian and upwards of 500 Honduran, Nicaraguan, Costa Rican and Paraguayan troops, forming the OAS sponsored Inter-American Peace Force (IAPF) under the command of the corpulent Brazilian General Hugo Alvim. General Palmer was instructed by Washington to become Alvim's American deputy commander, while retaining command of the American forces component of the IAPF. The OAS had been established in 1948 and was headquartered in Washington, D.C. to facilitate regional political leadership by the United States. Through schools, defense councils, joint exercises and other conferences and training programs, it was designed to ensure a continuing U.S. influence on regional security matters. It would serve this purpose in the Dominican Republic by endorsing Washington's policies and actions through the IAPF. Along the ISZ/LOC, however, things were less political and more down to earth.

Despite carefully sandbagged positions for protection and flood-lights facing out toward the rebels to both blind and expose them as much as possible, the paratroopers had to endure random sniper fire at all hours both day and night. This constant irritant of possible death from an unseen enemy grated on every soldier's nerves and was very tiring. Nonetheless, things appeared to have stabilized considerably until the 15th of June when a group of rebels not under firm control of Caamano's leadership attacked a number of the paratroopers guarding the LOC. Palmer ordered York to carry out a punitive attack to subdue the rebel's strong points and secure a more defensible line along the LOC, which the latter did, seizing 30 city blocks and even the city's vital electric power plant to boot.

Using aerial photomaps of the city as guides and avoiding the streets and alleyways to keep from being hit by snipers and cross-fires from Caamano's machine gunners, the paratroopers blasted their way through buildings, blowing holes in the walls with engineer satchel charges, anti-tank rockets and 106mm recoilless rifles. Other paratroopers, with their newly issued, fast-firing M-16 rifles, scaled the sides of buildings to go over the rooftops. These tactics enabled the men to penetrate into the center of a building, outflank the rebels on the ground floor and then clear the rest of the building's upper floors. The paratroopers who had scaled the rooftops often found them open and exposed to fire from adjacent and taller rebel-held buildings. Unfortunately, it was on the exposed rooftops that the airborne infantry took its heaviest casualties during the campaign. Nonetheless, the LOC was now widened and defended from both sandbagged rooftop and street positions. Even so, some rebels still attempted to harass the outposts by lobbing grenades down upon them from unguarded rooftops. The new M-79 grenade launcher, with its 40mm high explosive grenade firing out to ranges of 400 meters, was devastatingly accurate, especially when combined with a trip flare which announced the presence of a sniper on a rooftop. When some snipers would fire from an open window and then disap-pear back into a building, closing the shutters behind them, one 40mm grenade would be used to blow the shutters off the window and the next would explode inside the room where the snipers were hiding. It was an effective technique, which many rebels would come to regret.

The 82nd promoted the innovative use of a number of its assets. Besides conducting reconnaissance and evacuating wounded, the UH1 helicopter was used to lift troops, sandbags and even 106 recoilless rifles onto rooftops to gain tactical advantage. The experience of the previous year's training with the 11th Air Assault Division was now paying off. Since rooftops did provide considerable observation and fields of fire, this was a significant advantage which the 82nd Airborne exploited to the fullest. Another weapon of sorts which proved its worth in this particular situation was the use of the brigade counter-mortar radar section to determine who did what to whom. Imbert's forces took great pleasure in shooting up Caamano's rebels from the formers' positions in the northern part of the city. From time to time loyalist troops would randomly shoot high angle mortar fire into the downtown area, indiscriminately inflicting numerous civilian casualties. Of course the paratroopers were bitterly blamed by the rebels for these violations of the truce. Unbeknownst to Imbert's forces the radar section was able to plot by map grid the firing point of their mortars, as well as the angle and arching path of the round. Finally the truth came out and the firings stopped.

When all was said and done, the American show of force and the ease with which the 82nd Airborne Division had carried out its clearing operations, reducing in size the rebel enclave and inflicting some 70 dead and another 300 wounded on his forces, made a strong impression on Caamano. Not only did he make the effort to gain fuller control of his forces, irregular and otherwise, but it also contributed to his acquiescence in the results of negotiations that would be taking place in the immediate future which would determine to a large degree the destiny of the Dominican Republic for the remainder of the century.

As the summer wore on American strength was gradually reduced, leaving some 6200 soldiers of the XVIIIth Airborne Corps and about 1600 Latin-American soldiers as members of the IAPF. The majority of the 82nd Airborne Division returned to Fort Bragg, leaving behind the 3rd Brigade and A Battery of the 1/320 Arty. Lieutenant-Colonel Richard Pohl, the 1/320 Arty's commander was promoted and eventually given the command of the 101st Airborne Division Artillery. The rest of the 320th settled in once again at Fort Bragg.

Having guaranteed the impossibility of a rebel victory by force and demonstrating its overwhelming strength, the United States now assumed the role of the main mediator in the negotiations for a peaceful outcome to what had been a bloody revolutionary uprising. While both the Imbert and Caamano factions in the Dominican conflict had requested the United Nations Security Council to order the withdrawal of the Inter-American forces, the United States refused to withdraw until a broadly based anti-Communist coalition government had been established. In late August the loyalist and rebel leaders, at the insistence of the United States negotiator Ellsworth Bunker and the OAS, recognized Hector Garcia-Godoy as the provisional president of the nation on 3 September. This, it was hoped, would lead to formal general elections the following 1 June 1966 or nine months later.

Garcia-Godoy had been the Foreign Minister in the old Bosch cabinet and was a respected figure throughout the Dominican Republic. Both of the contending political factions saw this a suitable compromise solution, hoping that with the advent of formal elections they would be able to acquire some of the objectives they struggled so hard for. For the loyalist leaders this meant continued influence and power as they had previously held under Trujillo and for the Constitutionalist rebels it meant some basic reforms that had not been realized during the ill-fated 1963 government of Juan Bosch. The political lines were thus drawn.

Still, it was not all that easy as General Wessin attempted to engineer a coup to overthrow the government during the second week of September, was found out, and forced to leave the country, becoming the Dominican Counsel General to the United States. In addition, with Imbert now without a job and in limbo, it was also convenient to have Colonel Caamano leave for England as a military attache. While this appeared to "clear the decks" of major political obstacles to the new provisional government, on several other occasions Garcia-Godoy would have to request General Palmer's assistance in putting down political disturbances of one sort or another.

Back at Fort Bragg the 1/320 Arty, like most units in the division, found itself once again enmeshed in the doldrums of garrison soldiering. During the next few months and on into autumn, the battalion lost many of its highly trained personnel, including NCOs and officers. These, in turn, were replaced with others, notably Lieutenant Colonel Melvin Johnsrud, who took over as battalion commander from Richard Pohl. Captain John Dooley, a Special Forces combat veteran from Vietnam, took over B Battery and Master Sergeant David Craig, who would train up and run the battalion fire direction center, was assigned to the Headquarters Battery. As this was taking place, events of some note continued to take place back in the Dom Rep.

In late September Juan Bosch was allowed to return to Santo Domingo and declare himself as the Democratic Revolutionary Party (PRD) candidate for the presidential election in June 1966. What he found was not so much a reform party but a coalition of liberal and left-leaning groups like never before. The events of the last six months had contributed to a significant radicalization among his Dominican supporters. Whereas the Dominican Communist Party had been left out and, as a result, was taken completely by surprise by the advent of the pro-Bush revolution in April, there was now a crescendo of fervent support for leftist movements. Springing up throughout Santo Domingo and in other large cities there were parties which now considered themselves to be "Moscow-line" and "Peking-oriented" supporters, as well as pro-Castro affiliates (the 14th of June Movement), all of whom were jockeying for influence and power in the politics of the moment.

What appeared to uniformly inspire them was their intense anti-Americanism due, in the main, from the landings and successful operations of the U.S. troops still on Dominican soil in the late summer and fall of 1965. This under-girding of nationalism, reflecting on the nation's historical memory of the 1920's U.S. Marine occupation and the Navy's running of the customs house as a receivership until 1941, provided a hotbed of animosity towards the United States continued military presence. "*Fuera Yanqui!*" ("Yankee go home!") could be observed as graffiti commonly scribbled and scrawled on the walls around Santo Domingo. With the failure of Caamano's Constitutionalists to recover the presidency in April and May and egged on by Fidel Castro's propaganda, which alleged that the United States was merely exploiting the Dom Rep for its own ends, many young Dominicans now turned toward Communism and Castroism as the only alternative to possibly another Trujillo-style government. Whether one agreed with them or not, this is what they believed and they were the ones confronting the IAPF and its component of American paratroopers. Ameliorating the situation considerably was the move of the armed Constitutionalist rebels from Ciudad Nueva in downtown Santo Domingo to the 27th of July Barracks on the other side of the Ozama River near Sans Souci. This took many of the weapons in use during the civil war out of the hands of the population and opened up the political space needed to permit the conduct of actual political campaigning for the 1 June election that next year.

Bosch found that campaigning in his homeland was not an easy affair. Hundreds of his active supporters were harassed and sometimes murdered both in Santo Domingo and in the countryside. His son was one of those shot and a bodyguard was killed. For the most part he waged his campaign as the PRD candidate out of his home where he lived in almost virtual seclusion, making frequent radio broadcasts. Bosch's opponent for the upcoming election was Joaquin Balaguer, familiar to Dominicans as Trujillo's secretary and vice-president during the last years of the dictatorship and then finally president of the country when Trujillo was shot and killed in 1961. Balaguer, like Bosch, arrived from Puerto Rico where he had been sitting out the revolution. Albeit diametrically opposed on many issues, they were actually personal friends. While Balaguer was the symbol of peace, tranquility and maintaining the status quo, Bosch was the symbol of revolution, constitutionalism, and socio-political change. Balaguer, in contrast and calling his party the Reform Party (Partido Reformista - PR), continuously traveled and spoke throughout the nation, running a very skillful and well-financed race. Despite having served as a personal secretary and speech writer for Trujillo and having developed propaganda tracts to exhort the dictator's greatness, Balaguer was accepted throughout most parts of the country as an honest broker, winning votes among women and rural peasants. Because politics in the Dom Rep could become volatile and with the upcoming election heating up popular emotions, General Palmer thought it might be a good idea to reinforce his peace keeping forces in country.

With it's A Battery left behind in the Dom-Rep to support the 82nd's remaining infantry, the 1/320 Arty now became a prime candidate to be redeployed back to Santo Domingo in support of Colonel John Hard's

3rd Infantry Brigade which had pulled the assignment of being the 82nd Airborne Division's contribution to the IAPF. Alerted in early October for planning as to what would probably happen, the battalion received its 30 October deployment order from the XVIII Airborne Corps. It would now be part of the IAPF conducting a peacekeeping mission. For the battalion it was more like a phase two of the original deployment which began back in April. Instead of the anticipated airborne deployment, the heavy equipment of the battalion and the necessary drivers, NCOs and officers were to be embarked in two Navy Landing Ship Tanks, otherwise known as LSTs.

Considered more economical than using a fleet of C-130s and the fact that the Navy was in need of training for its LSTs in terms of full cargo deployments, two LSTs met the battalion's heavy equipment at Sunny Point, North Carolina. Carefully stowed inside the LSTs were 93 vehicles and 12 howitzers, all configured and positioned to exit within a minute or so of landing. A few days later or around the 20th of November the LSTs put ashore the battalion's vehicles on a beach in the vicinity of Haina, a few miles to the west of Santo Domingo. The balmy subtropical climate with its intense humidity let the paratroopers driving off the LST's download ramp know in an instant that they were back in the Dom Rep once again. With our "Navy days" over, we could now get back to soldiering.

The convoy's movement across the city, over the Duarte Bridge and out to San Isidro to link up with the remainder of the battalion's personnel, which had been air lifted from Pope AFB as an advance party, was relatively uneventful. It did however give one a chance to see first hand the condition of the rural population or poor peasant campesinos, who made up the vast majority of something over three million people. The road to San Isidro was intermittently lined with cane-thatched *bohios* or rustic shelters which substituted for houses. As the artillery convoy approached, chickens, goats, pigs and cows scampered to both sides of the road. Running around naked among the bohios were children, often wallowing in the same grime and filth as their families' animals. Bloated bellies and numerous scars and infections over their bodies attested to the lack of basic sanitation and medical attention. Perpetually in debt and barely able to eke out a subsistence living, there appeared to be little or no hope for these poor, destitute peasant families who grubbed for clothing and food in order to survive. The lucky ones grew sweet potatoes, corn, yams and fruit and possibly had a small radio to listen to at night. Sadly, all this was to a considerable degree the legacy of the Trujillo dictatorship of the previous several decades.

The Dominican Republic itself is located in the eastern two-thirds of the island of Hispaniola, which it shares with its poorer Haitian neighbor to the west. The social structure in the Dominican Republic was comparable to those in other Caribbean island nations. In the middle 1960s, there was a small, white upper class of Spanish decent, a small, but emerging mulatto middle class, and a large and very poor mulatto and Afro-Dominican lower class. The wage earnings gap between the rich and poor was huge, with almost 80 percent of the population at large living near the poverty line.

Large mountain ranges and valleys dominate the western half of the country, while the eastern half, which includes Santo Domingo, is made up of a great tropical plain. As part of this plain, agriculture has generally accounted for about nine-tenths of the republic's export revenues, and, in the main, this consisted of tilling, planting, and harvesting various crops by hand. Sugar cane, concentrated in the central valleys and southeastern parts of the country, was the principal crop and traditionally grown on large plantations, cut by hand using machetes, moved from the fields by oxcart, truck or small-gauge railroad trains, and then processed into sugar and rum at a series of nearby mills and brewery centers. During the dictatorship the Trujillo family owned most of the sugar mills, which then passed into the hands of the government as an autonomous corporation in the early 1960s. During the cane-cutting season, from December to June, employment is high; during the rest of the year, it falls off sharply with the unemployment rate reaching almost half of the regular workers. Compounding the problem in the rural areas was the fact that roughly 80 percent of the people could neither read nor write. It was in this ambience of surrounding sugar cane and dire poverty that the 1/320 Arty was to be located.

The San Isidro Air Base and the nearby Ramfis Trujillo estate were surrounded by cane fields and it was the estate house, now under the control of the government, that became the location of the battalion's headquarters. The intelligence and operations sections (S-2 /S-3) found their offices located in what had formally been the bedroom for Kim

Novak, the platinum-haired American movie star of the 1950s and one-time girlfriend of Ramfis. While the paratroopers of the firing batteries occupied tents raised over wooden dunnage and walkways to protect against flooding from the sometimes severe tropical rains, the actual 105mm cannons were kept in full readiness for action and parked with their ¾-ton tow trucks in what had been formerly the Trujillo stables and multi-vehicle garages. The entire area was surrounded by a barbed wire barrier to keep out intruders. This was certainly different from the full field habitat that the battalion had experienced during the previous spring's civil war.

Since the battalion had deployed with a significant complement of untrained soldiers, much of the next few months after arrival was spent training up the fire direction centers, gun crews and newly assigned officers and NCOs. At the end of the train up, the battalion underwent a full ORT conducted by the 82nd Airborne Division Artillery's headquarters. Now and then a firepower demonstration was conducted, just to let people know that the 82nd Airborne still had some devastating capabilities readily at hand. Colonel Hard's infantry brigade, which the 320th supported, conducted its own training and even upgraded some of the Dominican army's infantry reconnaissance units. Apart from the artillery training, there were parachute jumps into the twelve-foot high sugarcane surrounding San Isidro and Sunday picnics to the Boca Chica beaches, where paratroopers learned how to navigate their inflated air mattresses along the coral fringed Caribbean coast. This tended to keep troop morale up, at least for a while.

At sunup every Monday through Friday, come rain or shine, the battalion did its physical readiness training, which in the main consisted of calisthenics and a one-mile run in combat boots along the main road to San Isidro. Captain John Dooley, who had just completed a one year tour of duty fighting Viet Cong guerrillas in Vietnam, was critical of the one-mile run policy. He explained that in order to succeed in combat soldiers had to be in top physical condition; as such, the one-mile run would not cut it. Under his tutelage the Bravo (B) Battery soldiers began extending their runs out to two and even three or more miles. The superior physical conditioning of B Battery clearly showed up in sports, wherein Dooley's "Bravo Bulls" consistently won out over everyone else in the battalion's athletic competitions. Soon the other batteries in the battalion began to follow Bravo's suit. Unfortunately, it would be another ten years before the Army picked up on John Dooley's insight into combat physical readiness conditioning and formally implemented the two-mile run throughout the service.

That January, Brigadier General Robert Linvill replaced General Palmer as the commander of the American forces and the IAPF's deputy commander. Ellsworth Bunker, directly representing the Johnson administration as a roving ambassador, remained in country to ensure that all went well. An effort by the top U.S. military leaders in the IAPF to get the 82nd Airborne soldiers to take off their red, white and blue "double-A" or All American airborne division shoulder patches in exchange for the blue and white U.S. Forces Dominican Republic (US-FORDOMREP) patch substitute was met with considerable defiance and derision. "Once airborne - always airborne!" was the paratroopers' cry and it quickly became apparent that it would not be wise for the "brass" up the chain of command to tinker with a primary symbol of airborne esprit de corps.

While the provisional government of Garcia Godoy attempted to keep the peace as the election period approached, there were from time to time demonstrations and marches by one faction or another which got out of hand. Even visits to the presidential palace could be eventful, as happened on the 9th of February when students from the Autonomous University of Santo Domingo attempted to make a visit to bring to the president's attention the need to follow through on the promised payments from the government's educational budget. The supporting march by 800 other faculty members and students became disorderly and a firefight broke out between some armed students and the national police, guarding the seat of government. Throwing teargas grenades and firing rifles and submachine guns, the police repelled the students, killing seven and wounding thirty others. Events such as these contributed to a perpetual tension which always seemed to exist within the city and caused the 320th Artillery to keep a close eye on what was going on, generally keeping one artillery battery on constant standby in case of need. Nonetheless, the most frequent type of disturbance during this period was the burning of tires in the streets as part of a series of demonstrations and barricades to obstruct traffic and permit the passing out of propaganda leaflets. Despite U.S.-sponsored cleanup operations, the alternating hot sun and torrential rains, in conjunction with the garbage which littered the streets, contributed to the resulting unpleasant smells and general squalor of the city.

On the 1st of March the formal presidential election campaign between Bosch and Balaguer began in earnest. While Balaguer was favored by the American Embassy, as well as the Johnson administration in Washington, Bosch did have some strong support from younger Dominicans, and in particular students. The Federation of Dominican Students (FED) had been founded shortly after the assassination of Trujillo and included both high school and university students. Through the federation the students won autonomy for the university in Santo Domingo, participating in numerous demonstrations, strikes, parades and rallies. Over time, the schools where the FED operated became highly partisan, resulting in frequently violent political activities. With the overthrow of Bosch's Constitutionalist government in 1963 and the advent of the Constitutionalist counter-coup in 1965, a majority of the students became revolutionary leftists and radical nationalists, some more so than others. Sympathetic to Fidel Castro's overthrow of the Batista dictatorship, which they saw as a forerunner of the overthrow of the Trujillo dictatorship, and critical of the United States, they became avid supporters of Bosch's reelection. Any number of the causes the students espoused often coincided with those that the various Communist groups also advocated. One usually tried to avoid the student demonstrations and pep rallies that occurred from time to time around Santo Domingo.

As the battalion fire direction officer and a member of the battalion's operations staff (S-3), from time to time I was called upon to run liaison missions into Santo Domingo to the XVIII Airborne Corps headquarters at the Jaragua Hotel, sometimes staying overnight there before returning the next day. One afternoon in April I took advantage of one of these missions to break up the routine at San Isidro and run some documents over to the Corps headquarters. The liaison completed and it being late in the day, I instructed the jeep driver to lay over that night with the jeep at the headquarters company which had its quarters at the hotel. With some time on my hands, I caught a taxi to go over and visit some friends from AID who lived in the northwestern part of the city. It was here that one could pick up unofficial, but very interesting perspectives as to what was going on in and around Santo Domingo, which complemented and fleshed out the bits and pieces of generally incomplete information which Army intelligence provided to the battalion each week on the political situation as it affected the IAPF. Finishing dinner around 10 PM, it was time to go and I was picked up by another taxi to head back to the Jaragua Hotel.

The driver of the taxi was an engaging chap and he promptly informed me that the direct route down to the coast and then over to the hotel further east was blocked due to a political procession. He showed me on my Texaco road map that there was another way, a bit longer, but safer. Waving his arms, he assured me that the way was "Good good!" Was he right or was he wrong? Or was this just another way to gouge a Gringo (a derogatory term for an American) out of some additional Dominican pesos by taking a roundabout way back to the hotel? I wasn't sure, but with sufficient pesos in my pocket, I decided to take him at his word.

The new route that the driver had decided upon was a remote roadway through a series of tall, dry sugarcane fields, the stalks being some eight to ten feet high and lining both sides of the road. The aroma of rotting sugar cane filled the balmy evening air as we rolled along about 40 miles per hour. After a few minutes the otherwise pitch-black night changed into a warm orange-colored glow from a series of bond fires, not only straight ahead but also to the left and right of the road itself. We had blundered into a high-spirited pep rally being conducted by some hundreds of highly aroused and fired up FED students! These now swirled around the taxi, chanting political slogans and pounding on the top of the car with their fists, while wondering what it was doing there and who was inside (Juan Bosch perhaps?).

Only the glare of the reflection of the flames from the bond fires off the side windows kept them from seeing who besides the driver was inside, or better said the *Yanqui* in the back seat. Dressed out in my short sleeve tropical-style fatigue uniform and resplendent with all the uniform's colorful airborne patches and insignia, I was the perfect "victim" for a militant "Yankee go home" rally. I dreaded the thought of what would happen to me, let alone the taxi and its driver, if I was found out. Being clubbed to death or burned up in an overturned taxi due to student excesses also crossed my mind.

Indeed, this was not a good situation. The driver had now slowed down to about one or two miles per hour and said something about having to stop. "We had better keep moving through the crowd if we intend to work our way out of this" I thought to myself. As the driver slowed the taxi down to a virtual stop, my stomach tightened and I jammed my M-1911 Colt 45 automatic into the back of his neck, hissing "Go! Go! Go!" Feeling the hard, cold steel of the muzzle pressing against his neck and hearing the click of the hammer being cocked back, the driver quickly got the point and accelerated a little more or to about two miles per hour, gradually working his way forward. There must have been over a thousand students chanting and hollering and some still banging on the car. I had but eight cartridges in the pistol's magazine, which was hardly enough to put up a fight for very long. Hunkered down behind the driver's seat, the smoke from the bond fires now obscuring the windows, which in turn reflected the light of the bond fires back into the eyes of the students, and the slow but steady advance of the taxi enabled us to break free of the demonstration. The driver looked back at me with a sweaty smile on his rotund, unshaven face: *"Muy bien senor, muy bien!"*

The closer one got to the elections, the more hazardous the trips into Santo Domingo became, and the liaisons were made roundtrip within the same day. Over to the XVIIIth Airborne Corps headquarters in the morning and returning that afternoon, became the standing operating procedure. On occasion this did not always work out as smoothly as one would have liked. Leaving out one morning in early May, my driver and I crossed the Duarte Bridge. At the far or western end of the bridge the houses looked like Swiss cheese from the .50 caliber and 106mm recoilless rifle hits. Atop one six-story building a lone paratrooper on sentry duty hollered out: "All the way Sir!" I replied with the standard reply: "Airborne!" With my "Christmas tree"-style uniform, it was obvious that I was an officer. Dominicans had also made the same observation.

Several minutes later the jeep turned down El Conde Street and headed towards Independence Square, attempting to follow a different route from previous ones of the last several weeks. Some blocks up ahead there appeared to be a large number of people milling around in the street and, to be safe, I told Sam, the private first class driver, to go another two blocks and make a left turn at Espaillat Street, which would then take us to George Washington Avenue along the coast and on to the Jaragua Hotel. A block later it was all too obvious that the crowd had spotted us and was running pell-mell down the street, directly towards our Army jeep with its white, five-pointed stars duly painted on the hood and sides. Shouts were being hollered from the windows and rooftops overlooking the street and a rain of bottles, stones, brickwork and other debris came pouring down upon us. While the jeep was normally driven with its top down, that day there had been intermittent rain showers and the faded canvas top was up and tightly stretched. With bottles and bricks bouncing off the hood and top, Sam gunned the motor and we sped towards the next corner. It was a close call as we beat being intercepted by the crowd by about five seconds. With the mob hollering epithets in Spanish and "Yanqui go home," we had narrowly missed becoming a political target of opportunity for one of the Communist 14th of June Movement's pep rallies held from time to time at Independence Park.

Turning down George Washington Avenue along the Caribbean waterfront appeared to have been the right move, but, as it turned out, not necessarily so. Passing by an open field on the right-hand side of the Avenue there were a dozen or more teenagers and men playing baseball. Dominicans tend to be outstanding baseball players and the sport is as much a national pass time in the Republic as it is in the United States. One youngster saw our now badly battered jeep passing by and demonstrated his pitching prowess by hurling a piece of jagged coral the size of a fist at us from about a hundred feet away.

With the jeep having passed by the ball players and my attention focused on down the avenue, I next heard the loud cracking sound of rock striking metal. The kid had a dead shot aim and I would not be writing this book but for a small, but sturdy metal flange which stuck down from the jeep's roof support structure, protecting my right temple from an otherwise perfect throw. The force of the blow had bent the flange inward about a half inch, but still saving my life. It was a lesson learned that one could never be too careful when on the streets of Santo Domingo. A different route was taken back to San Isidro that afternoon. Over time other security measures that had to be taken to protect vehicles and their occupants included the welding of wire cutters in the form of a grooved, vertical steel bracket to the front bumper. The bracket, standing about a yard high, would catch and otherwise cut the strands of piano wire, which unrepentant rebels from time to time would stretch across side streets and alleys, hoping to strangle, if not decapitate, unsuspecting military vehicle drivers in movement.

As the elections approached, a military intelligence briefing team of the 519th Military Intelligence Battalion from General Linvill's headquarters came out to San Isidro to "brief the troops" of the 1/320th as to what was transpiring and what they should expect from the election process in terms of who might win and what threats could develop as a result. Interestingly enough, the team made it quite clear that they fully expected Juan Bosch to win the election. Ironically, the troops were ecstatic! Since Bosch had asserted throughout his campaign that, if elected, the first thing he would do would be to remove all foreign soldiers from Dominican soil, it meant that the IAPF peacekeepers, including the 82nd Airborne soldiers would be going home shortly. Had there been a soldier vote, Bosch would have won hands down. Life for the average trooper in the Dom Rep was getting monotonous and he more and more felt it was time to go home.

Despite the briefers' opinions that Bosch would most likely win, all their data had apparently come from sources inside Santo Domingo and a handful of towns immediately to the north. Other sources known to myself indicated that, while Bosch was overwhelmingly strong inside Santo Domingo, he was rather weak elsewhere, indicating that Balaguer was much stronger than he appeared to be. The fact that the majority of the populace had sat out the April 1965 revolutionary uprising and ensuing civil war and not thrown their hats into the fray on the side of Bosch-supporting Constitutionalists indicated that he actually might not have the wholehearted support of most of the population, as had occurred in the December 1962 election. I remained somewhat skeptical about Bosch's chances, knowing that the election results would tell the tail one way or another anyway.

The election of 1 June was relatively orderly and quiet, which suited the paratroopers just fine. When all the votes were finally counted the results were announced, sure enough, Balaguer was declared the winner. Bosch had been soundly defeated, with Balaguer earning 57 percent of the vote to his 39 percent. Dominicans, apparently tired of bloodshed and the trials and tribulations of civil war and fearing that a Bosch victory might lead to further revolution and chaos, had voted for Balaguer. A number of Dominicans known to myself said that the real reason that Bosch had not won the election was because "El no tiene huevos!" (He doesn't have any balls! - meaning guts). Indeed, many of Bosch's followers were incensed that he had sat out the Constitutionalist uprising to place him once again in power as the legitimately elected president. That he did not go to Santo Domingo to assume the political leadership of the revolution during the first several days of the crisis and that he remained safely on the sidelines in nearby Puerto Rico, caused him to be viewed as a coward by many who felt he was letting his party's rank and file fight his battles for him. On the 1st of July Joaquin Balaguer officially assumed the presidency of the Dominican Republic, and the provisional government of Garcia-Godoy was dissolved. Operation Power Pack had for all intents and purposes come to an end.

As the 1/320 Arty flew back to Fort Bragg, North Carolina, the soldiers of the 82nd Airborne Division could feel assured that their mission had been successful: prolonged civil war had been averted, democracy had been restored, American citizens had been protected, and a potential Communist takeover of the Dominican Republic quashed. Through all this there had been a cost. Although an estimated 2,850 Dominicans were killed, twenty-six Americans, mainly Army paratroopers and Marines died during the conflict. Another 154 had been wounded. By the 21st of September the last units of the American contingent of the IAPF had left the Dominican Republic.

*　　*　　*

The American peacekeeping effort in the Dominican Republic was a success. Despite the fact that the 82nd Airborne Division had been thrown into the middle of a chaotic civil war, the extraordinary discipline and training of the paratroopers paid off. That the division came out of a complicated STRICOM exercise, reorganized "on the run" and successfully deployed into an otherwise vague combat situation was tribute to the flexibility, innovation and adaptability displayed by the officers, NCOs and soldiers alike. The division deployed piecemeal and by increments, which is normally not how you want to go into combat. The

Colonel. Francicsco Caamano Deno was the military leader of the 1965 constitutionalist rebels' revolt to place former president Juan Bosch back in power. (Listen Diario photo)

Major General Robert York commanded the U.S. Army's 82nd Airborne Division during the 1965 invasion of the Dominican Republic. (82nd Abn. Div. Museum Photo)

Juan Bosch found himself overthrown by the Dominican military in 1962 and then denied the presidency again in the open democratic election for 1966. (Listen Diario photo)

Joaquin Balaguer, an old-guard holdover from the Trujillo dictatorship, defeated Juan Bosch for the presidency in the democratic election of 1966. (Listen Diario photo)

division's forte was massed parachute assault, which it would ultimately get to carry out in Panama some twenty-five years later. Nonetheless, the aggressive, common sense tactics employed by the junior leaders saw the division through a myriad of situations with a relatively low number of casualties. The paratroopers were able to contain both the rebels and the loyalists, restore stability, and support the provisional government and the electoral process, leading to the 1966 elections which resulted in the restoration of democracy. In addition, the division conducted a variety of humanitarian missions with army doctors treating over 58,000 Dominicans by the completion of the mission in the fall of 1966.

The division's success apart, there begs the question as to whether the peace keeping mission was even necessary at all, had the nature of the revolutionary uprising and ensuing civil war been clearly understood by Washington and its Embassy in Santo Domingo in 1965. Despite the fact that the Communists inside the country were initially made up of several competing factions, were not a powerful or united force, and had not even been included in the Constitutionalists' plans for revolt, the Embassy and the Department of State (DOS) had a tendency to tar the entire effort to restore constitutional, democratic government as part and parcel of a Castro-inspired Communist conspiracy. The propensity for the American diplomatic corps in Santo Domingo to remain isolated from the rebels and their leaders at the onset of the revolt contributed to the distorted picture of what was actually transpiring and ignored the fact that the pro-Bosch forces had pulled off a virtually bloodless coup.

Had the United States supported this initiative to restore genuine democracy and the lawfully elected president in the beginning, the political objectives of the revolt would have come to fruition and military intervention on the part of the U.S. would likely only have involved the evacuation of American and foreign nationals, a perfectly justifiable and legitimate action which the Marine Corps had carried out in an admirable way. Interestingly enough, the United States was being given a second chance to make amends for its failure to fully support a popularly elected leader and an orderly transition to a democratic system in 1963, which the U.S. sponsored Alliance for Progress had called for just two years earlier. Instead of remaining neutral in 1965, the U.S. tacitly at first and then openly supported the loyalists, exacerbating the situation considerably. The United States brought the OAS into play to give Operation Power Pack a veil of regional legitimacy and to provide a political instrument by which a democratic process could be brought about, without it being too obvious that the Americans were all the while pulling the strings and calling the shots. The OAS was viewed with contempt and seen as nothing more than a useful tool, with Lyndon Johnson remarking during this period: "The OAS couldn't pour piss out of a boot if the instructions were written on the heel."

During this time it was Juan Bosch who made the monumental political blunder of his life, remaining in Puerto Rico while the revolution ran its course. He represented the moral high ground for the Constitutionalists and, had he but arrived on the scene, they could have proclaimed a full, legitimating victory for their cause. His arrival in Santo Domingo during those early days of the revolution would have presented the United States government with a *fait accompli*, causing the U.S. Embassy, DOS and Lyndon Johnson to accept the re-imposition of legitimate democratic rule and Bosch as president, since no other reasonable course of action would have been open at that time. But Bosch failed to show up until too late, prejudicing not only the initial Constitutionalist revolutionary effort and his attempt to be reelected in 1966 but also *all* of his five future efforts to become an elected president of the Dominican Republic over the next several decades. In the five other elections which he also contested Balaguer for the presidency, he lost every one. Bosch died a bitter man at the beginning of 21st Century, complaining: "This was a democratic revolution smashed by the leading democracy in the world."

It is also interesting to speculate as to what might have happened to the revolution if John F. Kennedy had not been assassinated and had been in the presidency at the time the Constitutionalists conducted their counter-coup to reinstate Bosch. It is likely that Bosch would have had Kennedy's sympathy, since the former represented the ideals of the Alliance for Progress. Even so, Bosch would have had to arrive in a timely manner to claim the presidency, which was, in any event, the key factor enabling the Constitutionalists to achieve full legitimacy. Nonetheless, with all said and done, democratic governance at least for the present has been achieved in the Dominican Republic.

Juaquin Balaguer, elected president in the summer of 1966, set up the equivalent of a constitutional dictatorship, ruling in an authoritarian manner. Successfully running for the presidency five more times over the remainder of the century, he implemented a number of reforms. His paternalistic qualities, developed during his many years with Trujillo, came to the fore as he established massive public works projects in order to reduce unemployment. He also encouraged foreign investment and tourism, with the country becoming a low-wage haven for foreign companies. The United States supplied half of the nation's imports and purchased three-fourths of its exports. More than a hundred U.S.-based companies dominated banking and manufacturing, especially the textile, nickel mining and food processing industries. Over time, tourism actually replaced sugar as the top foreign exchange earner.

An astute politician, Balaguer's appointments covered the political spectrum, with both the left and right being represented in his governments, keeping his opponents divided and off balance. Even members of Bosch's PRD party served his cause from time to time. The military was kept in check by involving them in projects whereby the higher ranking members of the institution could acquire wealth - in essence bribed to remain in the barracks. In short, the strategy to deal successfully with the military and preserve democratic governance at the same time was to provide the former with well-paying jobs and periodic arms purchases. When there was some doubt as to the continuance of Balaguer's rule, elections were rigged and ballot boxes stuffed. Sometimes he was found out, as happened in 1978 and again in 1996, but, in each case, the sitting president agreed to hand over the power to an opposition leader.

In the Dominican Republic the president is viewed as a *patron* in the sense that, as the national leader and *jefe*, he must grant favors in the form of jobs, deals and construction projects, in return for loyalty and service. In short, allegiance is given to the leader (*caudillo*) rather than the party program or ideology. This is a traditional value-entrenched authoritarian approach to governance inherited from Spanish colonial times.

For the better part of the twentieth century inside the Dominican Republic the United States promoted democracy *for* the people rather than *by* the people. For this reason the value is weak and not well ingrained into the nation's psychic. During the 1920s U.S. Marines tried to create a professional armed force to maintain order and obey civilian authority and other Americans wrote electoral laws and constitutions in the belief that these structural institutions in themselves would hold the key to the democratization of the country. In 1966 another iteration of nation building took place as the democratic process was implemented once again. Despite the apparent success of this more recent enterprise, Dominicans do not readily conceive of government that works for the general good of the people and not for its own interests. People run for government office to get rich and promote the welfare of their families and friends and not much else. For most Dominicans, honest government has become a contradiction in terms. If Balaguer's conservative party groups were corrupt, as indicated by the vote frauds of 1978 and 1994, Bosch's own PRD was equally so.

Whether one party or the other was in power, labor unrest and political dissent were often repressed by harsh means. While the president controlled about half of the nation's jobs, 70 percent of the country still lived in a state of poverty. Plagued in the main by adverse economic conditions, food shortages and the breakdown of essential public services (electricity, telephones, and water) during the several decades since 1966, over a million Dominicans voted with their feet, fleeing the Republic for a better way of life elsewhere. The United States, as well as other countries, have benefited considerably from these new "pioneers."

Upon completion of my assignment in the Dominican Republic and after an interlude of some five years off and on fighting in the Vietnam War,* I received orders in 1971 from Washington, assigning me to the Green Berets or what was then known as the U.S. Southern Command's 8th Special Forces Group (Airborne), supporting special action operations inside Latin America.

*For this period see the author's Battle Captain: Cold War Campaigning With The U.S. Army In Vietnam, Cambodia and Laos 1967 – 1971

Chapter 2

Green Berets in Guatemala
1972

As the Vietnam War for the American military began to close down during the early 1970s, the professional soldier corps of the U.S. Army looked elsewhere for employment. Some officers and NCOs opted for assignments to West Germany and the North Atlantic Treaty Organization (NATO) forces guarding the Free West's frontier against the Soviet and Warsaw Pact armies, while others looked to South Korea and related Army units arrayed against possible invasion of that country by the North Koreans through the Demilitarized Zone along the 38th Parallel. Yet there was another battleground of the Cold War to the south of the United States inside the Western Hemisphere, which had evolved over time with the 1959 advent of the Cuban Communist guerrilla leader, Fidel Castro. Castro's genius had been to initially present himself as nothing more than an armed nationalist, avoiding the obvious trappings of Marxist-Leninism and Communist connections. Having "liberated" Cuba from its dictatorial past, Castro then went to work to consolidate his own position and authoritarian, caudillo-style government, all the while fervently fomenting and supporting Marxist-Leninist revolution and guerrilla warfare throughout the Americas. This new type of revolutionary battlefield involved much of what was known as Latin America and, as time went on, the insurgency situation throughout the region grew in intensity.

President John Kennedy inherited the Castro threat to the Americas in 1961 from his predecessor, President Dwight Eisenhower. Also inherited was a plan which was very much in the final stages of implementation with the objective of overthrowing Castro and his fledgling Communist government in April of 1961, thus ridding the Caribbean, as well as the Americas, of one of the most obvious Communist subversive threats to the region. Unfortunately the plan, incorporating the use of an invading two-thousand man liberation brigade made up of Cuban ex-patriots and exiles and supported by the CIA and the U.S. Navy, was poorly conceived and implemented, and in the end failed miserably, much to the immense consternation and embarrassment of Kennedy and his new administration.

A year or so later in October of 1962 the Cuban missile crisis and confrontation between the U.S. and the U.S.S.R. took place. While the Soviet Union did withdraw its threatening nuclear missiles from Cuba in the face of American military might, it did so with the understanding that the U.S. would never again attempt to physically invade Cuba to forcefully overthrow the Castro government. To this end, Castro's base of operations was now reasonably well secured by this great power, Cold War agreement, which seemingly awarded him a veritable carte blanche to continue his operations throughout the Americas.

Upon reviewing this new situation, Kennedy thought that the most effective method for checking further Communist subversion and guerrilla warfare in Latin America was to fight it on two fronts, the military and socioeconomic. Through fundamental reforms and a supporting doctrine of counterinsurgency these two thrusts of the Kennedy offensive were supposed to work in tandem. The doctrines were multifaceted and encompassed a variety of economic, social, political, psychological and military activities that required the coordinated supporting action of a number of U.S. government agencies, as well as acceptance by the targeted host country. For example, the Agency for International Development (AID) would oversee economic assistance to Latin American countries, the Office of Public Safety would train indigenous police forces, the United States Information Agency (USIA) would work to neutralize Communist propaganda by assisting host country governments improve their image at home and abroad, the Departments of Defense and State would coordinate counter-guerrilla or military training, and the CIA would gather intelligence and engage in covert and paramilitary activities.

All these agencies and others were to come together to work under the auspices of and in conjunction with a program known as the Alliance for Progress, which was to promote social reform and economic growth through improved financing and technical advice for better public health, education, agricultural research and development, land reform and more effective tax systems. And it was the Alliance for Progress which set the tone for the Kennedy Administration in Latin America, with the president stating in March 1961 that the program's objective was "to satisfy the basic needs of the American [Latin American] people for homes, work and land, health and schools." The Alliance was intended to be a ten-year program which would expend $20 billion on behalf of U.S. interests throughout the region to assist those people who were ill-housed, ill-clothed, ill-fed and illiterate. Unjust structures and systems of land tenure and use were expected to be replaced by an equitable system of property distribution and backed by readily available credit to facilitate the small, peasant-capitalist land owner's new start in life. The goal of all this was to show that the U.S. could offer a model of development and social welfare that would defeat Castro on his own terms. In addition, liberalizing elections were supposed to open up authoritarian, dictatorial regimes to allow for greater participation by the people in general, expression of civil and political rights, and competition on the part of the previously disenfranchised mass of the Latin American population. An accompanying Peace Corps program, aimed at attempting to penetrate into remote and otherwise neglected rural areas, whose populations could otherwise be co-opted by anti-government, revolutionary forces, was also brought into play as an additional check to Castro's aspirations.

After Kennedy was assassinated in Dallas, Texas, towards the end of 1963, Lyndon Johnson took over the programs and by the early 1970s under the Nixon administration the World Bank and the Inter-American Development Bank had also been brought into play for promoting development in Latin America. In short, the successful implementation of these programs throughout the Americas was supposed to serve to inoculate each and every country against Castro-style subversion; the creation of *peaceful change* being preferred over Castro's style of violent, revolutionary change. Nonetheless, during his time in office Johnson eliminated two of the Alliance's original goals, democratization and structural change, in favor of concentrating more on economic development and the anti-Communist counterinsurgency program to repress any and all guerrilla activity.

Working in tandem with the Alliance for Progress, the counter-insurgency doctrine found its implementation in the form of Military Assistance Advisory Groups (MAAGs) or Military Groups operating in eighteen Latin American countries, each of which received a State Department-funded military assistance program (MAP) with an emphasis on internal security and the handling of domestic subversion. Additional foreign military training for the region was to also be provided by the U.S. Army's School of the Americas (USARSA), located at Fort Gulick in the Canal Zone (Panama). To enhance the training provided in place by formally assigned U.S. military advisors to each country, small Mobile Training Teams (MTTs) and Technical Assistance Teams (TATs) from the various Army Special Forces units (Green Berets) could be dispatched at the request of a host country to provide specialized training in civil affairs, civic action, psychological operations, engineering and construction, medical assistance, intelligence and interrogation, as well as counter-guerrilla tactics and techniques.

Two Special Forces units or groups had been designated for this type of duty. One group, the 7th Special Forces Group (SFG), was located at Fort Bragg, North Carolina. The other, the 8th SFG or Special Action Force for Latin America (SAFLA) was located inside Fort Gulick (along with the U.S. Army School of the Americas or USARSA) at the Caribbean end of the U.S. Canal Zone in Panama. The 8th itself came directly under the control of the United States Southern Command (USSOUTHCOM or SOUTHCOM), which was in turn located at Quarry Heights at the southern end of the Canal Zone in the vicinity of Panama City on the Pacific Ocean (the Panama Canal running 52 miles north-south through the middle of the Isthmus of Panama). SOUTHCOM was responsible for all U.S. military affairs taking place in Latin America to the south of Mexico (whereas the United States Atlantic Command at Norfolk, Virginia was responsible for the Caribbean and Cuba).

Assignment to the 8th SFG in January 1972 brought me into contact with an interesting group of officers and NCOs who had served with the Green Berets in Vietnam. Many of these soldiers not only had combat experience operating along the Ho Chi Minh Trail and training and leading civilian irregular defense counter-guerrilla groups inside Vietnam, but some of them had also participated in the ill-fated 1961

Bay of Pigs invasion of Cuba. Besides being blooded in combat, among their many strong points was the fact that they were for the most part native Spanish speakers and understood the Latino culture better than anyone else in the Army. As a "Gringo" with only a five-month basic Spanish language course taken during the latter part of 1971 at the Defense Language Institute at Monterrey, California, behind me, I had some catching up to do in terms of learning the proverbial "ropes" in Latin America. The 8th SFG was commanded by Colonel B.J. Pinkerton, who, as a Vietnam veteran, had directed some of the clandestine special operations inside Laos and was held in high esteem by his men. Backing up Pinkerton was a veteran Command Sergeant-Major Paul Darcy who had made quite a reputation for himself, carrying out these operations and otherwise irritating the North Vietnamese Army with clever psychological ploys along the Ho Chi Minh Trail.

While the Green Berets stationed in the Canal Zone over the years had conducted dozens of training missions throughout Latin America, involving bridge construction and well digging, field medicine, water purification, communications, intelligence and the establishment of counter-guerrilla tactics schools of one sort or another, it was the 1968 operation inside Bolivia that had given the 8th its stellar reputation as a highly effective organization. In pursuing Fidel Castro's concept of creating "Vietnams" all over the Americas, the Argentine revolutionary known as Che Guevarra had been sent from Cuba to Bolivia in 1967 to foment revolution among the Quechua and Aymara Indian populations located in the high Andes. In carrying out this endeavor, Che either had not done his homework or was badly informed about the actual political situation there and had failed to realize that, some years prior to Castro's take over of Cuba, Bolivia had actually undergone its own socioeconomic revolution.

In 1952, led by Victor Paz Estenssoro and his multi-class National Revolutionary Movement (MNR), Bolivian workers, peasants and displaced middle class groups participated in one of the most profound social revolutions in twentieth century Latin America. The revolution overthrew the old order of a handful of monopoly tin mining and large hacienda land owners who as an oligarchy or elite group had essentially ruled the country with an iron hand for over a hundred years. In place of the old order a land reform program came into play in 1953 with each and every Indian peasant in the Andean region receiving full title to his or her own piece of private property, thus ending a centuries-long system of Indian servitude. In addition, for the first time universal suffrage enfranchised virtually the entire population, which meant that the workers were no longer excluded from the political process and their demands for improved working conditions could be heard and attended to. It was against this backdrop of basic reforms that Che attempted to exhort the Indians to revolt and overthrow their government. His effort was nothing less than an outright failure and a blunder that would cost him his life.

Alerted by the Bolivian government that there was a potentially serious insurgency attempting to establish itself in the Andes, SOUTH-COM responded by sending a counter-insurgency training team under the command of Major Arthur ("Bull") Simons to help deal with the situation. After training up a couple of Bolivian counter-guerrilla units called "Rangers," Simons helped coordinate their employment to first detect the whereabouts and then track down Guevarra and his band. Che, in turn, found that the Indians were unimpressed with his revolutionary program and promises of basic reforms, which they already had procured from the government. In the end the Indians showed the Bolivian army's Rangers where Guevarra was hiding out and he was captured and then summarily shot. From beginning to end the mission sponsored by the 8th SFG to rid Bolivia of its guerrilla threat was a textbook case of how a counterinsurgency operation was supposed to work. The key to this success was not only the training provided by Simon's Green Berets, but also the fact that the local Andean inhabitants supported their effort. The basic reforms provided by the Paz Estenssoro government had, in fact, won the Indians' allegiance, inoculating them against the Communist subversion of Castro and his Argentine protégé.

While the 8th SFG consisted of a dozen distinct, twelve-man A-Teams, which were its bread and butter for conducting counter-guerrilla operations, it also had organic to it an engineer construction company, a military intelligence detachment, a civil affairs detachment, a signal detachment, and a psychological operations (PSYOPs) battalion. It was to the 9th PSYOPs Battalion's Research and Analysis Section (RAS) that I had beem assigned at the beginning of 1972. Instead of artillery, tanks, rifles and machineguns, the PSYOP soldiers used radio broadcasts, loudspeakers, printing presses and propaganda leaflets to disseminate information in such a way so as to influence both the enemy guerrillas and friendly civilians alike in the pursuit of a host nation's military and political objectives on the insurgency battlefield.

It was a unique organization in which Army specialists versed in the Spanish language, local dialects and related cultures helped write scripts and other forms of propaganda to be directed at the "target audiences" of interest. The RAS of the 9th PSYOP did analytical work to determine appropriate themes, targets and vulnerabilities, which might be exploited in favor of the 8th SFG's counterinsurgency operations, as well as obtaining feedback from the field to determine the effectiveness of our own and the enemy's propaganda efforts. This required an intimate knowledge of the socioeconomic and political conditions of the targeted country, as well as an understanding of the culture, attitudes and language base of each and every ethnic group within the country.

Commanding the 9th PSYOP Battalion at the time of my arrival was Lieutenant Colonel James Dandridge, one of the Army's consummate psychological operations professionals. The Executive Officer (XO) of the battalion was one Major Edward Lesesne, whose great uncle and Confederate Civil War hero The Citadel, located in Charleston, South Carolina, had named its main entry gate after (The Lesesne Gate). Ed himself actually had gone to Wofford College in South Carolina and then on into the Army's Officer Candidate School (OCS) program where he was commissioned; later finding himself as a captain in the late 1960s commanding and leading Special Forces reconnaissance teams on and around the Ho Chi Minh Trail. Ed's exploits, which included snatching NVA soldiers as prisoners off the Trail, were well known and resulted in his being badly wounded on a number of occasions. When Ed completed his time as the XO, he was replaced by Major Manuel Granado, a Cuban-American airborne veteran of the unsuccessful 1961 invasion of Cuba. With only about 90 men in its complement, the 9th PSYOP battalion had other sections besides the RAS or what the professionals in the field called "teams," including a propaganda development section, a mobile printing capability for leaflets and pamphlets, a loudspeaker and radio-television capability, and the normal administrative, maintenance, operations and logistical staff functions found in any Army battalion of the day.

The operational mission of the 9th PSYOP was to use propaganda and other measures to influence the opinions, emotions, attitudes and behavior of hostile, neutral, or friendly groups in such a way as to support the achievement of U.S. national or host country objectives. In short it was to persuade an individual or group to embrace a particular point of view, form an attitude, or take a particular type of action that you wanted it to carry out. This type of persuasion could be conducted at the national or strategic level to affect an entire population or at specific tactical levels, targeting selected local groups or organizations.

Usually PSYOP messages fell into two distinct categories of either a divisive or cohesive nature. Divisive operations generally meant dividing and discrediting a guerrilla enemy by creating amongst its supporters a sense or feeling of hopelessness, doubt, fatigue, apathy, frustration, panic and even outright hostility against their sponsor organization and its leaders. Cohesive operations were usually conducted on behalf of the host country and were designed to unite, uplift and create a patriotic spirit and willing allegiance on behalf of the population in support of the national government's interests. In short, PSYOPs inside Latin America was about the traditional battle to win the hearts and minds of the people, all the while trying to undermine the morale and cohesion of the enemy's guerrilla forces. This was indeed a very subtle and unique form of war fighting.

As we understood our mission, all PSYOP operations were directed towards a person or a group known as the "target audience" and it was the perception of this audience, rather than the perception of the propagandist, that in the end would determine the success or failure of the effort. Consistent, credible and designed to appeal to the needs and aspirations of the target group, propaganda was the art of persuasion designed to influence the opinions, emotions, attitudes or behavior of the group and reminded one of commercial advertising campaigns conducted inside the United States. If a population group was illiterate in the sense that it could not read, then the means of transmitting the intended message would have to ignore traditional printed matter such as newspapers and written leaflets and rely on voice transmission or perhaps the use of symbols in the form of picture-style leaflets that had special meaning in the local culture. Poor people might not have televisions, but they quite often had daily access to radios. If not radios, then loudspeakers mounted on jeeps, trucks or helicopters and airplanes might be required. When all was said and done face-to-face communication might even have to be employed to convince the target audience of the credibility of the message through actually observing and judging the propagandist as a communicator.

To accomplish all this the communicator had to be able to speak the native dialect fluently and understand the local culture, as well as the feelings and attitudes of the people. Our own experience in Vietnam and the Viet Cong's use of PSYOPs had demonstrated that the face-to-face technique of propaganda communication was considered to be the most effective when dealing with an uncommitted civilian population. While all the theories and doctrine for PSYOPs had their validity in one form or another, in the Americas Fidel Castro had cast down the gauntlet of revolutionary guerrilla warfare and our challenge now was to assist in meeting and defeating it.

Castro's daring defiance of the U.S., confiscating approximately $1 billion in North American property and investments inside Cuba, had won for him and his revolutionary mandate a considerable number of admirers throughout Latin America. As such, early on in his efforts to consolidate his power inside Cuba he claimed that: "The only thing that can resolve the problems of hunger and misery in the underdeveloped countries is revolution." As an example to the rest of the countries in Central and South America the revolution inside Cuba was portrayed as placing maximum emphasis on education and health care. Over the decade of the 1960s the number of Cuban teachers tripled, schools quintupled and illiteracy virtually disappeared on the island. Education was free from nursery school through the university level. Albeit the process served to indoctrinate Cuban youth in the values of Castro's Marxist state, children, whose parents were poor peasant sugar cane cutters with little or no hope of ever breaking out of their poverty, now found it possible to become doctors, teachers and lawyers or otherwise achieve esteemed positions in society which previously had been unattainable. In terms of medicine, all medical services were free and doctors became available in the countryside for the first time in significant numbers. In general it appeared that for the majority of Cubans life had improved and that the government had eradicated illiteracy, hunger, destitution and unemployment. All these reforms Castro used to good effect in his efforts to propagandize the rest of Latin America as to what could potentially be done through the revolutionary process of violent change.

Despite Castro's early successes, throughout the first half of the 1960s there were numerous attempted uprisings against the Cuban government, emanating out of the Escambray mountains of Las Villas Province. In time six provinces sported some dozens of insurrectionary bands, totaling over a thousand men, but this was hardly enough to confront and defeat the Cuban armed forces who easily prevailed over their armed opposition. As a result, at the Uruguayan conference of Punte del Este II in 1962, the U.S. moved to isolate Castro by severing diplomatic ties and imposing a series of trade embargoes.

By 1963 Cuba's attempts to aid Venezuelan guerrilla-terrorists had backfired and led to the severing of diplomatic relations and trade with it by every Latin American country except Mexico. Still, Castro persisted in exporting or supporting revolution in the Americas and in 1966 convened the Tri-Continental Conference which included subversive groups from the Third World's Asia and Africa, as well as Latin America. A virtual mutual admiration society, all the participants were exhorted to spread revolution throughout the world as best they could. By 1972 there were armed groups of a serious nature in South America's Brazil, Argentina, Uruguay, Chile, Ecuador and Colombia and in Central America's Nicaragua and Guatemala - all of which received some sort of training and logistical support from Cuba.

For us in the 9th PSYOP's RAS a key figure in the spreading of revolutionary insurgency throughout the Americas appeared to be Manuel Pineiro Losada, whose office of Cuban intelligence or G-2 (DGI or *Direccion General de Inteligencia*) and later known as the "America's Committee" coordinated much, if not most of the insurgency support for revolutionary activities inside the Americas. Known as "Red Beard," he was a sort of nemesis of ours due to his competence in successfully placing his guerrilla-revolutionary instructors (called by the Cubans "*muchachos*") in a number of the targeted countries. Fanning the fires of revolt across Latin America was Pineiro's goal and, unfortunately, he was frequently able to find fertile ground. His effort was perpetuated by Communism's compelling ideology and propaganda which attempted to turn frustration over perceived injustices into sustained, effective action.

The example touted was that set by Castro himself, who had demonstrated that the Havana-based Fulgencio Batista dictatorship had been overthrown by a small group of bold militants, called a "*foco*" (focused effort). Operating initially in guerrilla-style hit-and-run operations, the efforts were eventually fused together to overwhelm and defeat the opposing government and its military. Latin American militants, intellectuals and political cadres who visited Cuba looking for guidance and inspiration came away awestruck by Castro's perspectives on the merits of revolution and were further imbued with the idea that they too could replicate what had transpired inside Cuba. The arms, training, money and equipment supplied to a guerrilla movement were merely the icing on the cake of revolution. What really counted was said to be a revolutionary imperative and the will to win. Castro and Pineiro promoted revolution without boundaries and propagandized the inevitability of such revolutions which were encouraged to sweep local dictators, oligarchs, their armies, and the United States before it.

At the beginning of March 1972 the 9th PSYOP Battalion received an alert from SOUTHCOM through the 8th SFG headquarters to be ready to provide a psychological operations training team (MTT) to Guatemala for an undetermined amount of time in support of the Guatemalan army. Containing over one-third of Central America's population or about eight million people and the most powerful and dynamic economy in the region, Guatemala was considered a "tough" country where, already from the mid-1960s into the early 1970s, the guerrillas operating inside the cities and out in the countryside had assassinated or kidnapped a U.S. ambassador, a military attache, and a military group commander, as well as the German ambassador and a number of prominent Guatemalan government officials and citizens. A guerrilla movement, known as the Revolutionary Armed Forces (FAR) had been identified in intelligence reports as one of the main perpetrators of the insurrection.

With this in mind and while Lieutenant Colonel Dandridge made a short visit to Guatemala City to conduct a pre-deployment survey, those of us, including myself, who had been designated as part of the MTT began an all-inclusive study into what was causing the insurgency situ-

ation and what the history and dynamics of the country's society were all about. Essentially we were conducting what the Special Forces called an "area study" or an analysis of the socio-economic and political conditions of Guatemala, which was expected to give us an idea of the nature of the insurgency that we would be confronting and why it had come about. To do this required an all-source input of data and information based on a perusal of all available intelligence files and any books, periodicals, or other information we could come up with from around the Canal Zone. What we found out was nothing short of astounding and our findings would influence how we would proceed in-country.

To understand the roots of the insurgency condition inside Guatemala, one could actually go a considerable ways back in history to the country's feudal origin and its medieval Spanish colonial heritage. During the first century (1500s) of Spanish colonial rule, a feudal-patrimonial system of land ownership and lord-peasant relations had developed throughout Central America underneath an authoritarian, hierarchical structure of political authority which had been imposed over the Mayas or what had been one of the most advanced Indian civilizations to have ever flourished on the American continent. The Spanish system was founded on a rigid system of classes, estates, rank orders and purportedly God-given inequalities inherited from the Spanish conquest. This buttressed an economic system which was both exploitive and monopolistic.

The early Spanish elites were the conquerors who secured land grants for themselves and their descendents, which included the rights to all of the local Mayan Indians who happened to be living on them. Under Spanish colonial law, a Spaniard received the Indians found to be living on his land as an entrustment (*encomienda*), to be protected and Christianized. In return he could demand tribute in the form of full time labor. The Spanish used a number of scams to consolidate their position, forcing the native inhabitants into the role of subservient workers. If the Indians could not show legal claim and title to their communal properties, which as uneducated illiterates they of course could not, the land was then seized. The Indians paid tribute by working the land for their white Spanish overseers. Because there was a considerable amount of intermarriage between Europeans and Indians over the centuries, a mestizo class of large landowners gradually appeared. Thus a "new race" had now evolved, blending the European and Indian.

Nonetheless, the indigenous full-blooded Indian masses remained at the bottom of the social scale and were expected to serve their betters in return for protection and a modicum of food and lodging. As such, they were expected to plant, tend and harvest the landowners' crops in the form of sugar, corn, wheat, tobacco, indigo, and cotton; guard their goats and cattle; mine their silver and gold; and to wait upon them in their homes - virtual slaves. A three-part corporate structure thus evolved in this class-structured system under Spanish rule, with the landowning elite classes providing for the economy, supporting military forces providing for the enforcement of law and order (the suppression of any and all Indian revolts), and the Catholic Church providing a moral cloak and justification for the process by looking out for "the best interests of the Indians." The Church preached resignation to the masses, reinforcing the position that if God had made them poor, it would be a sin to question why. Poverty was also said to have its reward in the next life.

The isolation of this part of Latin America from the outside world during the next several centuries after the discovery of the Americas, combined with the immense distances required for travel and communications by ship, horseback, or on foot, meant that Guatemala was largely unaffected by the powerful modernizing forces stirring elsewhere in the Western Hemisphere, with their thrusts toward representative government and participation on the part of the local population. In contrast to the North American colonies and England and their evolving concepts of limited and representative government, religious and political pluralism, and new, capitalist-based enterprising middle classes, the Captaincy-General of Guatemala essentially remained authoritarian, feudal, and elitist in every respect. While the wars for independence from the Spanish crown swept most of Latin America from 1807 to 1824, these were wars of separation rather than genuine social revolutions and the basic structures of authority and society continued as they essentially had been doing for centuries.

Initially led by caudillo-style men-on-horseback leaders, the new countries of Central America adopted the forms of democracy but not its substance. Constitutions often provided for representative and democratic institutions, separation of powers, and bills of rights in societies where these traditions were largely lacking and where the dominant structures had always been closed, authoritarian and highly centralized. The constitutions thus failed to serve as a check on those in power. Rather than instituting democratic rule, as had taken hold in the United States to the north, the founding fathers in Central America were chiefly concerned with preserving existing hierarchies, privileges, and their authoritarian and non-democratic institutions of the past, which they fully intended to dominate and exploit. In turn, concepts of land ownership and labor evolved from that of the encomienda with its tribute-paying Indians to that of the *hacienda* whereby the Indian workers were bound to the landed estate through debt peonage. With the throwing off of the reigns of Spanish crown control, there was no longer a state to look after Indian interests and they now found themselves under the jurisdiction and at the complete mercy of the land owner or *hacendado*.

Amidst the insecurity caused by a series of civil wars which followed independence in Central America, the Guatemalan hacienda stood firm, a bastion for its owner and a refuge of sorts for its many inhabitants. In addition, the local power structures tended to remain intact and unchanged from the previous centuries and slavery for the Indians was replaced not by freedom but by servile labor. Two political parties, Conservative and Liberal, came into play towards the latter part of the 19th Century. The Conservatives tended to ignore the Indians and the Liberals, apart from the desire to exploit them for their labor potential, regarded them as impediments to national development.

Under the caudillo-rule of Justo Rufino Barrios during the early 1870s modern capitalism was introduced into Guatemala in the form of large-scale exportation of coffee. Indian communal holdings, planted in corn, beans and other staples, were found to be some of the best land suited for coffee farming and duly appropriated by the state and private parties interested in expanding their coffee plantation holdings. In their stead a coffee elite or oligarchy rapidly developed. In addition, a system of railroads was constructed to accelerate coffee production and, by linking the coffee plantations to the Atlantic and Pacific Oceans, integrated Guatemala into the world market more closely than ever before. Spiraling coffee production soon diminished the amount of land, labor and capital available to produce food for local consumption and a coffee monoculture became the dominant characteristic of the economy.

Continuously stripped of their communal lands, the Indians now became little more than menial wage laborers. Contract wage labor in turn became debt peonage, tying the Indians and their descendants to the landowner through debt. The wages paid for such labor never really quite sufficed to liquidate the debt. Indian sons inherited their father's debts, which they in turn were forced to pay off in a subtle system of virtual slavery. To maintain the system, the familiar corporatist structure of the rural aristocracy or landowners, the Catholic Church and the army worked in tandem to preserve their respective class privileges, prestige, wealth and power.

Landlords tended to be patrimonial chiefs who ruled family, servants, workers, tenant farmers, sharecroppers, and peasants living on their lands and in the vicinity of the plantation with absolute authority. Peasants were expected to not only grow and market cheap food products but also to sell their labor skills cheaply to the local landowners. The vastness of most of the estates, their relative isolation from the seat of national government, the relative weakness of the local or provincial bureaucrats that existed and the propensity of the government to side with the landed class all strengthened the landlord's power over the Indians. In short, the liberalism of the day, which promised a theoretical garden of happiness, became of jungle of perpetual poverty. Indians were viewed as barbaric at worst and childlike creatures at best, to be exploited at every opportunity. The landowners justified their attitudes toward the Indian masses, which made up at least half of the Guatemalan population, by characterizing them as slow, lazy and despicable, and incapable of self-direction.

During the latter part of the nineteenth century, a revolt by one Indian tribe in reaction to their lands being placed in the hands of a newly arrived mestizo group (called "ladinos") by a state-appointed provincial governor spread to other provinces, but was brutally put down. From that point on, or from the 1870s on into the early 1940s with little interruption, iron-fisted, brutal, thug-like dictators, such as Manuel Estrada Cabrera, tended to rule Guatemala for periods sometimes lasting up to twenty years. Yet, throughout this period and despite their many hardships, involving chronic deprivation, a hand to mouth existence and no apparent solution to their problem, large numbers of Indian groups clung tenaciously to their own indigenous beliefs and culture.

A major break in the situation came about as a result of the world-market crash of 1929-30 and the ensuing decade of the Great Depression which created a considerable amount of dissatisfaction amongst the small, but gradually rising mestizo middle classes over the apparent failure of the traditional elitist system of control to deal with the crisis. During this time, in an effort to appease the coffee growers and energize the Guatemalan economy, the government of General Jorge Ubico imposed a mandatory work law on the Indian population, which from

1936 to 1944 ensured that all Indians who were not titled owners of five acres of agricultural land (most were not) would be declared vagrants and would have to work in the form of manual labor at least 150 days a year. Even those with some land had to work 100 days or enough time to cover the three month coffee harvest period. Each Indian carried a passbook in which their work record was recorded. In effect. Ubico had nationalized control of the Indian labor force. This now provided virtually free labor for coffee and sugar plantation owners. Incredibly, as World War II came on, the majority of the people in the Guatemalan society were still toiling as their ancestors had done for some four hundred years under the feudal yoke of a handful of elite farmers.

But what was the Catholic Church's role in all this? Simply put, the Church's morality stopped at the collection plate; the coffee growers could afford to tithe the Church and the coffee pickers and workers, the Indians, could not. For this reason the Church had decided it was not going to prejudice its assured source of income over the issue of the treatment of God's multitude. Moral justification for its position was rationalized by declaring that inequality in Guatemala was "divine permission for the wealthy to be masters and fathers of the less fortunate."

Following the Great Depression, Guatemala found itself exposed to the values being promulgated by the United States as part of its World War II propaganda campaign to seize the moral "high ground" and rally all of Latin America in support of the Allies and the just cause of democracy against fascism. This extraordinary outpouring of wartime propaganda in favor of U.S. democracy and the American standards, values and way of life was characterized as "democracy versus tyranny" and was orchestrated by Nelson Rockefeller's Office of the Coordinator of Inter-American Affairs (OCIAA). By the end of the war, the Latin American press, radio and the film industry had been heavily influenced and otherwise penetrated by these U.S. values. While the traditional interests of the United States in Latin America had been geopolitical and strategic in terms of defense against external attack or internal subversion by a foreign enemy, it was argued early on in the war that democracies in Latin America would be more stable, peaceful and friendly than dictatorships.

Accordingly, it was the promotion of democracy and its related liberal reforms and values that was in the long-term strategic and economic interests of Washington. Guatemala, with its tradition of authoritarian and often brutal dictatorships, fell neatly into this effort as a naturally targeted country. Impacting heavily on Guatemala's middle and lower sectors of society, as well as some parts of the military, were Franklin Roosevelt's war-time propaganda in the form of the "Four Freedoms," which espoused freedom of speech, freedom of worship, freedom from want, and freedom from fear. These basic human rights espoused by the United States contrasted blatantly with the tyrannical systems of government and society that the country had known for most of its existence.

Basing their movement on the ideas of freedom and democracy espoused by Roosevelt in the early 1940s, his New Deal programs of the 1930s, and on the example of liberal social and economic reforms promulgated by the presidency of Lazaro Cardenas in Mexico during the late-1930s, the small Guatemalan middle class of ladinos, consisting of doctors, lawyers, teachers and students among others, and a group of young, reform-minded army officers sponsored a series of rebellions to oust Ubico and his supporters from the government and form a new nation based on the principles of justice. The end result of the process was the open election of Juan Jose Arevalo as president in 1945 with over 80 percent of the vote.

Arevalo's government, which sought constructive domestic reform, went to work to eliminate the semi-feudal systems of peonage and forced labor and in their place establish a system of judicial procedures and laws in the form of labor codes to protect workers' rights. The right to strike, collective bargaining, restrictions on child and female labor, minimum wages and a sixty-hour week were to be adjudicated by special labor courts whose purpose was to resolve labor-management disputes. One law obligated large landowners to lease uncultivated land at low rates to landless peasants (called "campesinos"). Legal support was also given to the formation of cooperatives and labor unions as well as to organizations of professionals and business people.

By 1950, the government had enacted minimum wage and severance pay laws and even established a social security system, which provided injury compensation, maternity benefits and health care. Trade unions were created and the political system was opened up to encourage multiple political parties and interest groups to organize. Indicative of the growing strength of the rural workers and campesinos was the election of Indian mayors in about half (twenty-two) of the forty-five predominantly Indian communities in the highlands. In addition, Arevalo encouraged a free press. Parallel to this were the ongoing efforts through a literacy campaign to provide a basic education through the establishment of a government-sponsored, rural school system and the enhancement of the overall health of the diverse Indian tribal groups so that they might be better incorporated into the larger body politic; thus enhancing the concept of a single nation of Guatemalans. To bring this about the government established a series of agencies in the rural areas to foster patriotism and nationalism.

Nonetheless, while all these reforms were readily in accord with U.S. standards, they were perceived as very threatening to the privileged ladino minority and especially the landowning coffee elites and their supporting conservative wing of the Guatemalan army, who saw their control of the political system and its status quo being gradually eroded. As a result there were almost two-dozen assassination attempts against Arevalo before he finally turned over his presidential office in 1951 to Jacabo Arbenz, a reform-minded army colonel who was also democratically elected with about two-thirds of the popular vote. It was the first time in Guatemalan history that a democratically elected candidate in an open election had succeeded another democratically elected president!

Arbenz was from the nationalist, reformist wing of the Guatemalan military who accelerated the pace of the reform effort, picking up where Arevalo had left off. When he came to office he was confronted by a situation in which only 2 percent of the population or roughly 300 families owned 70 percent of the best arable land. Of that land, only a quarter was actually under cultivation and was worked by Indians who for the most part only earned around $100 annually or something less than $10 a month (about 40 cents a day or 4 cents per hour). He perceived his presidential mandate as being one of promoting political reforms in tandem with economic reforms to uplift Guatemalan society and its standard of living as a whole and to transform the nation from a predominantly feudal economy into that of a modern, capitalist one. In this regard he knew that an expanded democracy could only work if economic reforms provided land for the destitute rural workers. Economic growth was to be primarily capitalist, but influenced and controlled from the national level initially.

This essentially meant that each and every campesino worker could now become a capitalist, landowning farmer, producing whatever crops he wanted, and disposing of them in any manner he wanted. To this end Arbenz sought to break the economic and political power of the coffee elite who controlled the countryside and the international or foreign interests who owned and operated the nation's largest public utilities and agricultural properties. As such, the centerpiece of Arbenz's own program, an extension of the reforms initiated by Arevalo, was agrarian reform which was passed into law in 1952. The land reform was egalitarian and all encompassing and *everyone* would have to comply with the law.

The Agrarian Reform Law stated that all uncultivated land on estates over 250 acres, where less than two-thirds of the estate was under cultivation, would be subject to expropriation and redistribution, with compensation being paid against the declared real estate tax value in the form of government bonds. No one, not even the president himself, was to be excluded or exempted (Arbenz's family had 1,700 acres expropriated by the government under the law)! As such, it was probably the first time in Guatemalan history that it had been acknowledged that no one was above the law.

As a result Indian communities began to petition the government for land and by 1954 some 100,000 families or about a half million out of Guatemala's three million Indians began receiving titled land totaling some 1.5 million acres. This often amounted to about 10.5 acres per family or enough to make an adequate living. In addition, access to credit was provided by the government to provide tools, seeds and fertilizers. The agrarian reform program, in conjunction with those reforms of the Arevalo government, caused Guatemalan exports to jump from $20 million in 1943 to over $100 million in 1954! The synergistic affect of the Arevalo-Arbenz reforms was a virtual emancipation proclamation akin to what Abraham Lincoln had brought about for Afro-Americans inside the United States at the time of the American Civil War. As in

America, it was one thing to proclaim emancipation with suitable supporting laws, but it was another to make it stick.

Over time more than a thousand coffee and cotton plantations had to exchange excess land for ten-year government bonds as compensation. The agrarian reform law also gave resident workers on all estates with excess land first priority for settlement on those lands expropriated under the law. This, of course, brought them into head-to-head confrontation with the large landowners who not only resented the potential financial loss to themselves but also the fact that their prestige and social status of being big land holders was being diminished. That the campesinos were now being elevated to a coequal status in terms of also owning land was too much for the elite coffee growers to accept; given that they had been accustomed to obeying the laws of the land only insofar as they deemed them convenient, but otherwise ignoring them at will (*Obedezco pero no cumplo* - "I obey but I do not comply" was an enduring cultural value that had been passed down over the centuries from Spanish colonial times, acknowledging the government's authority without enforcing its will). With Arbenz's virtual revolution in capitalism and human rights-based laws inevitably reaching out and touching almost all of Guatemalan society, the reform effort was now perceived by the coffee elite as being a direct threat to themselves and everything they stood for. In turn they lashed back as best they knew how, forming violent vigilante groups and conspiring to overthrow the government.

The coffee elite was well-connected with the U.S. Embassy in Guatemala City and it cleverly used its numerous contacts to conjure up and allege that it was a victim of a massive plot on the part of Arbenz to steal its privately owned lands as part of an insidious Communist revolution which was now giving power to the workers. In addition, the elites many contacts within the Guatemalan army were utilized to build an anti-reform opposition throughout portions of the officer corps and play on the latter's fears that they too would be victims of the Arevalo-Arbenz policies. The army at this time was increasingly concerned that Washington would not sell it any weapons and equipment left over from World War II. Further reinforcing its concern was the fact that almost from the inception of Arbenz having been elected president, the U.S. Department of State had been attempting to isolate Guatemala diplomatically.

Despite the top-down authority that the president of a Latin American country was normally able to wield on behalf of his interests, Arbenz unexpectedly came up against an unforeseen nemesis in the form of the international banana plantation monopoly inside Guatemala known as the United Fruit Company (UFCO). In addition to its immense land holdings in the southeastern portion of Guatemala of up to a half million acres and the nation's biggest land holder, the Boston-based company also controlled the only overland transportation route and railway between Guatemala City and the Caribbean coast. As part of its carefully built up infrastructure which had evolved over a period of thirty years, the company also owned the Puerto Barrios docking facilities at the terminus of its railroad and most of the ships which serviced the port as part of its banana shipping fleet. Another UFCO investment was in the form of subsidiaries of the company which controlled a major portion of the country's electrical energy and international radio communications systems.

Of its extensive land holdings of some 550,000 acres only about 140,000 acres were actually employed to grow bananas; the remainder of the land being fallow. The Arbenz government wanted to expropriate the unused portion of the company's lands and offered UFCO $1.2 million in compensation, based on the company's earlier self-assessed, but considerably undervalued real estate tax valuation of the land at $3-an-acre. UFCO wanted $16 million, claiming the land was worth at least $75-an-acre, but the government remained intransigent and insisted on paying the lower price. In addition, Arbenz was working to counter the company's monopoly control and ownership of transportation, electricity and port facilities by announcing his intention to build electrical plant facilities for Guatemala City to supply energy at cheaper rates and build a new road out to a new Santo Tomas port facility on the Caribbean coast to compete with UFCO's own railroad lines and port facilities. In pursuing its goal of forcing all foreign businesses to respect the Guatemalan government's laws, a first ever audit of UFCO's railroad company's books revealed that the company owed over $10 million in back taxes.

UFCO responded to the government's initiatives by placing its full weight behind an anti-reform press campaign with appeals to Washington for help. If it could not get its $16 million, then its basic idea was to discredit Arbenz and ultimately bring about his ouster in order to recapture its now potentially lost lands from the agrarian reform program and to maintain its dominance over Guatemala's Caribbean focused transportation and port systems. Assisting UFCO in its efforts was Secretary of State John Foster Dulles and his brother Allen who was serving as the Director, Central Intelligence Agency (CIA); both of whom had done legal work on behalf of UFCO as part of the law firm, Sullivan and Cromwell during the 1930s. At this time John Moors Cabot, an Assistant Secretary of State for Inter-American affairs, had actual holdings in UFCO and his brother Thomas had served as president of the corporation in 1948. In addition, the U.S. ambassador to the United Nations, Henry Cabot Lodge was a stockholder. While UFCO's connections to the Dulles brothers and the Washington establishment were extensive and undoubtedly influenced U.S. policy towards Guatemala, the Cold War's ideology and driving imperative of anti-Communism stemming in part from the virulent McCarthyism of the day decisively formed the ubiquitous perception that Arbenz's land reform was an attack on private property. Egged on by the coffee elite who hoped to bandwagon behind UFCO in calling Arbenz a "Communist," the major landowners throughout the country preferred security to change and were not prepared to risk their social and economic predominance and status for the sake of benevolent reforms for the poorer masses.

In addition to his problems with UFCO, Arbenz's decision to legalize the Guatemalan Labor Party (a Communist party), as part of the opening up and liberalization of the political system to any and all parties, also caused him to bring several of the Labor Party's elected leaders into his government to assist in the implementation of the agrarian reform program; thus creating the basis for exacerbating his confrontation with the United States. Albeit the Labor Party only had a limited following and just four of its members in the fifty-six member national congress, Arbenz's actions now provided an open excuse to those in Washington to cast him as a "Communist" who was attempting to subvert Guatemala. John Peurifoy, then the U.S. ambassador to Guatemala, made the slanderous comment to that effect, claiming that "if Arbenz was not a Communist, he will certainly do until one comes along." Peurifoy had tried to get Arbenz to get rid of some of the democratically elected, Communist leaders of Guatemala's labor unions. The latter refused, saying that Guatemala was a democratic country and he could no more do that than the president of the United States could do that to the elected leaders of the American Federation of Labor (AFL) and Congress of Industrial Organizations (CIO).

Also damaging Arbenz's image in Washington's eyes was a May 1954 Soviet-bloc shipment of Czech-made weapons for the Guatemalan army, which had been under a six-years long American arms embargo from any purchases from non-Communist countries. With U.S. pressures also denying Guatemala access to arms suppliers in Western Europe, Arbenz had turned to Czechoslovakia as a last resort to equip his army on a par with the other countries in Central America. As the arms shipment came to light, the CIA's Allen Dulles deliberately misconstrued the arms shipment to signify that the Guatemalan government was now a threat to the Panama Canal. Despite the similarities between Roosevelt's New Deal and Arbenz's reform programs, the U.S. government had arbitrarily decided that the Guatemalan president would have to be removed from power one way or another. The die was now cast, as the Washington diplomatic community, including the CIA, concentrated on turning the Guatemalan military against their president.

Using a CIA-sponsored PSYOP's campaign of clandestine radio broadcasts out of Honduras, commencing in May 1954, the Agency convinced both Arbenz and his army supporters that the Guatemalan government was facing an invading army supported by the full might of the United States. In turn, the army's officers were given the coercive alternative by Peurifoy of changing sides (against Arbenz) or suffering the consequences. Given that the United States had weighed in against the government, the Guatemalan army's officer corps felt they had little choice in the matter. Brilliantly conceived and executed, the propaganda effort conjured up the image of some 5,000 troops backed up with flame throwers crossing the Honduran boarder into eastern Guatemala. In reality the force consisted in the main of about 150 old men and boys, led by two former Guatemalan army officers opposed to the Arbenz reforms. These were supposed to link up with another 150 paramilitary members who had been sponsored by anti-Arbenz elements within the

Guatemalan army and were scattered throughout the country. With a handful of mercenary pilots running psychologically damaging aerial bombing raids to cause panic and intimidate the army and Arbenz's supporters, the Guatemalan government fell apart at the end of June. Arbenz then resigned and went into exile. An obscure army colonel named Carlos Castillo Armas, the leader of the invading "army" and sponsored by the United States, now took control of the government.

While the CIA's operation to bring down the Arbenz government had been eminently successful, it was based on a tragic misreading of Guatemala's nationalist, reform aspirations and a gross misunderstanding of the socio-economic condition of the mass of the people. In short, the Arevalo-Arbenz democratic initiatives, which had finally brought Guatemala out of its feudal past and for the first time in its history had given real hope to the majority of its population for a better life, had been sabotaged. There would be no four freedoms, no political and economic equality, no uplifting of society, and no emancipation of the masses. Castillo Armas now became the new president, promising to make Guatemala a "showcase for democracy." Unfortunately, this was not to happen and his administration rescinded most of the reform laws, requiring virtually all of the new small land owners to give up their properties. In essence, the U.S. government had helped destroy democracy in order to save it.

The immediate aftermath of the quashing of the ten-year reform movement, once again saw the resurgence of the rigid hierarchical structures of society, feudal patterns of land ownership and the ruthless exploitation of the Mayan Indian communities. The right to vote was restricted to only the literate citizenry, thereby disenfranchising the vast majority of the Guatemalan population and annulling their participation in national life. In addition, the flourishing labor unions, agrarian committees and political parties which had developed under the Arevalo-Arbenz administrations were declared illegal, dismantled by the hundreds and ruthlessly suppressed, setting the stage for a militant left that drew the conclusion that no peaceful, middle road to reform was possible inside Guatemala. The end result of the Dulles brothers' efforts meant that any manifestation of grass-roots Guatemalan nationalism or economic independence, any desire for social change, any intellectual curiosity, and any interest in liberal reforms would be categorized as "Communism" and subject to repression in one way or another.

Virtually all of the reforms initiated during the ten years from 1945 to 1954 had now been reversed and the social structure of Guatemala remained built around land, owned by the fortunate few and worked by the miserable many. Thus ended the "ten years of spring" and the first genuine democratic movement in Guatemala's history. Two years after Arbenz was driven out of Guatemala, the American Federation of Labor was reporting that the plantation workers were once again living in "conditions of servitude if not actual slavery," working sometimes up to 80 hours a week and earning only 50 cents a day. It was not a good situation and only awaited a revolutionary catalyst to spark a violent alternative.

Ironically during the early 1960s, John F. Kennedy had discerned what this type of situation could lead to, stating that: "Those who make peaceful change impossible, make violent change inevitable." As such, he promulgated the Alliance for Progress, which advocated almost with out exception the same reform programs that had been put in place in Guatemala just ten years earlier by Arevalo and Arbenz! The Department of State too was now advocating reforms involving labor codes, land reform, the right to vote, systems of law and justice, and social equality for all people throughout the region. Kennedy's program also had a parallel counterinsurgency component. In addition to seeking out and destroying guerrillas, the public image of the host country's army was to be enhanced by promoting a new spirit of cooperation with the people in the form of community development, which stressed civic action in which the nation's soldiers would promote community development in the form of construction projects involving roads, wells and irrigation projects among others. Nonetheless, the question as to how much damage had actually been done to Guatemalan society as a whole by Washington's anti-Arbenz policies and how the overthrow of the legitimate Arbenz government might foment the development of a revolutionary backlash was soon answered in the years that followed.

During the early 1960s and inspired by Fidel Castro's successes in Cuba, disaffected army officers joined by other disillusioned reformists founded Guatemala's first modern guerrilla-insurgency organizations, which were initially focused on the eastern part of Guatemala near the

Honduran frontier. In the main these were the former ladino Arevalo-Arbenz reformists who had lost faith in peaceful, legal methods of social and economic change for their society and, out of frustration, had begun to accept the necessity of armed struggle as the only solution to a series of newly-formed military dictatorships. When Castillo Armas was assassinated in 1957, General Miguel Ydigoras Fuentes became president. There followed a coup in 1963, led by Colonel Enrique Peralta Azurdia, that successfully blocked any chances of Juan Arevalo from returning to the presidency in a democratic election. The string of military presidents ruling as dictators continued until 1966 when Julio Mendez Montenegro was elected as a civilian president in response to pressures from the Alliance for Progress.

During this time the army took full advantage of U.S. military assistance for Guatemala to gradually turn itself into a formidable counterinsurgency force. In this case its primary attention was turned to the eastern part of Guatemala where, as Fidel Castro and Che Guevara had advocated, the new insurgency was concentrating its forces in *focos* or groups; the largest of which, known as the MR-13 (November 13 Revolutionary Movement), was located in the area of the town of Zacapa. Responding to intelligence reports as to what was going on and an earlier guerrilla ambush which resulted in the deaths of twelve soldiers, Colonel Carlos Arana's forces surrounded Zacapa and then proceeded to literally wipe it off the map, lock, stock and barrel, killing in the process several thousand or more men, women and children. The campaign was extremely brutal, but very effective in exterminating the 400 or so MR-13 guerrillas located in the region and crushing in its path the anti-government resistance in that part of Guatemala. The remnants of the surviving guerrilla forces dispersed for the most part into the capital area and other large towns. Every member of Arana's brigade received a silver "ZACAPA" badge, that he wore over the right-breast pocket of his uniform.

Conservative elements of Guatemalan society responded to the influx of the guerrilla remnants into the cities with political death squads made up of anti-reform and anti-Communist militants who had the backing of the army, police and business elites. Called the "White Hand" (*Mano Blanca*) a vicious series of murders and counter-murders took place in what was rapidly taking on the appearance of a civil war, affecting both the urban and rural areas alike. Over time another death squad, called "An Eye for an Eye" (*Ojo por Ojo*) also appeared, kidnapping and murdering suspected subversives at will. Professors, lawyers, students and moderate, reform-minded politicians were cut down by the dozen.

Throughout this time Guatemala was enjoying an unprecedented prosperity, very little of which trickled down below the middle class. As part of the aftermath of the overthrow of the Arbenz government and beginning in 1956, the follow-on governments to Castillo Armas championed the interests of the agro-export sector. Their initiatives, combined with the economic support garnered from the Alliance for Progress and other economic development programs of up to $200 million annually, fostered the introduction of new crops for export and modern technologies and industries. These processes resulted in a diversification of the economy away from its traditional export crops of coffee, cotton and bananas into sugar, cattle and meat products for American-based fast-food chains and opened up Guatemala to foreign investments in banking, mining, food processing, pharmaceuticals, oil refining, paper and metal tubing. Even in the highlands region the Indian population benefited to some degree from the appearance of new textile industries, producing clothing and tapestries, which were then sold to the ever growing influx of tourists as indigenous works of art. But when all was said and done, the new economy saw considerable modernization, but without social reform. In the highlands regions over a million people worked 14-hour days and endured back-breaking work, all the while suffering malaria, dysentery, pesticide poisoning, miserable rations and unsanitary living conditions in exchange for miserly wages.

By 1970 Colonel Carlos Arana Osorio, who was described by the Guatemalan reformists and writers on the left as the "butcher of Zacapa," had been elected president. Once in office he began a systematic effort using army, police and paramilitary forces to root out the guerrilla cells. It was a no-holds-barred situation and the guerrillas responded in kind with terrorist assassinations and kidnappings. Arana was a hard core anti-Communist who had sworn to eliminate all the guerrillas even "if it is necessary to turn the country into a cemetery in order to pacify it!" He made good on his pledge by declaring martial law and raiding the National University where several professors were murdered and another 1,600 people were arrested. Nonetheless, his attempts to wipe out and otherwise coerce the guerrillas and their supporters in both the urban and rural areas into a passive role in the face of the military dictatorship were not working. It was in the face of this situation that the U.S. Embassy in Guatemala city, in an effort to produce some sort of harmony and stability inside Guatemala and put a new face on the counter-guerrilla war, had pushed for some assistance from SOUTHCOM's 8th SFG, through the Department of State's International Military Education and Training (IMET) program.

In reviewing the implications of our area study for Guatemala, the big question for us was the Indian population. Where did it stand at this point in time: neutral, for, or against the government and its security forces? There were other questions concerning the identified insurgencies inside Guatemala. Besides the FAR elements inside the urban areas, there were indications that some guerrilla elements in the northeastern province of El Peten were operating, as well as other elements in the southern part of Guatemala and also in the northwestern highlands regions. In the main these appeared to be ladino guerrilla movements fighting against the government, while the Indians, who made up over half of the population and generally lived in the cooler highland regions, appeared to be generally uncommitted at this time.

Nonetheless, it was obvious to us, that having been granted basic freedoms, a new place in society in terms of social equality, and a taste of what it was like to be a real capitalist farmer under the agrarian reform programs of the early 1950s, and then having had all that taken away from them, the Indian masses had gone through a significant sociological awakening, involving increased expectations and a heightened political consciousness, that only needed to be tapped. To this end they only awaited another catalyst in the form of charismatic guerrilla leaders to mobilize them into action against the government to right the injustices that they had habitually endured. With an illiteracy rate of over 90 percent, working in abysmal conditions and earning less than $100 per year, the persistent poverty and discrimination that they faced made the rural Indian populations inside Guatemala a natural target for the formation of a formidable insurgency. Thus, in our minds, these indigenous groups of Mayan heritage would very likely be the key center of gravity in terms of winning or losing the guerrilla war. Whoever, be

The 9th PSYOPs Battalion, 8th Special Forces Group, mission to Guatemala during the spring of 1972. Left to right: the author, Capt. Leo Sanchez, Lt. Col. James Dandridge, Capt. Luis Santos, and Lt. John Buford. (U.S. Government photo)

it the government and its army or the guerrillas and their cadres, won the hearts and minds of this over one million people in Guatemala's rural outback would win the insurgency war. This was perhaps the most important aspect of the challenge facing our PSYOPs mission to Guatemala.

Jim Dandridge returned from Guatemala and informed the rest of the team, which included myself, Captains Leo Sanchez and Luis Santos, and Lieutenant John Buford and Sergeant First Class James Shavers, that we would be conducting our training mission in two phases. The first or instructional phase was to be a formal, two-week course in psychological operations conducted for all the operations officers (major, lieutenant colonel and colonel levels) of the Guatemalan army, navy and air force, as well as some military instructors from the army's Center of Military Studies inside Guatemala City. In all it was expected that there would be about thirty officer students taking our course. Because the second phase of the MTT, called an advisory phase, would involve developing a series of PSYOP area studies and related programs for selected regions of Guatemala, it was thought that the principal operations officer for each region would be best suited to undergo the course and sufficiently strong enough in terms of influence and rank to introduce our PSYOP concepts and ideas to their respective commanders and staffs. In addition, each member of the MTT would circulate into designated portions of the country to assist in the initial formulation of each of the regional PSYOPs programs. The two phases were intended to compliment each other and depended for their success on the ability of each team member, working with his former student(s), to see the initial effort through to fruition.

Unquestionably Jim Dandridge was the most knowledgeable about PSYOPs and a superb trainer. For that reason he was the strongest member of the team. He was followed by Luis Santos who had attended the Peruvian military academy in Lima, Peru, and had received a battlefield officer's commission in Vietnam from the 1st Infantry Division's Major General Bill DePuy. Leo Sanchez was born and raised in Texas and was of Mexican descent. Both Sanchez and Santos were native Spanish speakers, which was a welcome advantage for our mission. In John Buford's and my own case, we were only school-trained linguists, speaking Spanish with a typical mid-western accent, although I kidded John about his "Indiana twang." As we prepared and rehearsed our lesson plans, completed our informal area study and attended to the myriad of details that go into a deployment of this nature, we were informed that we would indeed deploy into Guatemala on the 4th of April or about a month after our original alert. On schedule we arrived at Guatemala City via a U.S. Air Force C-130 Hercules aircraft and began teaching our course some days later.

It was obvious to us upon arrival and in our initial presentation to our students in Guatemala City that we were going to learn as much about them and Guatemala as they were going to learn about ourselves and PSYOPs. Dandridge led off the course with an overview of where we were headed. It became readily apparent to the students almost from the onset of the course that PSYOPs was very interested in dealing with the potential key center(s) of gravity which could influence decisively the outcome of an insurgency war - the people's leaders at the grass roots. We were very definitely dealing with a battle for the minds and allegiance of the local population and at the same time attempting to diminish the ability of the Guatemalan insurgents to convince them that their goals and aspirations were identical to those of the guerrilla cause. As such, we explained and attempted to demonstrate over those first several days that an insurgency occurs only where an environment of discontent can be utilized by subversive elements to foment an active revolt.

As part of the justification for their effort inside Guatemala at that time, the guerrilla groups were asserting that the people's interests were not being served by the government and its supporting elites. To this end the insurgents were seizing upon perceived government corruption, nepotism, incompetence, lack of justice, and especially the latter's use of vicious repression in order to maintain the status quo as the fundamental elements of a *just cause* for revolt. That the indigenous Mayan Indian groups appeared to be economically marginalized and unable to break out of their perpetual condition of relative abject poverty, were excluded for the most part from the political process, and had had most if not all of their aspirations for socio-economic and political progress quashed at virtually every turn, contributed immeasurably to an impression that the government was indeed unworthy of their confidence and, worse, unworthy of leading them. This loss of legitimacy on the part of the government was a guerrilla agitator's dream situation, ready for exploitation. If a charismatic leader could provide a logical, if not militant plan to rectify the perceived injustices, and the plan was acceptable to a popular following, the insurgency would then be underway.

In terms of our students it was important for each and every member of our course to return to their respective regions to accurately analyze, assess and identify the susceptibility of the various socio-economic and ethnic groups to PSYOPs and to determine against whom, as target audiences, the government and military could effectively direct propaganda to achieve both national and military aims. They would also have to determine the causes of popular discontent and potential areas that could be readily converted into discontent by an insurgent force and used against the government. Of particular interest in this regard were causes of friction and animosity between workers and plantation owners and cultural clashes between distinct ethnic groups. It was not so much an issue of identity that bothered the Indian groups inside Guatemala, but obtaining justice and achieving economic and political equality with the rest of society. And this had to be taken into consideration. They had achieved these uplifting goals for a few years under the Arbenz administration of the 1950s, only to find them abruptly quashed and their society returned to its former conditions of servitude. On this note we noted other potential causes of discontent, involving the lack of interest on the part of the government at both the national and local levels to the needs of the people. This meant that the attitudes of governing elites needed to be evaluated in terms of how they looked upon their fellow countrymen, and the military itself would have to undergo a critical self-examination to analyze its own relationship to Guatemalan society.

As part of their respective regional area studies each student was to determine to as large an extent as possible who the key communicators were by individuals or groups and what media (face-to-face voice, radio, or printed matter) was most suitable to reach out to them as target audiences. A key communicator was typically a person who was superior to the remainder of the target group in terms of age, social status, intelligence or some other kind of competence, or a combination of these attributes and served as a role model of sorts for the community in question. The more people respected, admired and otherwise identified with the key communicator, the more persuasive influence the PSYOP operator would potentially garner by working through and convincing the key communicator that the operator's (e.g. the army's) perspective was correct and in the best interests of his followers.

As the course went on and the students began to delve into what would constitute an area study, we realized that the Guatemalan Indian society was actually fairly complex, with some *twenty-one* distinct Mayan linguistic communities having been identified; the largest of which were the Quiches, the Cakchiquels, the Tzutujils, the Mams, and the Quekchis among others. In every case the village was the primary reference point and the focus of loyalty for most of the highland Indians. Village life revolved around those communal lands that still existed, providing food, a sense of security, and connecting the people to their gods. Apart from their native tongues, these communities had an illiteracy rate of over 90 percent. Nonetheless, an Indian identity was beginning to evolve with distinct styles of clothing delineating the region from which the wearer was from. The few educated and literate members of this community formed a corps of Spanish-speaking Indians who often served as leaders for their various groups and were thought to have a broader perspective on life. These were potential key communicators. Unfortunately, a few of the better educated Indian leaders were also reported as being part of the insurgency effort inside Guatemala.

Nonetheless, the pure Mayan communities as a whole did not trust the ladino or mestizo communities and the latter looked down upon the former. With ladinos running much of Guatemala it was easy to see that frictions among the two primary ethnic groups could easily form and potentially be exploited by any subversive force so inclined. As our initial MTT area study had depicted, Guatemala's feudal organization of society from colonial times still found the country divided into the conquered (Indians) and the conquerors (ladinos). The ladino landowning elites, especially the coffee plantation elite, looked to the government and its military to maintain law and order and keep the indigenous Indian workers in line. In turn, Indians were considered as beasts of burden who should be treated with animal brutality in order to preserve society's structure of elites and masses. To change or even modify these attitudes and the corresponding socio-economic and political condition would be a major challenge for our MTT, and far greater than what we could have ever imagined.

An important aspect of a successful PSYOPs effort involved the individual Guatemalan soldier and his comportment towards the local population within the region where he served. His individual actions toward the civilian population would generally spell the difference between success and failure - success if he was soldierly, fair, helpful, and kind; and failure if his actions were heedless, thoughtless, and cruel. In short, it was the creation of good will between the military and the civilian population that needed to be brought about, developing among the people a confidence in the legal government, instead of the all too often traditional relationships of distrust and outright fear. To do this the individual soldier needed to understand and visualize the situation of the target audience. In the case of the Guatemalan army, the individual soldier tended to mirror the attitudes of his leaders, and especially those of the officers above him. In short, the officers were key communicators for the rank and file down the chain of command. And here was a prickly point of concern for successful PSYOPs inside Guatemala.

The Guatemalan officer corps of approximately a thousand officers was generally the product of their national military academy (Escuela Politecnica) experience, which promoted unquestioning obedience to higher authority and patriotism above all else. As such, the cadets spent much of their four years preparing themselves for military command and, as the historical situation might provide, even rule of the Guatemalan state as the president of the nation. Every "*tanda*" or annual graduating class was expected to be ready for this eventuality. Nonetheless, there were no courses in public administration, management, systems of legal justice, economics, or even the law of land warfare. Training for the most part was geared to physical readiness preparation and infantry tactics, including those taught under the auspices of USARSA, which sponsored for many of the graduating classes a course in jungle operations and tactics at the U.S. Army's Fort Sherman inside the Canal Zone.

As part of the indoctrination process at the military academy, cadets tended to look down upon their ladino civilian counterparts as disorganized and incompetent. This developed a "we-they" attitude of disrespect towards an important segment of Guatemalan society. Undoubtedly this attitude stemmed in large part from the great disparity in salaries, whereby a new second lieutenant could expect a salary of less than a $100 per month, compared to the $400 or more earned by his civilian contemporary in the commercial sector. This attitude was reinforced by the fact that a colonel with over twenty years in service was earning little more than $500 per month. Certainly it was not a great incentive to look forward to in terms of a prosperous career and most officers only grudgingly accepted their economic situation as part and parcel of their patriotic duty to the nation, moderated from time to time when the opportunity of obtaining a government position with offsetting perks presented itself. Accustomed to exemptions and immunity from the jurisdiction of civil courts, in the tradition of the old Spanish *fuero militar,* attitudes towards civilians in general were not good and attitudes towards Indians were far worse.

The great mass of the Indians as an ethnic group and class were not only looked down upon as inferiors, but also as a negative element within the social fabric of the country. The dehumanizing value of ladino society which stressed that Indians did not count for anything and were but chattel to be exploited was reflected in attitudes further reinforced at the military academy. It became immediately apparent to us that these were especially negative attitudes and a challenge that the PSYOPs course would have to meet and hopefully change, if our approach for dealing with an insurgency was to be successful. We would somehow have to change the core values and attitudes of our students and, in turn, the army officer corps from that of a "we-they" perspective of superiors and inferiors to one of genuine concern for the interests of each and every member of the population and a shared value that all members of Guatemala's society were equally important and worthy of mutual support and respect.

To fight the evolving insurgencies inside Guatemala we advocated as part of our course the winning of the population's willing cooperation and denying the guerrillas their sympathy. To accomplish this required an imaginative program of village assistance, properly backed by the military and civilian authorities, which in itself would constitute a form of psychological operations. Specific measures to be implemented involved the formation of a village doctor and the construction of a medical clinic, which would support a general sanitation program to eliminate disease, waste and garbage, as well as provide for potable drinking water; the initiation of a basic educational program for both adults and children, using bilingual teachers to better establish a language tie between the people and the rest of Guatemalan society; the teaching of proper agricultural techniques (use of fertilizers, irrigation and crop rotation etc) to further develop farming and productive capacity to the maximum; and improve the general infrastructure and market access of the villages via rural road networks, electrification, and a system of cheap transportation. Keeping in mind that there is always resentment to change, all this would have to be done with tact and respect for indigenous customs, as well as working through the key communicators within each village and regional group.

In addition, the government would have to see to it that the Indian's interests and rights were protected in the same manner as the rest of society. This would also have to include the right to vote and participation in Guatemala's political processes at all levels: village, municipal and national. The end result of a successful effort over the long term would be to gain and retain the active support of the general population, all the while building national morale and confidence in the government and isolating the insurgents from the people who represented the latter's primary source of recruits, information and supplies.

While our students could see the logic in our approach to dealing with the Guatemalan insurgency situation, it also meant that there would have to be a pro-active change in attitude on the part of the Guatemalan national government and the military in terms of sponsoring reform and convincing the economic elites, especially the plantation owners, that welcoming the Indian population as an equal and integral part of society was not only critically important but beneficial as a whole. It meant shifting away from the previous methods of coercion and repression to those of actually trying to uplift society as a whole. In short, we were teaching a top down, comprehensive approach to PSYOPs, which had to begin with a national development program that would eventually reach out to each and every community throughout Guatemala. Guatemala City as the seat of government would have to link itself through the various provinces (departments) to the society's grass roots with meaningful reforms. Winning the guerrilla war in itself was not enough. It was *how* one went about it that made the difference. As one student astutely observed, we were advocating an "Arbenz solution" for dealing with the guerrilla wars inside Guatemala - and how right he was!

After a weekend break that marked the mid-point in the course, one of the older colonels returned that next Monday morning brimming with enthusiasm, if not outright joy. He informed us that in discussing with his family the thrust of our course and our ideas for reaching out to the population as a whole, much to his surprise he had positively touched a sensitive chord amongst his wife and daughters, winning considerable admiration and approval for himself and breaking down what had been a wall of little or no communication between them, which had been getting worse over the years. If nothing else we had at least one convert to PSYOPs in Guatemala.

The second week of the course found the students continuing to work on their respective area studies, while at the same time they learned about PSYOP campaign planning and how to focus the various mediums of communication on their target audiences which in general consisted of the Guatemalan government and its personnel, the civilian population, and the insurgents. A certain element of esteem and respect had been developed between the students and ourselves as instructors and this was important since we were about to shift into our advisory role and would have to depend on our former students to help convince the remainder of the officer corps key leadership that through a PSYOP approach the insurgency could be defeated and the nation brought together as a cohesive and united whole.

There was not a great deal of fanfare at the graduation ceremony at the end of the last day of classes. As we bid the students farewell, one could see in their eyes a certain sense of determination and the realization that the task ahead was not going to be an easy one. We had taught but *one course* in PSYOPs to less than 3 percent of the officer corps of the Guatemalan army and the question was: how receptive would the other 97 percent be? What about the rest of the government? What about the plantation owners and the rest of society? Only time would reveal the answer.

On the 24th of April the four of us fanned out over Guatemala for a period of about two weeks as part of the Phase II PSYOPs advisory effort. With Guatemala being an area about the size of Tennessee, we had to travel extensively by road and sometimes by plane in order to reach out to the half dozen or more military regions concerned. To this end we had been tasked with completing on site the area study for each of our respective regions being visited, which had been initiated during the PSYOPs course, developing and implementing an intelligence collection plan, and assisting and advising our Guatemalan counterparts on the development of a PSYOPs plan for their particular area. Jim Dandridge remained behind to work with the Guatemalan army general staff to promote the concept of a national PSYOP plan, which would provide a clear focus as to what would be expected nationwide, lay down guide lines and responsibilities for subordinate units to develop their own PSYOPs-related plans and operations, and generally coordinate the effort between civilian and military agencies. Nonetheless, the one member of our MTT who had the most difficult challenge was Captain Luis Santos.

Captain Santos arrived on 25 April in Poptun, the headquarters of an army infantry brigade in the southern part of the relatively remote, jungle covered province of Peten. This was a vast, tropical area which included the famous Mayan ruins of Tikal, but was otherwise sparsely inhabited by Ket'Chi speaking Indians. It was also an area known for its mahogany wood, chicle and oil exploration. As a mere captain in rank, Luis immediately found himself having to deal with two hard-nosed Guatemalan army colonels (Castillo and Marroquin) who held tenaciously to the belief that the best PSYOPs program in the country constituted a bullet being drilled between the eyes of each and every guerrilla.

Nevertheless, there had been few contacts with the guerrillas and it was known that there was some discontent among the *campesino* farmers over the government's land distribution program. In addition, the only radio stations that could be listened to inside the Peten were Radio Belize and Radio Havana. Neither the colonels nor any member of their staffs had attended the MTT course in Guatemala City, which was a clear disadvantage to promoting PSYOP. Nevertheless, through persistent and ultimately convincing presentations about the value of PSYOPs for fighting guerrillas, Santos not only established his credentials as a full-fledged professional but also convinced the colonels sufficiently so as to allow him to demonstrate by example how a PSYOP campaign could actually be conducted.

Relying heavily on his own personal reconnaissance, understanding of the culture and the intelligence information reported by the various unit staff officers and some civilians throughout the region, Luis worked in close cooperation with the operations (S-3) section in Peten to develop a campaign, targeting the guerrillas suspected to be members of the Rebel Armed Forces (*Fuerzas Armadas Revolutionarias* - FAR) in the outback. To accomplish this they had to identify the sociological, economic and political factors that had influenced the individual insurgents to join together and fight, all the while enduring a multitude of hardships. The idea or theme, which was the link between the propaganda opportunity as revealed by the intelligence collected and the behavior pattern which these psychological operators were attempting to understand, was to focus on the guerrilla's hardships. These concerned short-term susceptibilities, involving a lack of supplies, adverse living and medical conditions, unsympathetic leadership, and a longing to return to their loved ones and families. It was hoped that this would have the affect of depressing their morale, reducing their combat efficiency and ultimately encouraging defection. As time went on it was found necessary to make use of the U.S. Embassy's Julio Mendizabal (one of the principal supporters of the Green Beret PSYOPs effort inside Guatemala) and his United States Information Service (USIS), which taped a number of key messages and native music under ideal acoustical conditions, thereby precluding the distortion or background noise which one frequently encountered in this type of endeavor under field conditions.

Having completed their preparations and using 250 watt loudspeakers mounted in a Cessna aircraft, PSYOPs messages were broadcast by Santos and his Guatemalan counterparts for some days throughout selected zones of the Peten. Using native speakers in both the local Spanish and Ket'Chi dialects, both taped and live voice broadcasts were made over the targeted jungle areas where it was suspected that the guerrillas maintained their secret base areas. In addition, a simultaneous campaign was also conducted, using descriptive pictures or "pictorial language" and the dropping of thousands of leaflets on the otherwise illiterate population in selected areas. This had never been attempted before and the feedback over the ensuing weeks, long after Santos left the Peten in mid-May, indicated that the campaign had struck home and the FAR was not happy. In short, the loudspeakers had become an extension of face-to-face communication, even though the speaker was not always visible. While daytime operations enabled Santos and "his boys" to pinpoint their target audiences to a greater degree, it was found that the sound of the loudspeakers carried even further at night and were more clearly understood. At night the broadcasts were also somewhat unnerving to both the guerrillas and the populace, with the "voice out of the dark" beaming down upon them with nowhere to run or hide to escape the penetrating messages. As Luis Santos left the Peten, he recommended that the campaign continue with an emphasis on an amnesty program for the defectors and surrendered insurgents, rewards for information concerning guerrilla activities, and a policy of good treatment of prisoners by the army and national government.

My own activities focused on several zones to the northwest and north of Guatemala City and encompassed Quetzaltenango, El Quiche and Coban, areas known for their rich, volcanic soils and moderate rainy seasons which were conducive to producing some of the best coffee in the world. I was being given about four days to complete my mission in each region but, unlike Luis Santos' situation, within each of the zones of interest I was to be met and supported by a former student of the PSYOPs course who also happened to be the operations officer for that region's respective army brigade. In Quetzaltenango Colonel Manuel Sosa gave myself and his S-3, Lieutenant Colonel Carlos Aboyave, complete freedom of action to establish a PSYOPs section, involving members of the intelligence and operations staff. In addition, special patrols were sent out to begin to determine first hand where the basis of discontent lay among the various elements of the population. It was known that some insurgent groups were forming, but it was unclear as to what was motivating their operations and how many adherents they had. Working conditions in the coffee and sugar plantations of the area were notorious and this could serve as a starting point. Aboyave briefed the patrol leaders as to what information he was looking for. It was clear that finding out base causes of popular dissatisfaction, potential key communicators, and the ethnic makeup of the workers in the plantations were important items of information being sought. It also became increasingly clear that we could not finish the area study for this military region until such time as we had all the required key data in hand.

It was thought that to best reach the Indian population, the S-3 would have to work with the former's culture, folklore and traditions, being careful to respect them, but at the same time emphasize the need for citizenship and national unity. There were five radio stations in the city of Quetzaltenango and it appeared that they were for the most part willing to spare about 20 minutes a day to permit the broadcasting of messages, which could be exploited as part of a PSYOP plan being developed by Aboyave and his men. This was very promising for us as it appeared that the Indian population, which was the most vulnerable element to the insurgents' own propaganda efforts, was in the main 90 percent illiterate and therefore best reached as a mass by radio.

While the indoctrination of the soldiers in the brigade to treat the population with kindness and respect would have to be inculcated throughout the ranks over time, I also placed emphasis on meeting with the city and town leaders to obtain feedback as to their actual feelings and concerns and to develop ideas in terms of civic action and municipal development projects that the army might be able to support. Meeting with elected officials, civil servants, the clergy, newspaper editors, business and agricultural leaders, labor union leaders etc (all potential key communicators) was all part and parcel of reaching out and establishing contact with Guatemalan society in the region. Colonel Sosa had to admit that this was a new idea in so far as he was concerned, but potentially very valuable for establishing a solid public relations and contact program between the army and the people. He also noted that with over 1500 troops, the brigade had a manpower resource that should also not be allowed to go to waste. At bottom there was a need to evaluate adequate housing, sanitation, educational and working conditions to serve as a baseline of need for the army's help. Despite the good will and apparently positive attitude displayed towards PSYOP, I noted a hesitancy on the part of the brigade commander and his staff to go into great detail in terms of PSYOP planning and wholeheartedly embrace and execute a real program until such time that a uniform national PSYOP plan and respective guidelines had been promulgated as official policy by the government and its military in Guatemala City.

Upon reaching El Quiche at the end of April as my next area of interest, I met Colonel Chester Reyes, the military zone commander, whose wife immediately became enamored with the idea that I would be a perfect candidate to marry one of her two teenage daughters. It took considerable persuasion to convince her that I was really on a very serious military mission and not just merely an ambassador of good will (and promising matrimonial candidate). Be that as it may, the Quiche region was a very complex demographic situation, requiring a great deal more information for the military zone's area study to become complete. To obtain the information as rapidly as possible, the brigade intelligence officer recommended that each *municipio* or village develop its own area study under the guidance of a member of the brigade staff, the results of which could then be integrated into the brigade's own work as a whole. With living and working conditions on the various coffee plantations being a problem, it was also thought that a medical civic action team consisting of some nine doctors and paramedics, then on station and working in the area, could be of considerable service not only to the population, but also to the brigade in terms of providing feedback as to the actual feelings of the people at the grass roots level.

Lending an element of urgency to fulfill this requirement was the fact that in the northwest corner of that part of Guatemala, fronting on the Mexican border, a new insurgent group calling itself the Guerrilla Army of the Poor (*Ejercito Guerrillero de los Pobres* - EGP) had been recently established. Still estimated as being fairly small in size and made up of a mixed group of ladinos and Indian elements, it was the first time that a modern insurgency of any significance had come into play in this part of Guatemala.

It appeared to me that the army needed to establish in El Quiche a similar type of troop indoctrination and public relations and contact program as I had recommended for Quezaltenantgo. In addition to this recommendation, I noted that there were two radio stations functioning in the region. I thought that the S-3 and his intended PSYOPs section could make use of native speakers (perhaps even some of the key communicators) from each of the ladino and tribal Indian groups to reach out to their respective communities in their own dialect during the evening hours when they tended to be at rest and possibly more available to listen to whatever radio station was available to them. One way or another, this type of communication, be it face-to-face or via radio, would require one propaganda development and broadcast team for *each* ethnic group's dialect (at least six had been identified) in order to develop the specialized propaganda that was needed to attain the desired psychological effect.

This meant that the army brigade in the region had a great deal to do in terms of PSYOPs organization, research of its target audiences, and the implementation of influential propaganda. On my last day I outlined what I thought the program ought to look like and bid adieu to Colonel Reyes and his family. While I was headed over to the east (Coban), they were departing for Guatemala City in their land rover-style jeep. I noticed that everyone, including Mrs Reyes' daughters, had an Uzi submachine gun cradled in their arms. They were obviously concerned for their safety, as well they might, since one could be waylaid and killed by any number of groups inside Guatemala: the guerrillas, death squads, organized criminals, and even amateurs, preying on anyone who happened to come their way. I did not know it at the time, but this was symbolic of the hard times that would eventually befall not only El Quiche, but also all the rest of Guatemala.

Upon reaching Coban, the capital of the province of Alta Vera Paz, on the 6th of May, I conducted an informal PSYOP orientation for staff members and company commanders of the infantry brigade under Colonel Carlos Enriquez. This was one of the Guatemalan army's better combat brigades and one that conducted long range patrolling along the Mexican frontier, which included the Rio Salinas, running along Mexico's border with the southwestern part of the Peten. Once a patrol was dispatched on foot, the only real communication over extended distances was by C-47 or Cessna aircraft which dropped messages and supplies by parachute and received messages by short-range radio from the patrol. Some patrols lasted longer than a month and were usually commanded by graduates from the army's Kaibil commando school. For some reason Guatemalan army compasses for land navigation were in short supply at that moment, so I "lent" my own wristband compass to a needy red-haired reconnaissance platoon leader, who informed me that compasses were illegal on the open market inside Guatemala for fear that their availability would aid the guerrillas. I wondered whether this policy was really very logical, since the guerrillas already knew the territory reasonably well anyway. Coban was known for its hydroelectric projects, nickel mining and large cattle ranches, which included the *Franja Transversal del Norte,* a broad strip of land which included an access road used by higher ranking army officers to increase their personal landholdings at the expense of the rest of the population.

Similar to the other two zones I had operated in, PSYOPs planning was initiated almost immediately, including the use of the two local radio stations. The brigade staff was very interested in the use of fixed wing aircraft and even helicopters to broadcast propaganda against the insurgent bands operating along the Mexican frontier. In addition to the guerrilla bands of one sort or another found in the area, also taking place were a series of illegal smuggling and contraband operations. For the army lieutenants leading their long-range reconnaissance patrols in the vicinity of the Mexican frontier it was a dicey situation, whereby they either won or lost whatever fire-fights they happened to find themselves engaged in. As such, there was no aerial or artillery fire support, no medical support, and no hope for reinforcement or relief if you were in over your head in a do or die battle against a superior force.

As I concluded my stay at Coban and returned to Guatemala City, I summed up my mission by making a series of general recommendations that affected all three of the regions that I had worked in. One of these involved establishing a government commission to inspect all the coffee and sugar plantations to determine uniform minimum working and living standards for all workers. In addition, the commission was to establish minimum wages and ascertain whether the workers were receiving their salaries as entitled under Guatemalan law. I also thought it advisable that all new medical school graduates spend at least six months to a year on community service in the rural areas of the country under the direction (and protection) of the army or local health services to support a medical civic action program on behalf of the people. Lastly there was a need (and here a great opportunity) as part of a community service program to reduce illiteracy by establishing a broad system of rural schools, run by the new graduates of Guatemala's teacher-training institutions. All these programs were to be part of the national development plan for Guatemala and would support the National PSYOPs Plan that Jim Dandridge was trying to promote.

Captain Leo Sanchez worked inside Guatemala City with the army general staff to assist Jim Dandridge initiate a draft national PSYOPs plan and then deployed out to Pacific coast military bases located at San Jose and Sipacate. Lieutenant John Buford visited bases and units at Puerto Barrios, Zacapa and Jutiapa. In sum, they worked toward accomplishing much the same thing as I had been trying to do in my own visits to the west and north.

As we concluded our advisory phase and prepared to depart Guatemala, Jim Dandridge, a concerned look on his face, mentioned that he was afraid that we had just scratched the surface in our PSYOPs effort and not provided enough indoctrination at the top of the Guatemalan army's leadership structure to secure a permanent place for psychological operations in their own thinking and that of the institution as a whole. He had offered to teach a special short course to the general officers of the army, but had been told that the Department of State had neither the funds nor the interest (mandate) on the part the Guatemalan army for the additional instruction. Not only was this a serious mistake on the part of Washington, it was also a blunder of considerable consequences, given the potential that the program had to offer on behalf of the Guatemalan people as a whole. Although our PSYOPs training operation had been rated as a "success" by the American Embassy in Guatemala City and the SOUTHCOM headquarters in the Canal Zone (Panama), our Guatemalan army patient would eventually "die" as part of a unfolding tragedy which only became clear as time went on.

* * *

Upon return to Fort Gulick inside the Canal Zone our PSYOP training team went back to its normal routines within the 9th PSYOP Battalion, 8th Special Forces Group. Nonetheless, the Research and Analysis Section was able to monitor the events that followed in Guatemala. It appeared that there was some initial impact from our training mission. A national PSYOPs plan was completed, at least in part, and there were some attempts to implement our recommendations in regard to the population in general. A literacy campaign was undertaken in Santa Cruz del Quiche to the northwest of Guatemala City and a series of conferences and meetings had begun to take place in areas such as Quezaltenango, bringing Indian leaders and government officials together to discuss the formers' most pressing issues. Within the departments of Chimaltenango and Solola, Indians were elected as national deputies. It was the first time that this had ever happened and generated some expectations that Indians finally had access to power at the national as well as the local levels. At least for the time being, it now appeared that there was a genuine interest on the part of the government at the municipal level to begin to deal with local problems of a social and economic nature.

Guatemala as a state was very much militarized, with the army not only exercising power but also carrying out what were normally civilian functions. The army controlled some forty-six semiautonomous state institutions, including its own investment bank and pensions funds. For more than a decade one general officer after another succeeded one another in the presidency as a result of controlled elections which the army always won. In 1974 General Kjell Laugerud was Carlos Arana's hand-picked candidate. Supported by a military-civilian coalition made up of economic and political elites, he successfully ran against General Rios Montt. In this case the military was destined to win the election either way and, as it turned out, Laugerud reportedly won the election through extensive fraud, forcing Montt into exile. While the military now controlled the executive, the civilians were allowed to dominate Congress and manage the political parties, as well as the economy. Recognizing the need for national unity and social peace if Guatemala was to develop further and possibly influenced by the new approach to dealing with society that had been introduced by the national PSYOPs plan and our course teachings, the new president initially reduced the pressure on labor unions and allowed the development of rural cooperatives, some of which were led by local parish priests.

Unfortunately, an earthquake took place in 1976 - a disaster that killed an estimated 25,000 people and made homeless a million more - and destroyed dozens of critical bridges in less than a minute, forcing many of the relatively isolated communities in the outback to fend for themselves. Hardest hit were the Indian groups who were virtually left destitute in the quake's aftermath. As a result, a series of spontaneous grass-roots organizations began to sprout up in Guatemala's highlands to respond not only to the natural disaster but also to the precarious living conditions. Parallel attempts by urban workers to take advantage of the apparent liberal opening of the first two years of the Laugerud regime by forming labor unions were now abruptly curtailed by a government backlash and major crackdown. Inside Guatemala City death squads systematically murdered workers attempting to unionize the local Coca Cola bottling plant and other commercial enterprises.

Apparently the pressures for reform being generated among both rural and urban labor were seen as threats if not outright assaults on the traditional foundations of property rights and the structure of privileges that the plantation owners had been accustomed to. They in turn used their influence to convince the government that a benevolent, humanist approach towards labor or any other reform initiative was dangerous and aiding the budding insurgency. Complementing the repression taking place was the transversal road that had been constructed to make the recently discovered Guatemalan oil fields in the vicinity of the Chiapas area of the Mexican border more accessible. In so doing the road opened a corridor through a large region of Indian lands which hitherto had been largely inaccessible for farming. As a consequence, vast tracts of farm lands were now appropriated by army officers and their civilian political cronies, with the former Indian occupants being uprooted and otherwise driven away.

Bogged down in hopeless poverty and unmercifully abused by the ladino society as a whole, the only outlet for the Indians was a blind and unavailing rebellion. Deprived of their ancestral lands and forced to sell their labor for miserably low wages in the highlands and along the coastal regions in order to survive, the Indian population of the late-1970s finally decided to fight rather than remain passive. This moved Guatemala in the direction of a grim and complex civil war to the death, involving numerous confused and shifting alliances amongst the Indians and ladinos who eventually made up the guerrilla forces.

In response to this evolving situation, the government began to rely more and more on repression in the form of state-sponsored terrorism, often targeting the very people who represented the possibility for nonviolent reform of the political and social system - leaders of the Christian and Social Democratic parties, major trade unions, and Indian organizations throughout the country. Not helping matters were the special security or paramilitary guard forces that private families paid to maintain law and order on their plantations. Under these circumstances labor disputes were often settled by assassination rather than by arbitration. As the army attempted to repress the reformist efforts and community organizations, this led to a general defensive mobilization by the Indians to protect themselves from both the land owners and the military.

It was obvious that with the progress made during the first couple of years following the PSYOPs mission to Guatemala now having been quashed, it was time for an appraisal. Jim Dandridge had been correct in his 1972 surmise that we had neither penetrated deeply enough nor broadly enough to make a decisive impact on the thinking of the army in terms of utilizing reform-oriented PSYOPs as a means of winning over the Indian masses and neutralizing them as a source of support for the insurgency. The special course for the general officer corps of the armed forces and most importantly the army general staff, which Dandridge so very badly wanted to see brought into play, would have given our PSYOPs program a top-down approach within the military hierarchy and helped to foment a fuller appreciation for its value in befriending and helping the population as a means of dealing with the insurgency. In addition, follow-up PSYOPs training teams should have been sent into Guatemala in the fall of 1972 and again over the next several years to check to see if the programs in the various military zones were on track and functioning. Instead, the handful of trained Guatemalan army officers who actually went to the field to implement the program after completing their course often found themselves transferred to other assignments after only a year or so and then replaced with officers who either did not know or understand PSYOPs or were just not interested in what the program could offer. In the end, the Green Beret PSYOPs training mission to Guatemala was simply unable to breakdown and modify the countervailing racist attitudes and values in play amongst the mainstream of the Guatemalan army officer corps, especially the colonels and generals. Most of these officers saw the Indians as an alien force which could only be dealt with through brutal retribution.

During the mid-1970s, while at the U.S. Army's School of the Americas (USARSA) at Fort Gulick in the Canal Zone as both a student in the Command and General Staff Course and on the staff and faculty, I noted with dismay that the Guatemalan army officers (colonels, majors, and captains) were largely unaware of the Green Beret PSYOPs training mission to Guatemala and the efforts that had been made to implement a national PSYOPs plan. Furthermore was the fact that, in response to human rights groups complaints about the curriculum at USARSA, the Congress of the United States had passed a law prohibiting the teaching of intelligence and PSYOPs courses. In effect, this now eliminated the one last recourse that the U.S. Army had in its USARSA course inventory to help formally sensitize the officer corps of the Latin American military institutions to the need to treat their populations humanely in order to win their respective allegiances during an insurgency war. The U.S. Army's PSYOPs approach to dealing with an insurgency (guerrilla warfare) was human rights based and directed along the lines of the Alliance for Progress and the Guatemalan Arbenz government's efforts to bring about positive reforms to uplift society as a whole and thus inoculate it against the agitation and divisive influences that Fidel Castro's revolutionary efforts were bringing into play.

Nevertheless, it is possible that not even a PSYOPs course at USARSA would have sufficed in the case of Guatemala, since it is only the *saturation* effect which permeates an entire organization that will tend to offer the chance to bring about permanent institutional change in the member's minds, attitudes, and values. At heart, USARSA was an infantry training school during the last half of the 1970s and nothing more. As such, human rights groups inside the United States and elsewhere unfairly castigated the institution as the "school of the dictators," implying that USARSA was responsible for the development of the values, belief systems and corresponding attitudes leading to the plethora of cruel military dictatorships that had plagued Latin America for a generation. This notion was completely false.

Forgotten was the fact that Latin American military institutions, like similar institutions worldwide, tend to reflect the base values of their respective societies in which they were initially formed. In terms of indoctrinating the Latin American military in the U.S. Army's perspective on morality and war fighting at the tactical level, USARSA's influence and impact on most of its students was minimal and transient at best. As the students returned to their own countries and institutions they were once again re-immersed in their own dominating cultures and related authoritarian value systems, diluting whatever countervailing values of a democratic or liberal nature that had been temporarily imparted to them by their U.S. trainers. While USARSA could readily teach the tactical skills of counterinsurgency, emphasizing that the military who treats the local population with greater understanding and kindness will eventually gain the latter's loyalty or at least its benevolent neutrality, it could not change the fundamental psychic and behavior of a generation of Latin American military officers whose basic approach to dealing with an insurgency amounted to nothing more than brutal killing or repression.

Supporting democratic processes and respecting human rights can only emanate from a society's culture, traditions and value systems, which in turn tend to influence and mold the attitudes of the local military institution as a whole. Illustrating this point were the decades of outright U.S. occupation and direct influence in the running of the countries of Cuba, Nicaragua, Haiti and the Dominican Republic during the early part of the 20th Century, which indicated that democratic concepts and supporting human rights values must emanate from the heart and soul of a society and not at the point of a bayonet.

For an insurgency to succeed it requires four key elements to be in place and working in a synergistic manner. The first is a *just cause* or any number of concrete reasons for revolt in which significant portions of a society find themselves politically excluded from the governing system, economically marginalized with no real hope for material progress, and their aspirations for change in their favor quashed. Ted Gurr in his *Why Men Rebel* presents the situation as one where there are no effective channels to redress the perceived inequities and lack of justice in a society, and related dissent and complaints by those suffering are not tolerated by the ruling system. In short, it is frequently the callous attitude and the rigidity of the ruling system which frustrates evolutionary reform, thereby fostering attitudes of violence as the only practical path to change. According to Gurr, it is when men's aspirations for change in their favor, for which they know they are capable and deserving and which the system is able to grant but not willing, are quashed that gives rise to rebellion. One could amplify this perspective by adding that when a state or government through its incompetence or viciousness (repression) fails to provide and otherwise protect liberty, justice, economic opportunity and the ability of the population as a whole to influence government policy, it loses legitimacy in the eyes of the victimized people it presumes to rule over.

The next element necessary for an insurgency to take place is any form of charismatic or convincing *leadership* on the part of an insurgent cadre to show the affected population how badly and unjustly they have been wronged and galvanize them to action. This is normally followed by the insurgent agitator presenting a *plan* (guerrilla war and violent revolution) to resolve the adverse situation and otherwise enable the population to work its way out of its predicament. If the *population accepts* the plan as its only solution to resolving its problem and follows the insurgents lead, then the forth element is in place and the result is a full-blown insurgent war. This was what eventually took place in Guatemala.

Ever since January of 1972 the Guerrilla Army of the Poor (EGP) had been working with and trying to prepare the Indian workers in the western highlands region of Guatemala to accept violent revolution as their only alternative against further deprecations at the hands of the government's security forces and the ladino society in general. Albeit having trained scores, if not hundreds of members of EGP cadre in Cuba and infiltrated them back into Guatemala via Mexico, the insurgent leaders in the northwestern part of Guatemala initially found it very difficult during the early-to-mid-1970s to draw disaffected Indians into their cause. Their problem lay in the fact that for the most part they, the guerrilla cadre, were Spanish-speaking ladino student revolutionaries, former teachers and workers who were very much initially distrusted by the Indians, who were highly suspicious of the ladinos. This was a difficult situation for the cadres to overcome and one which the government should have be able to exploit, but did not. In addition, the EGP found that the Indians were not only fragmented as community groups and spoke a multitude of diverse Mayan dialects, but they also saw no real relevance in Marxist-Leninist propaganda as a solution to Indian oppression. To that end the EGP and its sister organization the Organization of the Revolutionary People in Arms (ORPA) changed their propaganda emphasis to that of focusing on cultural and racial oppression as the basic causes by which the Indians were being exploited.

The issue of land ownership was one key point which had considerable relevance for some Indian groups, another was wretched working conditions, and still another placed emphasis on ladino control of local trade and markets. In cases where coffee planters kept Indian laborers in debt bondage with miserly pay and raped their wives and daughters at will, EGP cadre stepped in and executed the perpetrators to demonstrate that "people's justice" could prevail. This type of direct action to met out an impromptu justice against selected plantation owners was designed to win the sympathy of the Indian workers. In retaliation and fearing that the aroused Indian workers would seek similar forms of justice to resolve their plight, the coffee plantation owners asked the Guatemalan army to intervene and exterminate the Indians involved. This eventually did take place, but by then the EGP cadres had moved on to other portions of the guerrilla battlefield, leaving the vulnerable, local Indian community to suffer the consequences. When all was said and done the Indian population as a whole maintained an innate distrust of the ladino guerrilla leaders and recruitment for the insurgency effort at this time proceeded very slowly, with little more than a thousand males having made the commitment to fight for their "just cause," while the Indian community provided some food, shelter, and intelligence information. This situation should have given the Guatemalan government and its army a huge advantage in terms of winning the hearts and minds of the Indian population and splitting them away permanently from the insurgency. Unfortunately, Guatemala's violence-prone ladino society and army frittered away this advantage well into the 1970s and eventually had to endure an intransigent insurgency for another fifteen years.

As General Romero Lucas succeeded to the presidency in a patently fraudulent election in 1978, the insurgency situation came to a head. A series of government sponsored death squads then initiated a campaign, attempting to exterminate anyone suspected of being against government policies and supporting in any form the guerrillas. In the urban areas terror and assassination took a significant toll of labor leaders, lawyers, journalists and opposition politicians, as well as students and faculty at the University of San Carlos. During 1980 alone at San Carlos, it was reported that 86 professors and 389 students had been killed by death squads; for all intents and purposes closing down the institution and forcing its rector into exile.

The Catholic Church was not immune to the government's retribution either and dozens of priests and laypersons alike were killed or forced to abandon their rural parishes when it was determined that they too had sympathized with the Indians plight. While the Church had been traditionally aligned with Guatemala's landowning elite, doctrine changed and a number of priests and lay workers found their calling assisting the rural poor. In an area known as the Ixil Triangle several hundred agricultural cooperative leaders, school teachers running literacy classes, and Catholic catechists and missionaries, who had been radicalized by the implacable exploitation of their parishioners by ladino plantation owners, were systematically hunted down and murdered by government security forces.

The involvement of the Catholic clergy in the guerrilla war inside Guatemala and elsewhere in Central America stemmed from Pope John XXIII's encyclicals of the early 1960s in which he stressed the need to honor human rights and create decent standards of living for all peoples. These had been followed by Pope Paul VI's concern about "institutionalized violence" which referred to the social and structural conditions of poverty that starved the poor. In short, the attention of the Church shifted from personal redemption and a maintenance of the status quo divisions within Guatemalan society to that of general social change and reform in order to end the violence. In a complete about face the clergy was now trying to help the poor and not toady to the rich. Out of this conversion and the effort to help the masses uplift themselves and even fight for their basic freedoms and human rights a concept known as "liberation theology" was brought into play. Encouragement for reformist activity was preached and lay ministers increasingly became involved in social action. Catholic Action, as an organization, focused on promoting literacy through a network of radio schools, encouraged the formation of local political parties that reflected Indian concerns, and organized independent farming cooperatives. This increased the sense of connection between villages and inspired a more active Indian population that was more and more willing to stand up for what it thought were its rights.

In the fall of 1979 a commission of Indians traveled to the capital to request that General Lucas put a stop to the military's heavy-handed repression in the Ixil area. As part of their grievances the commission intended to argue that while the government had promulgated a new wage scale for agricultural workers, raising their wages from $1.12 to $3.25 per day, the plantation owners by and large had merely ignored the new law. Refused an audience with the president, the group then went to a session of the national congress to present their demands, only to find themselves rebuffed again. Desperate and thoroughly frustrated over the futility of not being able to have their situation and demands addressed by governmental authority, the group decided to peacefully occupy the Spanish Embassy at the end of January 1980, in the hopes that this would attract international attention and some form of relief from their plight. The government's response was to deliberately massacre the entire group in a Dantesque nightmare of brutality by burning them alive inside the embassy, killing 37 people! As a result, the Spanish government broke diplomatic relations with Guatemala over the horrific incident. Another result of this tragic incident was that Indians in general could now see that they had little or no options left other than joining the nascent guerrilla war that was beginning to flourish countrywide.

In the countryside the army waged a systematic war against Indian workers and community leaders who supported the insurrection or were thought to be supporting the guerrillas. Urged on by the economic elites' Coordinating Committee of Agricultural, Commercial, Industrial, and Financial Associations (CACIF), the army began to carry out a series of operations using "Zacapa tactics" or the wholesale slaughter of entire villages in the highlands regions, including all men, women and children regardless of age, as part of a scorched-earth campaign. Entire villages in the El Quiche province, involving scores of thousands of people, fled to the Chiapas area of southern Mexico where other Mayan ethnic groups had been making their homes for centuries.

One celebrated case in May of 1978 illustrates the problem and this involved the army's reaction to 700 Kekchi Indians who had gathered at the town of Panzos in eastern Alta Verapaz to protest their not being able to obtain legal title to land that they had worked in some cases for as long as a hundred years. Their lack of formal titles had exposed them to having their lands encroached upon and used for cattle-raising by ladino cattle-ranchers. In some cases marginal Indian farmers had to give up their lands and become wage earners on land that they considered theirs. As the crowd swelled in the town square and the demonstration became more heated, soldiers began to arbitrarily massacre the crowd, killing at least 100, which included women and children. By 1981 human rights groups estimated that over 13,000 Indians a year were being systematically murdered by the army's draconian measures. But it was the Panzos massacre that marked a turning point in the highlands war in terms of the combative mobilization of the people that seriously began to take place throughout the highlands.

By the end of 1981 many Indians had finally decided that with no possibility of redressing their situation through local or national channels they had no other choice but to throw in their lot with the guerrillas. In so doing the regions of El Quiche became a hotbed of hit-and-run guerrilla raids and ambushes of army forces, with the town of Nebaj actually being seized for some weeks. ORPA conducted similar operations in the San Marcos area along the Mexican frontier. The majority of the militantly inspired Indians joined the EGP, the largest of the guerrilla organizations which operated in the capital and the provinces of Chimaltenango, Huehuetenango, Quiche, Sacatepequez, and Alta and Baja Verapaz. Others joined ORPA, which operated in San Marcos, Quezaltenango, Solola and Chimaltenango. A handful of Indians joined the FAR and the PGT (Guatemalan Workers Party [Communist]). The FAR retained its focus in the Peten region where additional petroleum reserves, as well as nickel and tungsten had been discovered, and the Indians had been forced by the government to relocate so their lands could be expropriated by multinational corporations operating with the consent of the government. While many people in the highlands now felt that the guerrillas could help change things for the better, there still was an inclination by some to only lend passive support and not necessarily join the insurgent ranks as a full-fledged fighter.

The Guatemalan army now found itself involved in an intractable guerilla war involving up to a half-million highland Indian people with ever increasing casualties and no end in sight. The some 7,000 actual guerrilla fighters were spread out over the countryside and found that they could not stand up to massed army forces. As a result and in addition to ambushes and raids, they preferred to cut telegraph lines, block highways with nails and fallen trees and generally create headaches for the government. All these actions, while not appearing to be very important, did have a cumulative effect on the economy which began to deteriorate rapidly. Worse yet for the army was the worsening relationship that Guatemala had with the United States.

President Jimmy Carter had announced during the late 1970s that the United States of America was eager to stand behind those nations which respected human rights and which promoted democratic values. While respect for human rights was a condition for receiving U.S. aid, Guatemala rejected both the conditions and the aid. With General Lucas rejecting Carter's terms, the U.S. Congress, responding to the continued reports of army sponsored atrocities and human rights violations, cut off all military aid to Guatemala in 1977 (lasting until 1983). While Carter had good reason for addressing the Guatemalan issue in this manner, General Lucas was able to work around the situation by importing ammunition, weapons and training from Argentina and Israel. During the 1980-81 period almost fifty local journalists were assassinated as a result of their attempts to report on the guerrilla war and its related atrocities. The attempts on the part of the Lucas government to suppress the news media's activities generated a widespread climate of fear, demoralization and the growth of a clandestine opposition both within and without the army. While the sale of weapons to the Guatemalan military was banned, the U.S. Agency for International Development (USAID), an affiliate of the U.S. Embassy's "country team" in Guatemala City poured millions of dollars in economic aid into Guatemala to assist in the resettlement of thousands of Indian refugees who had lost their lands in the Transversal and Peten regions. Nevertheless, in the end Carter's human rights policy only hardened the resolve of the Guatemalan military and death squads to deal violently with the Indian insurrection.

The overthrow of Nicaragua's Somoza dictatorship in 1979 raised the morale and accelerated the pace of the insurrections inside Guatemala, as well as throughout Central America. In turn, Fidel Castro in exchange for supporting the insurgents argued that they would have to unify their respective efforts in order to mass sufficient forces to overcome the Guatemalan army. Based on Castro's guidance and with the assistance of Manuel Pineiro, the Guatemala National Revolutionary Unity (URNG) was formed in the early 1980s to supposedly link all four of the distinct insurgent groups under one umbrella headquarters. A similar effort was also taking place inside El Salvador, one of Guatemala's eastern neighbors, where the guerrilla forces had been exhorted by the Cuban caudillo to further unify their efforts in order to win their revolutionary effort there. The guerrillas' efforts to gain unity and obtain better training and support out of Cuba came precisely at the time when the Guatemalan army underwent a major split within its officer corps.

Junior army officers were becoming increasingly concerned about the corruption and politicking among the institution's senior officers or colonels and generals, who were perceived as enriching themselves at the expense of the rest of the institution and even the country. Over time greed had overcome professionalism and the army had more and more become a "praetorian guard"-style military institution in which its involvement in national politics and the self-enrichment of its senior members was an all-consuming passion. Colonels and generals were now in direct control of public agencies, transportation, communications, electrical power, credit institutions, factories, and the ports, to include customs control of imports and exports, exploiting them all as part of an extensive system of graft.

Left to actually fight the war and possibly die in the rugged outback against an ever more capable guerrilla adversary now armed with automatic weapons smuggled in from Cuba were the young lieutenants and captains, all but forgotten by the senior military hierarchy in Guatemala City. Another concern of the junior officers was the fact that the war was not going well and the guerrillas appeared to be more than holding their own. Within miles of the capital, guerrillas actually controlled large tracts of land and were stopping cars, issuing "travel passes," and forcing people to pay "war taxes." Despite the fact that the army had practiced a scorched earth policy of burning villages, killing cattle and poultry, shooting down civic leaders and anyone suspected of collaborating with the guerillas, and otherwise bombing and strafing portions of the highlands population with helicopters, the insurgency had shown remarkable resilience and had endured. From the point of view of the junior officers the internal corruption within the army as an institution and Guatemala's international isolation stemming from international human rights concerns were not only hampering the fight against the guerrillas, but also jeopardizing the army's very survival.

In March of 1982 a successful coup was staged by the junior and midlevel army officers, demanding an end to electoral fraud and corruption and promising to restore democracy and continue a more focused war against the guerrillas. One of the complaints of the junior officers was that of some $450 million budgeted for arms acquisitions, $250 million had been embezzled, ending up in high-ranking officers' Cayman Islands bank accounts. The elections of that year saw General Lucas attempt to fraudulently manipulate the electoral process in order to impose his hand-picked candidate from his faction of the army on the country. When Lucas' plan backfired and his regime was overthrown, retired General Efrain Rios Montt was placed in power by the junior army officers. Rios Montt was an eccentric, new-born, fundamentalist Protestant, who promised to make the necessary reforms to eliminate corruption both within the Guatemalan government and its military institutions and elect a new democratically-based regime, as well as to forcefully prosecute the war against the guerrillas. While his time in power was short-lived, the general did bring into play a strategy for successfully defeating the insurgency, which set the course for Guatemala over the next two decades.

Rios Montt's strategy for dealing with the insurgency was essentially one of using a "carrot and stick" approach that alternated carefully measured benevolence with brutal repression to physically separate the people from the guerrillas by force, while at the same time taking care of their basic needs and indoctrinating them in how to become "good" Guatemalan citizens. Having failed to arrange an amnesty and dialogue with the guerrilla leadership shortly after the coup which placed him in power, the general declared a state of siege and an all-out offensive against the insurgency. Some 440 Indian villages in the provinces of El Quiche and Alta Verapaz were wiped out and razed to the ground, forcing their residents to flee to Mexico or be reintegrated into several dozen army and government-sponsored villages. A million people were displaced over the next few years, with the majority opting for the government-sponsored facilities.

These forced resettlement camps were established with the idea that the army would be able to wipe out the Indian support bases for the guerrilla organizations most active in the highlands and bring the four million Mayan Indians from the region under direct military control, whereby the army would administer every aspect of their lives. In short, the guerrillas were to be denied support and the Indians were to be incorporated into national life through participation in civil-defense forces and resettled into protected villages. As an army-sponsored civic action program, work, water, food and health care were provided for all males and females in return for the male population's recruitment into a mandatory system of local patrols. The patrols, as the "eyes and ears" of the army, were to monitor suspicious activities within their respective villages, patrol the approaches into the villages against guerrilla encroachment and to assist the army in defending their assigned areas against guerrilla attacks. Some villages became known as "model villages" whereby the people were taught how to read, write and master additional useful trades of one sort or another. Roads, schools and clinics were gradually constructed in most parts of the rural areas, with the schools having the aim of assimilating the Indians into the national or ladino culture and enabling the state to incorporate its values as part of the Indian culture.

Because about a fifth of the resettled Indian population in the highlands could no longer effectively farm their distant plots of land or seek employment outside the area, this portion of the population was totally dependent for basic economic survival on handouts from the state or military-controlled relief agencies. Not helping matters was the country's concentration on export crops (coffee, cotton and bananas) which had led to a decline in the production of basic foodstuffs and the need to import rice, beans and corn, products that had previously been produced locally in ample quantities. As a humanitarian effort, USAID provided substantial economic assistance in this regard with over $15 million to offset the shortfall in food and keep the resettled Indians from starving to death.

The counterinsurgency strategy and program became known as *frijoles y fusiles* ("beans and bullets"), which was described by Rios Montt himself in a simple and straightforward manner: "If you are with us, we'll feed you, if not, we'll kill you!" Those Indians who wanted to survive embraced the program (the "carrot"), those who did not took their chances in a bitter and very cruel war (the "stick") which took on the appearance of ethnic extermination. Entire campesino Indian families were wiped out and reports indicated that they had been machine-gunned, burned or even hacked to death with machetes. Indian villages which were deemed sympathetic to the insurgents were to be utterly destroyed. Others, which professed to be neutral or loyal to the government were integrated into the civil patrol system (*Patrullas de Auto-defensa Civil* or PACs).

As the cornerstone of the army's control over Indian communities, the PAC structure enabled the army and its informants to constantly monitor the activities and whereabouts of the villagers, making any sort of contact with the guerrillas or other political activity extremely difficult. Over time the program worked and numerous guerrilla members and their ardent supporters and sympathizers were rooted out. Eventually one million Indian males from age sixteen to sixty or about 50 percent of the adult male population from over 850 villages were involved in the patrols. At the same time the army doubled in size to around 30,000 men and redoubled its efforts in the outback to bring the guerrillas to battle.

Unfortunately, the Indians found themselves caught between two fires: those of the army and those of the guerrillas. Counterinsurgency and guerrilla warfare had effectively blurred the distinction between the civilian and the soldier. The guerrillas claimed that the insurgency was a "peoples war" and therefore every man, woman and child was a participant whether they wanted to be or not. The army countered that anyone amongst the Indian population even suspected of being a guerrilla was a fair target and would be dealt with ruthlessly. Working against the guerrillas was the sense of Indian community identification which complicated and exacerbated the divisions between the 21 distinct linguistic groups, which effectively blocked the possibility of a unified Indian struggle against the army and the state. This forced the guerrilla leadership to reassess its situation, which found that poorly trained and poorly armed villagers could not defend themselves against the army whose own brutality and threats of death, torture and mutilation frequently coerced some of the staunchest guerrilla supporters to reveal information about the location and identity of insurgent bases and members. When the army attacked, the guerrilla forces would retreat, as they had been trained to do when outnumbered and unable to deal with the situation. Nonetheless, while undoubtedly logical tactics from the guerrillas' point of view, this left the villagers to suffer the consequences of their ill-fated allegiance to the guerrilla's "cause."

As part of his programs for ruling Guatemala, Rios Montt did end most of Guatemala's urban violence, greatly lowered corruption in both the army and the government's national bureaucracy, and introduced Indian representation into the governmental advisory body known as the Council of State, which had temporarily replaced the shut down National Congress. Nonetheless, Rios Montt's own lust for power alienated enough business, military, and Catholic Church groups so that he too was eventually overthrown in 1983 via another coup by still another clique of military officers. The die was nevertheless cast in terms of the prosecution of the guerrilla war and the EGP was gradually scattered and reduced to small pockets of resistance.

In 1984 elections were held for a constituent assembly which began drafting a new constitution which, in turn, paved the way for democratic elections, leading to civilian rule through the end of the century and on into the next. Caught up in its dual status as institution and rulers, the Guatemalan military, riddled by intra-institutional frictions and strife and unable to deal with the deteriorating economic conditions of the day, returned to the barracks to tend to its wounds and attempt to regain a more professional focus. That the army was back in the barracks did not mean that it was out of the war and it prosecuted the beans and bullets strategy with a vengeance.

The Guatemalan insurgency or URNG, although not completely eliminated over the next ten years, was reduced to a scattered force of around 2,000 surviving guerrilla fighters. As the army's system of civil patrolling began to systematically sever the links between the guerrilla fighters and their popular base, guerrilla morale declined and relations with many of the Indians began to deteriorate. Over time the Indians were forced to provide and cook food for the guerrillas under duress, but with no compensation. Exacerbating this relationship was the fact that the guerrilla cadres constantly jeopardized the lives of scores of thousands of Indians who believed in the former's promises of a swift victory over their oppressors and the redressing of their centuries-old grievances.

Also contributing to this decline in guerrilla fortunes was the Esquipulas peace negotiations of 1986-87, which used Oscar Arias' skillfully developed, democratically-based peace plan for Central America as a basis for concluding the civil wars afflicting the region. With the late-1980s collapses of the Marxist-Leninist Sandinista government in Nicaragua, the Marxist guerrilla revolution in El Salvador, and the fall of the Soviet Union at the end of the 1980s, the URNG now found itself more isolated than ever. By 1996 it found itself negotiating a final settlement of its own just cause with a more responsive Guatemalan government. This concluded some 36 years of civil war and an estimated more than 140 thousand deaths, as well as the creation of some 60 thousand orphans.

A turn of the century (2000) study by the Archbishop's Human Rights Office (ODHA) in Guatemala City concluded that the army had perpetrated 626 distinct massacres of civilians during the civil war. Despite the tragedy that had befallen them, some Indian communities actually benefited from the decades of strife by the fact that much of the ladino power structure fled the highlands with the escalation of violence and had not returned. Since the war, lands have been sold to

Indians and others divided and distributed by the government. While the economy has been enhanced somewhat with over 300 U.S.-based corporations having invested inside Guatemala, it still benefits in the main a small number of the ladino rich.

This is not to say that Guatemala has resolved its problems involving societal cleavages - far from it. A coercive climate based on deeply rooted racism still pervades the country. This includes assassinations, extra-judicial executions, kidnappings and disappearances, harassment of popular organizations, violence and threats against judges, lawyers, and newspaper reporters and a rural power structure that still attempts to exploit its workers at every turn. Human rights abuses continue, if only on a smaller scale, and bitterness and hatred still endure in a population two-thirds of which lives in poverty. In sum a *caudillaje* culture has survived in which the pursuit of power has become the reference point for one's life activities. The army, Church, and agricultural and commercial elites still contend for influence and power as they can, although the army appears to be more supportive of the civilian government than ever before in order to enhance its legitimacy and international standing and the Church has generally become a human rights watchdog. As a multicultural and multiethnic nation, Guatemala is still searching to achieve the ideals of the Arevalo-Arbenz era.

THE BATTLE FOR CENTRAL AMERICA
1982-84

As the guerrilla war in Guatemala began to build to a climax towards the end of the 1970s, Communist-led revolutionary wars literally exploded throughout other parts of Central America, catching the United States' attention and highlighting John Kennedy's prescient observation that: "Those who make peaceful revolution impossible will make violent revolution inevitable." Both Nicaragua and El Salvador reflected the "inevitable" and became directly caught up in bloody conflicts, one preceding the other respectively, which more and more involved Washington until the situation reached a point where the decision was made by President Ronald Reagan in 1981 to make a serious security assistance effort within the region to defeat the Marxist-Leninist guerrilla revolutionaries. With Nicaragua eventually falling to the Sandinista insurgency movement and then, in turn, serving as a base and inspiration for further revolutionary activity, the focus for American economic and military aid to the region became centered on El Salvador and Honduras in a counter-insurgency effort which would last for some ten years and cost the United States billions of dollars. But it was Nicaragua with its population of about four million people that served as the early catalyst for the 1980s civil war in Central America.

— NICARAGUA —

Intense U.S. interest in Nicaragua during the twentieth century actually began in 1909 when it intervened with warships, troops and arms to back a successful insurrection to overthrow president Jose Santos Zelaya. The Nicaraguan president had made the mistake of threatening to construct a trans-isthmian canal to compete with the Panama Canal and was in the process of negotiating with Germany and Japan to this end. The intervention circumscribed Zelaya's plan and was then followed by an occupation of the country by U.S. Marines with only some brief interruptions until early 1933. While U.S. bankers Brown Brothers and Seligman replaced the British as Nicaragua's creditors, the Marines kept the peace, ran elections, and organized and trained a national guard (*Guardia Nacional*). In 1916 the Washington-sponsored, Bryan-Chamorro Treaty ceded the United States "in perpetuity and for all time" ownership rights to any Nicaraguan-proposed canal through its territory, in essence protecting the Panama Canal from any further competition. Nonetheless, despite decades-long American efforts to instill Yankee values at the point of a bayonet, the U.S. effort at fomenting democracy ultimately failed.

Beginning in 1936 Nicaragua fell under the suffocating control of first the father and then the sons of the Anastasio Somoza Garcia family. Led by Anastasio (Tacho) Somoza, a manipulating army sergeant who managed to get himself appointed to command the U.S. Marine-trained National Guard and then proceeded to use the Guard to propel himself into the presidency, a predatory family dynasty and political reign was created which lasted some forty-three years. While opposition political parties did exist during these years, the Somozas made sure they would never be allowed to play a central role in politics. No matter who won the subsequent façade of "elections," the Somoza family ruled the country. If legal limitations did not suffice, then a subtle repression took place, keeping most parties small, weak and divided.

Taking advantage of rigged elections, political cronies, personal inter-familial ties, patronage, and the power which stemmed from controlling the National Guard, the family created a virtual monopoly through which it eventually came to own a fifth of Nicaragua's richest farm lands, the national airline and maritime fleet, and controlling interests in transportation, meat processing, industry, banks, exports and control of the national treasury. No one could do anything involving a significant economic enterprise within the country without at least the tacit approval of the family and over time Nicaragua became known as the "Somoza ranch." It was monopoly capitalism mixed with corruption in a large sense and, as such, the Somozas regularly took their cut from any private investment or public aid package, further perpetuating their power, wealth and enterprises through extortion, racketeering, violence and fraud of all kinds. Greed, corruption, and brutality were the name of the game, as the family routinely ruled the country through surrogate "elected" politicians or directly by themselves. The Nicaraguan people were unable to exercise political power or influence, and the Guard dealt ruthlessly with anyone brave or foolish enough to try.

Family interests were shaken in 1956 when Tacho Somoza was assassinated by a young, dissident liberal and the country thought that there would finally be some respite from the ubiquitous Somozas, but it was not to be. Luis, the easygoing eldest son, stepped into the presidency and ran the country for another ten years before his younger and far more aggressive brother, Tachito, took power through a rigged election in 1967. This latter event dashed the hopes of the rising liberal middle class for a transition of sorts to some other form of rule other than the Somoza family.

Flaunting his wealth and power and the fact that he had the full support of the United States behind him, Tachito Somoza found everything still going his way in this virtual dictatorship until the earthquake of 1972. This quake reduced much of Managua, the capital, to rubble and further killed some ten thousand people and rendered another quarter of a million homeless. When it was revealed that Tachito and his cronies in the National Guard had absconded with large amounts of the disaster aid and food and medicine relief that the United States had sent to help out the post-earthquake victims and their families, a major scandal broke, resulting in a major break if not isolation of the family from the rest of Nicaraguan society and further eroding the legitimacy of the regime. This event represented a "great divide" of sorts which, when combined with the blatant political, economic and social corruption of the regime, set the stage for the revolutionary overthrow of the dynasty. It was now only a matter of time before someone would come to the fore to lead the effort.

The organization which took the lead to develop, dominate and otherwise control the effort to overthrow the Somozas was the Sandinista National Liberation Front (FSLN). "Sandinista" was the *nom de guerre* of the FSLN and was derived from the name of a Nicaraguan nationalist Augusto Cesar Sandino who had waged a five-years-long war during the late 1920s and early 1930s against the Washington-backed government and its supporting U.S. Marine occupation force. Unable to defeat Sandino and his guerrillas, Washington brought the Marines home in 1933 and Sandino ended his war, declaring victory. A short time later Sandino was assassinated on orders from Tacho Somoza, who feared that the former guerrilla leader and popular folk hero would outmaneuver him and win the presidency.

Originally founded in 1961 and led in part by pro-Castro, anti-Somoza dissidents such as Tomas Borge and Oscar Turcios, the FSLN looked to the marginalized farmers or *campesinos* of the remote mountain areas as the rural support base for their guerrilla operations. While it was assumed that land hunger on the part of the peasantry would be the critical driving force behind the revolution, providing guerrilla fighters with adequate support and a source of recruits, the assumption proved to be false. After the earthquake of 1972, while the guerrillas could get food from the poor peasant farmers or *campesinos,* they found themselves dependent on the urban areas for arms and ammunition, medicines and clothing, and money. Bank robberies and the hijacking of commercial airplanes did bring in some monies for the guerillas' coffers. Nonetheless, sensing the FSLN's dependence on the urban areas during the years immediately following the 1972 earthquake, the National Guard successfully counter-attacked the guerrillas, cutting them off from their urban lifelines, destroying their rural-based bands and generally suppressing their operations. It now appeared that Tachito Somoza had firmly secured his dictatorship.

The Sandinistas did not give up, however, and turned their efforts directly to the urban areas in an attempt to exploit the general animosity toward the Somozas on the part of the middle- and upper-class students at the university level. Nonetheless, there was still a certain lethargy and feeling of hopelessness on the part of Nicaragua's moderates and business community which kept them from throwing their full support behind the Sandinistas. These attitudes changed abruptly in January of 1978 when the highly respected and venerated newspaperman and anti-Somoza opposition leader Pedro Joaquin Chamorro was gunned down on the streets of Managua while on his way to work. Because the public at large blamed Somoza for the newspaperman's murder, no one felt safe from the wrath of the dictator, and this produced a massive outpouring of anti-Somoza feelings if not outright hatred from Nicaragua's elites which the FSLN astutely exploited.

Large scale unrest and demonstrations against the regime now became almost daily events in the towns and cities and the FSLN began to raid isolated National Guard outposts and barracks. An August 1978 commando raid led by the charismatic guerrilla leader Eden Pastora seized the National Palace, holding most of the Nicaraguan Congress hostage and representing the boldest action to date, which effectively captured the imagination of the Nicaraguan people, further unleashing additional forces for the fight against Somoza. This gave the FSLN a popular legitimacy all out of proportion to its wildest dreams and, with Pastora claiming he was fighting for democracy and free elections, civilian militias joined the FSLN by the thousands.

In September FSLN guerrilla units attacked directly into Masaya, Managua, Leon, Chinandega and Esteli in an effort to galvanize the population and ad hoc militia forces to action. Somoza's air force counter-attacked, bombing and strafing the towns while National Guard infantry cleared the buildings. The resulting chaos and the thousands of casualties in dead and injured suffered by the civilian population caused many of the urban dwellers to conclude that Somoza's 14,000-man army was out of control and had to go - and the only means of destroying it was the FSLN!

With the population now thoroughly aroused, if not radicalized, the FSLN opened its ranks to accept anyone who opposed Somoza. Nonetheless, the military leadership and control of the now rapidly evolving revolution remained in the hands of the original Cuban-trained, Marxist-Leninist guerrilla leaders of the FSLN. The groundswell of broad popular support, which now included many members of the Catholic Church inside Nicaragua, enabled the guerrilla cadres to build a broad-front alliance and emboldened them to begin operations countrywide to split up the Guard and eventually isolate and destroy it piecemeal. In just a year the FSLN would expand tenfold from roughly 500 guerrilla fighters to upwards of 5,000.

Now that the situation inside Nicaragua was rapidly deteriorating into outright civil war, the administration of American President James Earl Carter, using a human rights-based justification, charged that the Somozas were repressing freedom of speech, the press, political pluralism and meaningful elections, and further requested that Somoza give up control of the government in favor of a reform effort. When Tachito refused to hold elections or even step down to allow an open political process to evolve into a peaceful solution, the White House cut his regime off from all trade and military assistance of any kind. With the regime virtually isolated from any and all aid, the FSLN opened its final offensive of May-July 1979 which included calling for a general strike nationwide and uprisings in six of the most important cities and towns in the country. With local National Guard garrisons under siege and the roads sustaining the military's supply network interdicted, Somoza found his forces being attacked everywhere. The Guard's officer corps had been trained in small unit counter-guerrilla tactics at USARSA in the Panama Canal Zone but, while these tactics had generally proven successful over the years in Nicaragua's outback, nothing had prepared them for the FSLN's tenacious, urban-guerrilla fighters.

The highly motivated guerrillas were clearly fighting for a just cause and the Guard had nothing around which to rally, except its allegiance to the now morally bankrupt and obviously failing Somoza dynasty. That the Guard's soldiers would callously murder ABC television news reporter Bill Stewart, a civilian, in a summary execution before the network's own cameras in June 1979 stripped away the regime's last vestige of moral legitimacy in the eyes of the international community. Supplies for the FSLN now came pouring into Nicaragua from Cuba, Panama and Venezuela and more directly through neighboring Costa Rica to the south and Honduras to the west. At Washington's insistence Somoza finally resigned and fled to Miami in mid-July to open the way for a new government. A few days later the Guard dissolved and the rapacious dictatorship of over forty years had finally ended. It now remained to see how the new national unity government, the victorious FSLN Sandinista guerrillas and their nationalist supporters, would actually pan out. While the war had killed an estimated 50,000 people and terrible as it was, this was relatively benign in terms of the cost to what would ultimately transpire in El Salvador during the twelve-year civil war there (1981-1992) where over 75,000 people would eventually die and another 7,000 would simply disappear, never to be heard from again.

— El Salvador —

As was the case with Nicaraga, the roots of El Salvador's civil war of the 1980s could be traced back to the 1930s. In December of 1931 Major A.R. Harris, a U.S. military attache made a report which stated in part:

> "The first thing one observes when he goes to San Salvador is the number of expensive automobiles on the streets...There seems to be nothing between these high priced cars [Pierce Arrows - the Mercedes Benzes of the day] and the ox-cart with its bare-footed attendant. There is practically no middle-class between the rich and the poor. Roughly 90 percent of the wealth of the country is held by about one-half of one percent of the population.
>
> They live in almost regal splendor with many attendants, send their children to Europe or the United States to be educated, and spend money lavishly on themselves. The population has practically nothing."

Harris's conclusion was that "a socialistic or communistic revolution may be delayed for several years: ten, or even twenty, but when it comes it will be bloody one."

Ironically, about a month later and almost on cue, the Nahuizalco Volcano erupted in January, 1932, as a peasant uprising of Pipil Indians, led by the Communist revolutionary Augustin Farabundo Marti, took place. Scores of thousands of poor, destitute workers and farmers armed with little more than machetes, clubs and wooden spears came pouring out of the hills in an attempt to rectify the gross imbalance between the haves and themselves, the have-nots. The attempted revolution to recover ancestral lands and establish their basic rights was brutally put down by the army with some 10,000 peasants indiscriminately slaughtered in what became known as the great *matanza*. The military then took control of the country, enjoying the power of government, while the large landowners or elites enjoyed the fruits of the economy. The power structure was set in what had now become a culture of oppression. To ensure that their heads would never roll in a future revolutionary attempt and to preserve the status quo, the Salvadoran military propagated a series of seven consecutive military dictatorships with colonels and generals ruling El Salvador over a period of forty years.

With the advent of the Alliance for Progress during the early-to-mid-1960s, the Salvadoran economy boomed and an educated middle class began to flourish. Huge plantations, in the main belonging to some fourteen extended-family groups, produced coffee, sugar, cotton and cattle and very much defined the economy. Nonetheless, the modern mechanization of agriculture drove thousands of peasant workers off lands which hitherto had been their only source of income, leaving them for all intents and purposes destitute. For many even the smallest piece of land had provided some security in the form of a one-room hut or home and a tiny bit of space for subsistence crops. Now this was also gone and there was nothing left but the clothing on their backs. In an economic sense the competitive, large-scale capitalist market forces were working to squeeze out the lower-income producers and temporary workers, who seasonally picked coffee and cotton or cut sugar cane only four months a year and found themselves more and more paid at lower, unregulated wages. The dire poverty of the majority trying to eke out a survival existence on tiny plots contrasted blatantly with the luxurious opulence of the few, large landowners.

An example of the callous disinterest of the landowners in their workers' livelihood was explained to me in 1976 by Tom Rene, a former Army Green Beret lieutenant who had been employed during the mid-1970s as a manager of a medium-sized coffee plantation. According to Tom, the workers on his plantation often found themselves not receiving their paltry salaries of $30 to $40 per month for sometimes up to several months at a time and, even then, at the discretion of the landowner, were frequently only offered partial payments. On other plantations peasant workers demanding more pay or claiming that their wages were being stolen were shot by their bosses as an intimidating inducement to others not to complain. After about a year, Rene, thoroughly disgusted and fed up over not being able to change working conditions on the plantation, finally quit. In short, the rich were getting richer and the poor poorer in a country where, simply put, there was not enough land to go around. El Salvador's relatively tiny size, about the area of Massachusetts or some 21,000 square miles, contrasted considerably in comparison to neighboring Honduras which enjoyed six times the amount of land, but roughly about the same number of people (5 million).

In response to the seemingly endless perpetuation of military dictatorships and the generally adverse living conditions, the middle and the peasant classes formed a coalition called the National Opposition Union (UNO) and fell in behind Jose Napoleon Duarte, then the mayor of San Salvador and leader of the Christian Democratic Party, as a presidential candidate in the election of 1972. It was the first time in forty years that someone had been willing to seriously challenge the tyranny of the military and their landed-elite supporters in a bid for the presidency. Hopes for reform ran high. As the election results were being tallied and it was obvious that Duarte was winning a landslide victory, sweeping both the urban and rural areas, the electricity suddenly went off and the military suspended the ballot count. When it finally came back on some hours later, the military announced that their candidate had once again "won" the election. An attempted revolt by a small, reform-minded clique of military officers to reverse the fraudulent election results failed and shortly thereafter Duarte was literally run out of town, humiliatingly beaten up, and forced into exile. It was obvious to those interested in serious reform that peaceful political and economic change was now out of the question through elections and that the only recourse available would have to be in some form of coercion or even outright revolution.

The Catholic Church at this time materially changed its position from that of supporting the wealthy elites (they were the only ones who could afford to make significant contributions to the collection plate) because of their predatory behavior to that of helping the poor realize their political rights through deliberate organization to better confront the dictatorship. Over time the Church had become fed up with the abuse, injustice, poverty and neglect that its flock was suffering at the hands of the military and its supporting oligarchs. It was a moral stand which would be costly to El Salvador's Catholic clergy. Nonetheless, it did highlight the plight of the Salvadoran people at large who found themselves in a condition of being politically excluded from the decision making system through the closure of the electoral arena, economically marginalized (eking out a living in most cases on less than a dollar a day), and their aspirations for something better in life thoroughly crushed. This was truly a just cause merely looking for a charismatic leader who could articulate the cause into a plan for remedial, violent action which, in turn, would be acceptable to the people at large. The conditions for revolution were at hand!

Frustrated liberals, reformers and members of the Church joined hands in forming what became known as the United People's Action Front or FAPU. As FAPU's popularity and membership grew during the mid-1970s, President Jimmy Carter's call for human rights-based governments in March 1977 gave considerable moral support to the now increasingly militant reform effort, which now saw the United States government as being fully on its side, at least in spirit. While massive popular protests racked El Salvador during the mid-to-late1970s, it was the toppling of the Somoza regime in 1979 and the realization that wrong could be righted and abusive dictators overthrown through force that unleashed all the competing forces, right, center and left, in El Salvador. Boisterous, anti-regime demonstrations were now met with brutal repression on the part of the government's security forces, even to the extent of mowing down demonstrators by the dozen with machineguns on San Salvador's National Cathedral steps. Actions such as these brought the country to the brink of civil war and the battle lines were now being more and more clearly drawn.

With the situation now visibly out of hand and violence breaking out in most of the larger towns and cites, a group of reform-minded military officers staged a coup on 15 October 1979 and took over the government, ousting the military dictator of the moment, General Carlos Humberto Romero. This coup broke the old alliance between the military and the large, landowning-elite oligarchs and represented the first real challenge to the power structure in fifty years. While sweeping land reform and an end to repression were promised as part of the formation of a joint, civilian-military reform junta which was to serve as a provisional government, death squads ran rampant throughout the country in an effort by the anti-reform, conservative Right to stamp out the obvious revolution which was taking place under their very noses. In reaction to the indiscriminate killings, the civilians in the junta resigned in anger and disgust, leaving the military in charge of a reform effort that was now coming apart.

By 1980 the mass organizations of the left, including FAPU, joined forces, calling for armed insurrection. In an effort to advertise its potential for revolutionary power and further intimidate the ruling junta, over a 100,000 people from all parts of El Salvador joined together with FAPU on 22 January, the anniversary of the 1932 uprising, to march in a massive demonstration through the streets of the capital to express their dislike of the government. This event in particular had a great impact on Salvadoran society and the ripple effect of its actions, along with other demonstrations in other parts of the country also taking place over the next few weeks, brought the nation to the point of chaos. The escalating violence saw kidnappings, assassinations, building seizures, bank robberies, embassy occupations and hostage-taking on the part of the mass organizations occurring virtually every week.

While the Left appeared to have the numbers, the military had the guns. As the government's security forces and right-wing vigilante groups struck back with death squads, killing upwards of a thousand people a month, the Catholic Church's Archbishop Oscar Romero came out against the military's repression publicly, and for his efforts was in turn assassinated. The murder of Romero in mid-May 1980 further hastened the disintegration of El Salvadoran society.

While the revolutionary reformers and the left in El Salvador saw the Salvadoran Armed Forces (ESAF) as unredeemable, and therefore an element in society which had to be completely destroyed, the Carter administration thought it wiser to reform the military institution from within through a process of carrots and sticks (the offer of military aid as a reward for human rights reform or face a cut off of aid if reform was not forthcoming), rather than face the possibility of Marxist-Leninists coming to power, ala Fidel Castro's Cuba and Sandinista Nicaragua. After the failure of the second junta and in an ironic effort to reassert the reform process in the face of imminent Communist-led, mass guerrilla insurrection, Jose Napoleon Duarte was asked by the Salvadoran military in December 1980 to return from exile to take over yet another provisional government and lead the country into real reforms. Despite his animosity towards the military, Duarte accepted the challenge and tried to work within a repressive system to reform it. Many of his erstwhile friends, political allies and socialists of the 1972 era, such as Guillermo Ungo (Duarte's former running mate in the 1972 election), now formed the Democratic Revolutionary Front (FDR), which allied itself with the various militant and guerrilla factions working to overthrow Duarte's provisional reform government.

Duarte went to work as El Salvador's provisional president and his government promptly seized many of the large coffee estates in order to form peasant cooperatives for the masses of poor farm workers who desperately needed land. As land reform proceeded and 472 of the largest estates were dismembered in order to help provide land for scores of thousands of needy peasants, the government nationalized selected banks in order to provide credit and loans to this new farmer class. When the government took over the export industry to ensure that the cooperative and small farm exports would be able to get to the international market, the entrenched landed oligarchy began to realize that their previous power structure of absolute control over economy was now in jeopardy. When Duarte announced democratic reforms, including the rewriting of the constitution and future elections, the oligarchy also saw its political power structure directly threatened and struck back with their traditional methods of coercion - death squads.

Under the auspices of renegade ESAF officer, Major Alberto D'Aubisson, a psychopathic killer, and at the behest of the landed oligarchs, thousands of suspected reform sympathizers, members of the opposition, and militants were kidnapped, murdered, tortured and mutilated throughout the country; their bodies often unceremoniously dumped at the sides of rural roads. These included students, teachers, political leaders, newspaper reporters, businessmen, clergymen, and other professionals of one sort or another, in addition to thousands of peasant farmers and workers trying to take advantage of the land reform program. Despite Duarte's efforts to curb the violent excesses of the ESAF and the death squads, much to the dismay of Washington, they continued their deadly operations. The situation came to a head in December 1980 when four female American citizens, who were Christian lay workers and nuns, were murdered as suspected subversives by the military.

In the face of skyrocketing criticism from religious sectors all over the United States and Congress, Jimmy Carter immediately suspended all military and economic aid to El Salvador. Nonetheless, since Carter was a lame duck president and because the outspoken and newly elected anti-Communist, Ronald Reagan, was taking over the presidency in late January 1981, the ESAF and other Salvadoran security forces could still be fairly confident that the military aid faucet would be turned back on. They were not wrong.

Realizing that the moral force of Jimmy Carter probably would not remain behind them in the immediate future for 1981, the various guerrilla revolutionary factions concluded that they had better launch their "final offensive" to capture control of El Salvador as soon as possible, defeating the ESAF and accomplishing a *fait accompli* overthrow of the government before Reagan would actually come to power. They were confident of success, since the Spring of 1980 at the insistence of Fidel Castro they had unified most of their competing factions into an umbrella organization known as the Farabundo Marti National Liberation Front (FMLN). In exchange for unity of command, Cuba was now disposed to provide arms, ammunition and medicines via Sandinista-controlled Nicaragua. In addition, taking advantage of the Sandinistas' willingness to foment further revolution throughout the region from nearby Nicaragua, the FMLN established its headquarters in Managua, using a powerful command radio network to transmit orders to its guerrilla units in the field inside El Salvador.

The FMLN's unification of command and control brought together in one united effort guerrilla leaders from five major groups who believed in a variety of ideologies and strategies. Some believed in Maoist-style protracted revolution, others in mass, urban organizations, and still others in Vietnam-style guerrilla warfare as practiced by Ho Chi Minh or even Cuban-style armed uprisings or *focos*. Despite often incompatible strategies and tactics, a lack of cohesiveness, varying degrees of morale, discipline and most of all operational effectiveness, their common goal was to impose a Communist government on El Salvador along the lines of Castro's Cuba. For the remainder of 1980s the guerrilla groups continued to run their own intermittent wars, some striking inside the cities, others ambushing ESAF units in the countryside, raiding garrisons to steal ammunition and weapons, and still others blowing up roads and bridges to disrupt army communications and prevent export crops from reaching their markets.

The 10 January 1981 guerrilla offensive pitted some 2,500 guerrilla fighters and about 200 of their Cuban-trained cadres against the ESAF's 8,000 regulars and another 5,000 military-police of one sort or another. In addition to the military operations, a nation-wide general strike was called for in order to precipitate a massive uprising to bring down the government (a FMLN version of the 1968 Vietnam Tet offensive strategy and what they had also seen happen in Nicaragua in 1979). While the extent and violence of the roughly 40 guerrilla attacks country-wide virtually brought the army to its knees, the ESAF hung on in its garrisons and eventually sent the FMLN cadres and their troops reeling back into the countryside. Despite having demonstrated their power a year earlier with over 100,000 people marching in one demonstration alone, no major strike developed and the streets of the cities and towns were largely devoid of popular support. The insurgents, at that time particularly powerful in the cities and towns, lost many of their urban bases, being forced to retreat into the mountainous areas for sanctuary. The "final offensive" had failed!

In truth, the guerrillas had failed because they were unable to produce the mass popular uprising which was critical to their success; simply because the Salvadoran people at large believed enough in Duarte's promises of reform to take a "wait-and-see" attitude and not stake their lives in battle, thus generally opting out of the war for the moment. Nevertheless, an estimated 15,000 recruits did rally to the FMLN's cause and the revolutionaries ended up controlling a tier of several of the larger, northern provinces. In addition, some 600 tons of weapons and ammunition began to flow into El Salvador from Nicaragua, enough to equip and supply about 15,000 men. Conclusive evidence along these lines had been discovered in a captured guerrilla safe house inside San Salvador. At this point in time, success in the battle for El Salvador was now predicated by both sides on winning the hearts and minds of the people, for this was the key center of gravity which would ultimately determine the outcome of the war.

The response of the Reagan administration in early 1981 to the now stalled FMLN offensive was immediate and some fifty-five military advisors and $25 million in military aid were rushed to El Salvador. In addition, crash training programs were organized in the United States for several ESAF infantry battalions. Alexander Haig, a former Army general and now Secretary of State, declared that what was happening in El Salvador was a pattern of activities on the part of Cuba and Marxist-Leninist affiliates in Nicaragua to capture complete control of Central America - after the fall of El Salvador, Honduras would be next!

In March 1982, as a first step in the transition to democracy, elections for El Salvador's constitutional assembly took place. In a tremendous display of faith and confidence in the Duarte reform effort, over a million people turned out and voted in the country's first free election in 50 years. This was particularly meaningful as a test of Duarte's reform effort and the FMLN made a determined attempt to disrupt the process by directly threatening the people: "Vote in the morning and die in the afternoon!"

Despite having their lives threatened, sometimes being shot at and having election booths machine gunned and blown up, *campesinos* were observed coming in out of the hills of their own free will and walking up to fifteen miles to cast their individual ballots. Over time the elections would be seen as a turning point in the war. While Duarte had offered the FDR the opportunity to participate in the process, the guerrillas' political organ boycotted the elections. All the same, the success of the elections and the great popular display of resolute voters arrayed against them tended to demoralize the guerrillas. Ironically, the ultra-rightist and death squad advocate, Roberto D'Aubisson, running as the primary candidate for the National Republican Alliance (ARENA) party, was elected president of the constituent assembly.

The results indicated that the majority of the Salvadoran people had generally voted for a hard-line approach in dealing with the guerrillas, rather than the reform or soft-line, political approach. Nonetheless, with the U.S. Congress balking at providing aid to El Salvador due to reports of human rights violations and death squad activities being on the increase, the White House sent Army General Vernon Walters, then serving as an Ambassador at Large, to San Salvador to convince D'Aubisson to appoint someone else besides himself to head the government. Dr. Alvaro Magana, a moderate conservative and banker, was then appointed interim president of the country while the assembly prepared a new constitution. While this was taking place the guerrillas retreated to the mountains and began forming a disciplined fighting force more capable of challenging the ESAF.

— HONDURAS —

Having been designated as an Army foreign area officer specialist for Latin America, as well as trained in the Spanish language, which had been enhanced through previous assignments in Guatemala, the School of the Americas (USARSA) in the Panama Canal Zone, and Peru, I was assigned as a lieutenant colonel in mid-1982 to the position of Chief, Army Section of the U.S. Military Group (MILGP) in Tegucigalpa, Honduras. The geographic location of Honduras in the center of Central America gave it the appearance on a map of being a keystone in a Roman arch, in this case the arch being part of the isthmus connecting North and South America. Ordinarily a backwater "banana republic" with previously little or nothing of an international note ever happening, the country would quickly rise to a position of critical importance in terms of Washington's foreign policy initiatives unfolding within the region for the remainder of the 1980s. Overlapping for a few days with (soon-to-be promoted to colonel) Lieutenant Colonel Charles Frei gave me an opportunity to obtain a quick, first-hand overview of what was going on inside Honduras before going on down to Panama to visit the U.S. Southern Command (SOUTH-COM) for further briefings on the situation in Central America.

Charlie Frei was a Green Beret veteran and acknowledged special operations expert who had done a superb job in Honduras. In reaction to local insurgents kidnapping wealthy businessmen, taking hostages and hijacking airplanes, he had recommended to the U.S. Ambassador, John Dimitri Negroponte, that U.S. special operations forces be requested to train up a Honduran army anti-terrorist unit to deal with any further situations that might come to pass. The recommendation had been acted upon and training was on-going as I arrived in country. While not fully appreciated at the time, this was one of the best decisions made on behalf of Honduran national security and would bear considerable fruit over the next few years, as well as the rest of the decade.

SOUTHCOM was located at Quarry Heights in the Panama Canal Zone. Besides its primary mission of defending the Panama Canal, it was also responsible for all U.S. military activities and relations within Latin America, extending from Mexico's southern frontier as far south as the southern tip of Chile. Around mid-morning of the 1st of June I reported to the office of Lieutenant General Wallace H. Nutting, Com-

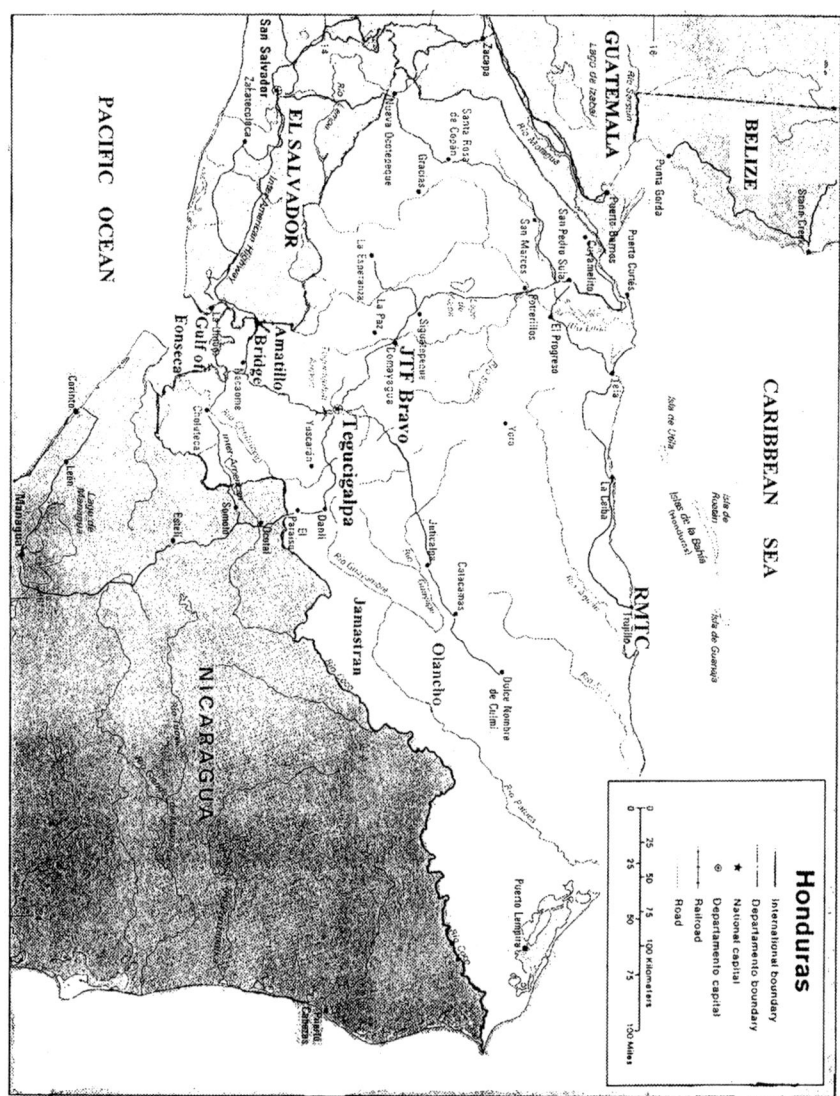

mander-in-Chief (CINC), USSOUTHCOM. Wally Nutting must have heard me introducing myself to his aide-de-camp for he came striding out of his office to greet me effusively. He had read my Army personnel record file and knew that I had been with the 11th Armored Cavalry (Blackhorse) Regiment in Vietnam. This had apparently impacted on him favorably as he too had served with the Regiment as a colonel and was its last battlefield commanding officer as it prepared to leave Vietnam in March 1971. So we had a combat soldiers bond which broke down the usual formalities between the general officer (himself) and the field grade level of rank (myself) which I held. Actually, I had run across the general in the Fall of 1978 while serving with the 5th Infantry Division (Mechanized) during a NATO-sponsored REFORGER maneuver exercise in West Germany, which pitted the 5th Mechanized against Nutting's 3rd Armored Division (as a major general, he was then a division-level commander). One of the 5th's tank company commanders, Captain Bernie Reiger, noting a gap in Nutting's defensive alignment, charged on through to capture Wally Nutting's headquarters and the general himself. While this was an embarrassing moment for the 3rd Armored and NATO, Bernie, now a "hero" of sorts, became known as "Rommel" Reiger due to his exploit.

The general, having long forgotten the incident, stood an impressive six feet, five inches tall and even appeared big when sitting behind his oak-wood, CINC's desk. In addition to my background with the cavalry and Green Berets, he seemed very interested in what I had learned from my first few days in Honduras and what I thought about the situation there in regards to the Sandinistas in Nicaragua.

Having been ushered into his office and now comfortably seated in a heavy, leather armchair, I waxed enthusiastic, explaining that, while I still needed to do a detailed analysis of what I thought would be needed in terms of equipment and training for the Honduran army, I had been toying with some ideas on increasing its mobility and firepower in the face of an obvious tank and mechanized infantry threat emanating from a buildup now to taking place inside Nicaragua. Given that security assistance funding at that time was not all that substantial, it appeared to me that the new Hughes 500MD attack helicopter, now available on the international arms market, with its periscope-like target acquisition sight and its two or four TOW (tube launched, optically guided warhead) anti-tank missiles with a two-mile range would give the Honduran military a cost-effective capability for defeating any mechanized force of tanks and armored personnel carriers that the Sandinistas could throw into a ground attack against it. The advantage of the Hughes 500MD configuration was that it could look for targets with its three-foot high periscope extending above its rotor blades while its mainframe and armament were completely hidden behind trees or ridgelines; thus enabling it to pop up and engage the enemy by surprise from a distance over which it could not be easily observed. The mountainous nature of much of the Honduran countryside adjacent to Nicaragua would, in short, enable the pilot and his gunner to engage in long range anti-tank ambushes from the front, flanks and even rear of the enemy.

Nutting cut me off abruptly stating, "Honduras ought to focus solely on its internal subversive threat and not worry about outside threats [Nicaragua], since the United States will provide the umbrella in the event of an outright invasion." He went on to state that he did *not* want to develop any kind of an "offensive capability" which might tempt the Hondurans to conduct cross-border conventional operations into neighboring countries. It was obvious that he no longer appreciated my observations on "the situation" and that the interview was getting a little tense if not down right testy as it rapidly came to a conclusion. Nevertheless, it did seem to me that everything taking place in Central America concerning Honduras, Nicaragua and El Salvador was synergistic in relationship and the activities taking place within each country were inherently related as part and parcel of everything else. In sum, the solution to what was taking place there involved a regional approach as well as country-specific approaches. The interview terminated with Wally Nutting personally giving me my mission statement: "Do everything you can to enable the Honduran army to defend its country." It was direct and to the point.

My conference with the CINC now concluded, I stood to attention, saluted, and did an about face to leave. At that moment Nutting rose from his desk and approached me from behind, placing his great, bear-like arm and paw of a hand around my shoulder, saying, "Sewall, I know you do not have much money to work with and I know that you are alone, but just do the best you can and I will try and help out from here." He was right in one sense: I was alone and very much "an army of one." While in my notes I made the point that the general appeared "naïve" in many respects about the situation in Central America, I was probably being far too harsh for Wallace Nutting was actually a very frustrated general.

Some years later I found out that, despite the Reagan administration having been in power for more than a year, the Sandinistas consolidating their revolution inside Nicaragua, guerrilla warfare raging in El Salvador, and an incipient insurgency developing in Honduras, the

CINC, USSOUTHCOM, had been unable to obtain appropriate guidance as to how Washington wanted him to deal with Central America. Neither the Department of State nor the Department of Defense had any concrete idea as to what he should be doing in terms of a strategy to support American interests in the region; thus the CINC did not really know what he should be telling me in terms of how to proceed in Honduras. But there was a reason for this, as I will explain later on in this chapter. My next stop at SOUTHCOM was to the offices of the J-2 (intelligence) and the J-5 (civil-military affairs).

At my intelligence briefing on Central America, I had the chance to interface with a number of other professional officers who had spent years studying the security situation in the Americas and in particular Central America. Fundamentally what they perceived taking place was a continuation of Fidel Castro's efforts to foment revolution in different parts of the world. Beginning in 1978 Cuba had placed major forces of up to 20,000 men in Angola and another 15,000 or so in Ethiopia. This Cuban Afrika Korps was operating as part of a Moscow-Havana Axis to support wars of national liberation throughout the Third World (By this time the Soviet Union was also involved in military operations in Afghanistan.). As a reward to Castro for his timely support, the Soviets had promised to guarantee Cuba's oil needs through the mid-1980s and were paying up to four and five times the world price for Cuban sugar. All told, the Soviet Union was spending upwards of $11 billion annually in support of its Caribbean ally.

The Americas Department inside Cuba was now running training camps for future guerrillas and sponsoring networks for the covert movement of personnel and materiel between the island and Central America. Of the some 5,000 Cuban advisors, teachers and medical personnel assigned to Nicaragua to work at all levels of the military and civilian infrastructure, an estimated 1,500 were actively providing military instruction and combat training. In addition, $28 million worth of military equipment had been received by the Sandinistas from the Soviet Union and its Warsaw Pact allies. This included tanks, light aircraft, helicopters, field artillery and anti-aircraft artillery involving surface-to-air missiles and automatic cannons, as well as tons of small arms and ammunition. And more was pouring in each month! Cuba's role in all of this was to facilitate the flow of arms from Vietnam, Ethiopia and Eastern Europe into and through Nicaragua to El Salvador and other parts of Central America, including Honduras.

I pondered what they were telling me in light of what the CINC had said was my mission. In response to some questions, the officers providing the briefing were not certain what Nicaraguan intentions were in terms of the use of the heavy forces now steadily building up on the other side of the Honduran frontier. They could be used for defensive purposes or as a deterrent to anyone contemplating an invasion of Nicaragua. While this was readily apparent as a potential use, they were not at all in agreement as to whether there was an intended offensive role for these forces in the future. In my own mind I imagined the FMLN guerrillas seizing the eastern portion of El Salvador, establishing a provisional government, and then calling for help from Nicaragua. I could further envision Sandinista tanks, mechanized infantry, and artillery rolling across the Choluteca coastal plain (later referred to as the "Choluteca Gap"), which ran along Honduras's Pacific coast region from Nicaragua to El Salvador, as part of an effort to support the "liberation" of El Salvador through extending military "aid" to a new insurgent government. It was not a happy scenario and I suggested to my briefers that they weigh its consequences if it should ever come to fruition.

The situation in El Salvador was depicted as evolving into a knock down drag out fight, with the FMLN guerrillas developing battalion-sized forces to try and overwhelm the ESAF. Honduras was depicted in the main as being a transmission belt or infiltration route for arms being sent from Nicaragua to El Salvador and for lesser amounts of arms being forwarded on into Guatemala. In short, while Honduras was not seriously regarded by SOUTHCOM in terms of threats, there was much more to the country and the role it would eventually play than was appreciated at that moment.

About two weeks after returning to Tegucigalpa, the Honduran capital, I was working in my hotel room on the outskirts of the city in mid-June when I heard the sharp report of an explosion from some sort of a bomb downtown. In the same instant as the sound of the explosion reached me, the hotel's lights and air conditioning went off. Sensing that this was something very much out of the ordinary, I dashed outside onto the patio to see if I could hear or observe anything more (automatic weapons fire, rocket explosions, shots etc). Nothing. A deafening silence appeared to reign at that moment. Automobile and truck traffic on the roads was still moving, camouflaging to some degree the true extent and significance of what had just happened. Nonetheless, what I had heard was the opening "shot" or blowing up of the Tegucigalpa electrical power generator as part of a formal "declaration of war" on the part of the Marxist-Leninist-inspired Honduran insurgency in what would become a vicious, internal, subversive war, lasting the better part of a decade.

The Honduran insurgents apparently had taken their cue for action from the FMLN inside El Salvador. At that time, as the Farabundo Marti guerrillas had begun to turn their forces into 500-men battalions for formal battle with the ESAF, the FMLN's leadership decided in the interim to put pressure on the government's reform effort by creating an economic crisis. Because a national economy works to maintain a nation's military in the field, it stood to reason that it should also be attacked. To this end the FMLN advocated economic warfare in order to destroy the Salvadoran economic infrastructure, which included sabotage of the electrical power plants, telephone lines, bridges, transportation of all types, and even the most important crops, such as cotton and coffee. By creating and then intensifying the crisis, it was thought by the Salvadoran guerrillas that this, in itself, might cause the governing regime to collapse economically, losing credibility over time and ultimately leading to a popular uprising on behalf of the guerrillas.

Sabotage operations in themselves are fairly economical and do not require a great deal of effort. As such, a few pounds of explosives detonated at key points in a critical infrastructure can create chaos. Undoubtedly this was also the expectation of the guerrillas inside Honduras and the attack conducted inside Tegucigalpa was designed to destabilize the Honduran government. As a terrorist act the guerrilla's bombing could be seen as a psychological attempt to destroy the solidarity, cooperation and interdependence on which societal functioning is based, leading over time to insecurity and distrust on the part of the people. Certainly part of their strategy was also political, so as to discredit President Suazo Cordova's government and then claim the moral right to govern. By undermining the democratic process in play and causing the government to declare a state of emergency or even a state of siege, there was also some cause for reasoning on the part of the guerrillas that military and police repression would ensue and that their armed struggle would then acquire a real reason for being - to save the country from military authoritarianism. But the guerrillas had miscalculated across the board and the chaos and destabilization created in the capital came back to haunt them in spades. In short, their effort boomeranged against them with important detrimental, long-term affects.

The bombing of the electrical grid in Tegucigalpa had a significant impact on all of society inside the city and its environs. As a dramatic act of violence, it did catch the attention of the people. Commerce was disrupted as banks and businesses had to revert to hand calculators to conduct transactions. In the local hospitals, some patients undergoing operations died on the operating tables for lack of electricity to adequately maintain the extensive lighting systems that the surgeons required to carry out their delicate work. But the impact was even more general. With the stop lights inoperative, traffic now became congested, snarled and generally unmanageable and accidents increased accordingly. Popular television programs, soap operas and even radio broadcasts could no longer be enjoyed by the people at large; university classes could not be taught at night; and life after sunset appeared to be governed by just how many candles one could find at home for light.

But what most affected the population in general was that their meat and dairy products were now spoiling in the supermarkets and household refrigerators. It is one thing to cause general inconvenience throughout society, but when it comes to food and survival one does not want to have the local housewives arrayed against you. The dismay of the housewives turned into full blown criticism if not wrath over the inconvenience of having to go to market every day in order to purchase that day's main meal - and the blame was placed squarely on the guerrillas! This negative reaction was an aspect of their sabotage operations that the Honduran guerrillas had not contemplated and they had fallen into a trap of their own making by not thinking through the consequences of their actions. Instead of rallying the people to their cause as part of an opening campaign to bring down the Honduran government, the guerrillas had accomplished just the opposite!

While Ambassador Negroponte worked frantically to alert the Department of State and the White House in Washington as to the seriousness of the situation in Tegucigalpa and the need to respond with an emergency power generation capability, Honduran police and army counter-guerrilla teams went into action with a vengeance. It wasn't that the security forces lacked previous experience. On the advice of Argentine and Israeli advisors and at the behest of General Gustavo Alvarez Martinez, then a hardnosed, no-nonsense Public Security Forces (Fuerza de Seguridad Publica - FUSEP) commander, the Israelis had trained a special strike force and para-military commando unit within the police force. This force in late November 1981 had successfully raided a guerrilla safe house on the outskirts of Tegucigalpa, killing two guerrillas, including a Uruguayan, and capturing a number of Hondurans and Nicaraguans, as well as automatic weapons, explosives and notebooks concerning training in Cuba. A week or so later guerrilla safe-houses in north coast La Ceiba and San Pedro Sula were raided, with arms, explosives and communications equipment being captured. Each raid had produced key pieces of information that clarified the extent of the insurgency effort inside Honduras and led to the next counter-guerrilla operation. Nonetheless, it was very difficult to determine exactly who was behind the attack on Tegucigalpa's power grid.

The insurgent groups as organizations inside Honduras tended to be numerically small and structured into cells, with usually only three to ten individuals in each cell and very much focused on the urban areas. While the cells formed networks, usually only one member of any one cell was fully aware of his or her cell's links to any of the other cells. This compartmentalization reduced the chances of other cell members identities being known in the event of capture. To further provide for security, a system of dead drops (mail boxes) or cut-outs (messengers) who merely passed information without knowing the identities and locations of the sending or receiving cells was sometimes employed. Some cells specialized in military action, assassinations or ambushes, others in sabotage operations, and still others in proselytizing, recruiting, running safe houses, and purchasing and infiltrating weapons and explosives into and through Honduras.

Apart from the relative security achieved, the great liability of the cellular system was that it could not readily expand into large numbers of guerrillas to conduct major operations without being compromised by police intelligence penetration. During the early 1970s the Uruguayan Tupamaro urban guerrillas had undertaken a similar operation, which ultimately failed when they tried to expand their organization. When all was said and done, an urban area was actually a very difficult ambience to operate in and the guerrilla or terrorist cells embedded in the population always lived in fear of being exposed by those who lived around them. For the security forces inside Tegucigalpa, this ultimately became a deciding factor which played to their advantage in the internal war for control of Honduras.

After about five days had passed since the bombing of the electrical grid in Tegucigalpa, exasperated housewives and others began to pass on to the police tips as to the whereabouts of some of the clandestine cells' guerrilla members. One such piece of information led the police force's National Directorate of Intelligence (Directorio de Investigacion National - DIN) to surround a kiosk or cigarette-soft drink stand which concealed a couple of the guerrillas. Attacking the kiosk with an anti-tank rocket and small arms fire, the DIN's counter-insurgency strike force, known as the "Cobras" captured the surviving members of a cell. Under intense interrogation the insurgents fingered other cells' whereabouts and the hunt was on. One after another, over the period of a couple of months, the police, assisted by the army, rounded up about a dozen cells inside the Tegucigalpa area alone. The counter-attack was so thoroughgoing that the back of the insurgent effort inside the capital was shattered in terms of the guerrillas being able to successfully execute another bombing along the lines of the power grid action. Placing icing on the cake was the fact that John Negroponte was able to coordinate the shipment into Honduras of a replacement electrical generator and even have it operational by a little more than a week after the original bombing had taken place. The ambassador's effort on behalf of Honduras was impressive and something that the Honduran government and its people would not forget for quite a while.

By this time there were enough captured documents and prisoners from the guerrilla war inside Honduras to obtain a fairly good idea as to what the government was up against. It appeared that out of the success of the Sandinista overthrow of the Somoza regime and motivated by the inspiration that military dictatorships could be successfully confronted, several or more insurgent groups in strengths approximating some 200 guerrillas each had formed inside Honduras itself. The Lorenzo Zelaya

Popular Revolutionary Forces (FPR-LZ), linked to the FMLN in El Salvador as well as to Nicaragua and Cuba, had established its headquarters in Tegucigalpa sometime around 1978. Its modus operandi was bombing and strafing embassies in general and especially, as the chance presented itself, the U.S. Embassy, American companies, and military personnel. Fortunately the Lorenzo Zelaya folks were not good shots, as was illustrated in September 1981 when they ambushed five members of an Amy Special Forces mobile training team (MTT) riding in a truck approaching the entrance to the MILGP's offices. Firing at pointblank range, assault rifle and sub-machinegun bullets splattered the truck from front to rear, passing in front of and behind the soldiers, tearing their clothing and equipment, but not producing any serious casualties. God was certainly with the Green Berets that day! The FPR-LZ then followed that action up in April 1982 when some of its members hijacked a commercial airliner in Honduras and escaped to Cuba.

The Cinchoneros Popular Liberation Movement (C-MPL), founded in 1980, was based in both Tegucigalpa and San Pedro Sula and became one of the most active of the guerrilla-terrorist organizations in Honduras. Linked to the Sandinistas and the Farabundo Marti guerillas, the Cinchoneros specialized in bombings, kidnapping businessmen for ransom, bank robberies, hijackings and hostage taking. Besides hijacking a New Orleans-bound, Honduran based airlines (TAN SHASA Airlines) in 1981, the C-MPL pulled off its most spectacular operation in September 1982 or about three months after the bombing of the Tegucigalpa power grid. The guerrillas brazenly took 104 hostages in a raid on a Chamber of Commerce meeting in San Pedro Sula and over the next eight days presented a series of demands for the release of dozens of political prisoners in El Salvador and Honduras.

While the police strike force or "Cobras" coolly stood by to await an opportunity to counter-attack, some 20,000 people brazenly demonstrated against the Cinchoneros in protest over their continued use of terrorist tactics and violence. The demonstration came as a shock to the guerrillas and appeared to demoralize them. After the army cut off their water and telephone communications and seeing that they were not welcome by the population, they dropped their demands one after another, finally settling for a plane and free passage to Cuba. It was the last major action on the part of the C-MPL for the duration of the war.

The third most important insurgent group was the Morazan Liberation Front for Honduras (FMLH), which was formed in 1979 and based in San Pedro Sula, taking its *nom de guerre* from the former Honduran military hero and president of Honduras during the 1830s, Francisco Morazan. Besides kidnapping for ransom, it attempted to build a series of armed groups and cells which could be called upon to foment a national uprising. All the guerrilla forces had but one thing in common: the overthrow of the Honduran government and the taking of power by force. All were inspired by the success of the Sandinistas in Nicaragua and the on-going insurgency in El Salvador. And all ignored the fact that Honduras was now governed in mid-June 1982 by a duly elected, democratic government, which was in the process of attempting to implement an agrarian land reform on behalf of the poor, Honduran *campesino* peasant farmers. Nonetheless, to further build their infrastructure, various guerrilla splinter groups were noted as being in the process of infiltrating the universities, labor unions, farmer cooperatives, and affiliated church groups and using their cadres to serve as social activists and catalysts for revolution. While the guerrillas in general were able to generate well over a million dollars for their coffers from the some 232 kidnappings perpetrated during the guerrilla war, some of these backfired. Hostages, such as eminent banker Paul Vinelli and entrepreneur Jacobo Larach, were murdered outright in retribution for the victims' families not paying the ransoms or in some cases not paying enough, further turning the population against the insurgents.

The Honduran counter-insurgency war fought against the guerrillas was for the most part conducted in a clandestine manner; a cloak and dagger-style affair which involved spies and counter-spies, kidnappings, assassinations, disappearances, torture, secret detention centers, ambushes and murders on the part of both sides. In short, it was a hard, cruel war, which unfortunately involved the innocent as well as the guilty and produced a series of human rights abuses and violations which only came to light over time.

In the truest sense for the military and the police, the insurgent enemy was very much ill-defined. The guerrillas encountered were often found to be students, priests, *campesinos*, labor leaders, university professors, factory workers, or in other words from all walks of life. In most cases none wore a uniform and merely blended into the population as a whole, which meant that the intelligence services had a major challenge in terms of attempting to obtain accurate information in order to ferret out who was who, target, and ultimately capture or kill the guerrillas before they could inflict further damage against the government and its people.

Complicating the issue of preempting guerrilla attacks on the part of the security forces was the myriad of concerned Honduran citizens and nationalists who like anyone in a free society saw it as a right and even civic duty to voice their opinions about what they saw as both good and bad about the government and society. Those who were vociferous in their criticism of Suazo Cordova and his policies sometimes found themselves also targeted by the security forces. As such, it was unfortunate that the intelligence services in play tended to equate all dissent with subversion. Nonetheless, it was the earlier evolution of Honduran society and its politics which set the stage to a considerable degree for the conditions leading to the guerrilla war effort.

During the first half of the twentieth century tropical Honduras was known as the "quintessential banana republic." Located about 900 air miles to the southwest of Miami (a distance shorter than Miami to Chicago for the purposes of comparison), it was the poorest (80 percent poverty) and least developed nation (50 percent illiteracy in a population of five million) in the region. Roughly the size of Tennessee (46,000 square miles) and with a national budget equivalent to that of Macon County, Georgia (about $200 million), Honduras was also one of the most mountainous countries in Central America. A limited road network connected the cities and towns of the western half of Honduras, as well as its Caribbean and Pacific coasts. As only about one-fifth of the country's land was suitable for agriculture, the bulk of the good land or the fertile, low-lying valleys and coastal plains was owned by large Honduran agro-export farmers or transnational companies. Its dozens of rugged, saw-toothed ranges ran from the Guatemalan frontier in the west out towards the Caribbean to the north and Nicaragua to the east. Only a flat, largely uninhabited tropical zone located in the northeast known as the Mosquitia plain provided a contrast to the ever present mountains and valleys. This terrain, coupled with its lack of rich volcanic soil as was typically found in its neighbors, meant that Honduras had had little to offer the world in terms of exports until the international fruit companies recognized the value of the otherwise uninhabited, tropical, north-coast lowlands as a prime banana-growing region.

Hundreds of thousands of acres of coastal land were obtained by the United Fruit, Standard Fruit, and the Cuyamel Fruit Companies at little or no cost from the Honduran government in exchange for building railroads, ice plants, generators, hospitals and port facilities, which generally benefited in the main the companies and their workers. By 1930 Honduras was producing one-third of the world's supply of bananas. In short the companies became self-contained and self-governing enclaves, looking out for their interests by bankrolling both of the country's Liberal and National Parties and otherwise bribing and influencing those who would become president of Honduras. If local political turmoil appeared threatening to the fruit companies, Washington would sometimes intervene directly to provide stability and preserve the peace "American-style."

This happened in December 1924 when warships were sent to the Honduran coast along with a contingent of Marines to occupy Tegucigalpa. With only three weeks notice the government was forced to call for an election. As a result, the Washington-backed candidate for president (Miguel Paz Barahona - the only one running in the election) "won" and was sworn in as the story goes, "with a U.S. Marine holding the Bible." Nonetheless, the frequency of changes in national leadership (126 changes of government and some 385 coup attempts since gaining independence) and the continuous political intrigues caused some writers to quip that the capital should be known as "Tegucigolpe" to reflect the large number of coups (*golpes* in Spanish). Honduran politics, deprived of national goals, became a kind of charade in which the only gains possible were those wrested by individual factions from the government's treasury, and that "treasury" depended to a large part on the handouts it could garner from the foreign owned export sector. Thus, control of the presidency was the only one sure way to achieve fame and fortune. Disgruntled plantation laborers who demanded higher wages and/or better working conditions and got out of hand in terms of labor unrest were put down brutally and forced back to work by government-controlled goon squads, and sometimes even the army.

The Great Depression of 1931 saw the government's financial situation deteriorate to the point that it was forced to borrow $250,000 from the fruit companies to pay the army. While this guaranteed stability for the American fruit companies, the country as a whole suffered and grinding poverty became the lot of most Hondurans (rural families lived in thatched huts with dirt floors and tended farms averaging two acres in size, typically earning no more than $250 a year). Including the banana company managers, only a handful of people actually lived in some luxury, while the rest of the country suffered primitive housing, inadequate diets, abysmal health and sanitation conditions, and an almost nonexistent educational system. This situation continued under the sinister and often brutal caudillo rule of Tiburcio Carias Andino from 1932 to 1949 and finally came to a head in the mid-1950s.

With an eye on the Jacobo Arbenz reform effort in Guatemala in 1954, the occasional labor unrest for that year over unmet wages and poor working conditions blossomed into a national general strike, involving some 55,000 workers in the banana, mining and tobacco industries. While an agreement was eventually worked out, the incident produced a national labor movement which came to the fore as a recognized entity in the form of the first union effort of any consequence in the nation's history. With the backing of the American Federation of Labor's (AFL's) American Institute for Free Labor Development (AIFLD) and the Department of State's Agency for International Development (AID) in 1961, the labor movement established its own worker's rights and created the basis for social stability for the remainder of the century. Ironically, while this was taking place, the CIA was exploiting Honduran territory to conduct its campaign to overthrow the democratically-elected Arbenz government in neighboring Guatemala. This was not the first nor the last time that Honduras would get caught up in Washington's CIA-sponsored border wars.

By the early 1960s Honduras was governed by the Liberal Party's Dr. Ramon Villeda Morales. Villeda was an anti-Communist progressive along the lines of John F. Kennedy who embraced the latter's Alliance for Progress, instituting an aggressive land and labor reform program under the auspices of the National Agrarian Institute (INA). Recognizing that private, family farming offered the greatest potential for enabling the poor peasant-worker to raise his standard of living, the government focused its efforts on 123,000 families who lacked access to productive farm land. As a result of the land reforms implemented and the availability of investment credits, beef, cotton, seafood (shrimp) and coffee became significant export products for the first time and a light industry focusing on metals, soap products, textiles, furniture and apparel began to develop.

Spurred on by U.S. funding and growing revenues stemming from a strong Central American Common Market trade, the Honduran president encouraged workers to demand higher rural wages and occupy idle land, some of it owned by the American banana companies. The president's popularity with the rural poor was offset by the hatred of the large land owners and banana companies. Nonetheless, the military inside Honduras backed Villeda up until he attempted to disband the national police force and replace it with a civil guard, independent of the army. At that point a military coup was staged in October 1963 and Ramon Villeda found himself overthrown by an air force officer, Colonel Oswaldo Lopez Arellano. The pending national elections were cancelled, Congress dissolved, and the constitution suspended as Lopez declared himself president.

Ruling as a military dictator and chief of state in the *caudillo* tradition of the early days of nineteenth century Central America, Lopez Arellano, the son of poor peasant farmers, forced most of the Liberal Party leadership into exile and then declared himself as the opposition National Party candidate for president in1965. Hard-eyed, venal, small in physical stature, and sometimes repressive, he ruled Honduras by rigging elections until 1975 (with only a roughly two-year interlude in 1971 and 1972 in which he unsuccessfully attempted to rule through a puppet president, Ramon Cruz). Distrusting the Alliance for Progress, he said he would only accept aid from the government of Lyndon Johnson if he could "institutionalize it," which inferred channeling the funds into the pockets of himself and his cronies. This attitude was not at all new in Honduran history and since 1700 had remained the primary characteristic and social value of Spanish colonial America in which public office at all levels was seen as a legitimate instrument to further personal, private interests over public weal. In short, lacking a tradition of civic service, government jobs were viewed as entitlements and rewards for personal loyalty to the national leader rather than as public trusts and responsibilities and, as a result, corruption and malfeasance in public office reigned supreme.

Although *campesino* radicals were suppressed and imprisoned from time to time during Lopez's tenure, he did pursue a moderate approach towards the *campesinos* in general (over 23,000 families received farmland) and labor, which included pressing ahead with some of the Villeda reforms, supporting labor unions, and diversifying the economy. Like most of his military predecessors, he attempted to exploit his new-found power to enrich himself, taking advantage of his close ties to the banana companies. For his cronies he offered "a deal" and for his competitors or those viewed as enemies he offered "the law." Nonetheless, the inherent corruption that tends to accompany power at the highest national levels caught up with him. In May 1975 when the U.S. Securities and Exchange Commission implicated the dictator in a $1.25 million bribery scandal with United Brands (the former United Fruit Company under a new name, which stood to save $7.5 million in reduced export taxes), a military triumvirate, under considerable criticism and pressure from the media, finally threw him out of power for good. Still, Oswaldo Lopez had not fared too badly economically, having looted the nation's treasury to the degree that he now held controlling interests in the national airline, banks, automobile dealerships, credit card companies and so much land that it would ultimately require a computer system to keep track of it all.

The ouster of Lopez in May 1975 unleashed a flurry of reprisals on the part of the large landowners and cattle barons who launched their own private armies of thugs against the poor farmers and peasant organizations. In the north-central province of Olancho the cattlemen and the military conspired the following June to capture and then cook to death in bread ovens nine of the peasant activists promoting land invasions for the poor. The "Horcones massacre" came as a shock to the otherwise relatively mild-mannered Hondurans and highlighted the feudal conditions that actually existed in many parts of the country. Possibly in an effort to show its good side the military junta, now ruling the country, authorized an agrarian reform program which promised over 350,000 acres of land to the campesino poor. Nonetheless, scandal tainted the junta and the press reported unbridled corruption, links to drug traffickers and embezzlement of government funds.

The coming to power of the Sandinistas in neighboring Nicaragua in 1979 and the unfolding civil war in El Salvador sent shock waves throughout Honduras. With considerable prodding on the part of the American Embassy, the junta leadership, seeing what was then transpiring inside El Salvador and facing a declining economy, agreed to hold elections as a way to hopefully immunize Honduras against revolutionary activity. Elections for president and the national Congress were set for 29 November 1981, with the swearing in of the president taking place in January 1982. As a result, the Liberal Party's Roberto Suazo Cordova, the country doctor and "farmer" from La Paz, became the next president, effectively renewing the Honduran democratic tradition and heading the country away from the dictatorial rule of the past seventeen years. About a third of the country had participated in the voting (1.5 million), which saw the Liberal Party decisively defeat the National Party. Nonetheless, while democratic elections in favor of civilian rule would continue for some time, it was the Honduran military that continued to dominate the internal politics of the nation.

Upon returning to Honduras from my visit to SOUTHCOM and my meeting with General Nutting, I took stock of what would have to be done to prepare the Honduran army to defend its homeland. Fundamentally, I needed to know in detail what the Sandinista threat was amounting to and how well prepared the army was to meet that threat. In essence, any shortfall in the army's capability to defeat a Sandinista offensive would have to be met in terms of organizing, equipping, manning and training the force. My threat analysis and the army's actual situation would drive any and all of my decisions as to what needed to be done.

The Sandinista army consisted in the main of a half dozen light infantry regiments totaling some 15,000 men and what intelligence reports also indicated was a developing motorized rifle division (MRD) organized along the lines of the Russian or Cuban equivalents. This stood to reason since the Cubans were training the Sandinistas in the use of the weapons systems for the MRD and were copying their own organization and tactical employment doctrine based on their experiences in Africa. The equipment for the MRD was essentially in place and training was ongoing as part of the Cuban effort to flesh out its structure of three motorized (armored personnel carriers) rifle regiments, one tank regiment and one artillery regiment. In addition there was an armored reconnaissance battalion, an engineer battalion and even some tactical bridging units. When all was said and done a MRD typically moved to the attack in two or more echelons or waves totaling some 200 tanks (T-55s and PT-76s) and another 200 wheeled armored personnel carriers (BTR-60/152s) in a formation extending out about a mile wide. In addition, it could attack over a distance of 200 miles before having to refuel.

These units were supported by 122mm and 152mm artillery pieces which were towed by trucks and BM-21 rocket launchers which could launch a devastating barrage of up to forty 122-mm projectiles out to a range of 12 miles. Additional support for crossing steams and rivers was provided by engineer mobile bridging and amphibious ferries, reportedly equipped with scissors (BLG-60) and cantilever (GSP/MTU-20) bridges launched from tracked vehicles. In Europe, there is a river 30 to 60 feet wide every six miles and one 60 to 300 feet wide every thirty miles. For this reason the Soviet army made sure that the MRD had as part of its organization river crossing equipment, which of course enhanced the forward mobility of its tanks and armored personnel carriers. The T-55 tanks sported a 100mm cannon with a range of 1,500 yards and the PT-76 tanks, which also had an amphibious capability, sported a 76mm cannon with a range of about 1,000 yards. The artillery could range out to 11 miles for the 152mm pieces and some 18 miles for the 122mm pieces. No other country in Central America had a force equivalent to what the Sandinistas and their Cuban advisors were putting together. In essence, it was a force that could either be used to punch through the Choluteca Gap into El Salvador or even traverse the several main roads leading from Nicaragua into the vicinity of Tegucigalpa.

The Sandinista light infantry units could be used in a conventional or unconventional manner and were armed with the standard assault rifles, machineguns and rocket propelled grenades found in the Soviet and Cuban inventories. While these troops could be trucked onto the battlefield for further commitment on foot, there was also an airmobile capability which one had to consider. The Sandinistas had been supplied by the Soviet Union with at least a dozen MI-8 HIP troop-carrying helicopters, which could also serve as gunships in a ground support role, firing machineguns and rockets. Equally as important, there were reports that the Soviets intended to provide some armor-protected MI-24 HIND-D attack helicopters. Known as the "flying tank," the MI-24 had seen service in Afghanistan and was noted for its extraordinary firepower in the form of its 128 air-to-ground 57-mm rockets, bombs, four anti-tank guided missiles and assorted machineguns and automatic cannons. In essence, the dozen MI-8s offered an air mobility potential to simultaneously lift some 140 soldiers to virtually any point within the southern part of Honduras or a belt of land 100 miles deep, adjacent to the Nicaraguan frontier. This helicopter lift capability gave the Sandinista infantry the ability to leapfrog over and behind opposing ridgelines and mountain defensive positions, cutting them off and otherwise assaulting them from the rear. It even meant that Tegucigalpa was potentially within range of direct attack. In sum, the offensive potential of the Sandinista army was considerable when compared to that of the Honduran army, which totaled some 11,000 men (about the size of a single U.S. Army light infantry division) who could only move by truck or on foot.

Having a good idea of what Honduras might be facing in terms of a ground conflict with Nicaragua, as well as its own internal insurgency threat, I conducted a series of visits to see first hand the condition of the army's infantry, armor and artillery units. My first visit was to the special forces anti-terrorist training school nearby Tegucigalpa. The last increment of some thirty soldiers (they had started out as a group of about 100 candidates) were completing their final phase of training before joining their unit. The U.S. special operations trainers had done a splendid job in putting together not only an anti-terrorist-trained force but also the equivalent of an elite Ranger strike force of some one hundred men for use against the guerrillas as well.

One of the trainers, who was still under deep cover and called himself "Tom," informed me that the training conducted in Honduras went well beyond the tolerances of what was allowed in the United States. To make his point we observed the final training exercise that every candidate would have to pass in order to qualify as a member of the Honduran special operations commando. As a candidate entered a room containing a series of hostages (dummies), he received a full kick in the chest from his American trainer, knocking him to the floor.

While still groggy and in pain from the impact of the kick and before he blacked out or threw up, the candidate had to draw his automatic pistol and shoot each of the several kidnapper dummies "dead" without hitting any of the hostages. It was a severe, if not brutal, trial by force, but Tom swore by it as the only way to truly weed out the weak from the strong. Over the next couple of years the army's special operations commando would prove its worth time and again. With an elite force like this in play I was not particularly worried about dealing with the guerrilla-terrorist threat inside Honduras.

The condition of the Honduran army as a whole in mid-1982 was another story and reflected its relatively recent history. The army had been at war about thirteen years earlier in 1969; the issue involving Oswaldo Lopez's forced ejection of some scores of thousands of Salvadoran migrant workers back into El Salvador. While the war only lasted about four days against the Salvadoran armed forces (ESAF), Honduras's lackluster performance had been caused in large part because its army's leaders had been involved in politics and the administration of the country, and not particularly focused on the institution's principal function of equipping and training for war fighting. As a result, partially manned (often only 50 percent of the infantry strength of any battalion was actually in place), poorly equipped and trained, and ineptly led soldiers took a licking from the Salvadorans, who quickly captured the western frontier town of Ocotepeque, while penetrating some twenty miles into the Honduran frontier areas. In addition, there was a failure on the part of the army's intelligence service to determine accurately and in a timely manner where and in what strength the ESAF was attacking. Neither Oswaldo Lopez Arellano, the commander of the armed forces, nor his top army commanders ever bothered to visit the battlefield to see first hand what the valiant Honduran soldiers were up against.

What ultimately saved the army from total defeat was the rugged, mountainous terrain which slowed down the ESAF infantry, sapping their strength and ultimately causing the ground invasion to fail. Another, possibly more decisive factor, was the Honduran air force which managed to bomb some petroleum storage tanks near San Salvador, destroying precious aviation fuel and thereby scaring El Salvador's national leaders into breaking off the war to prevent further damage to national resources. Some of the lessons learned from the 1969 war had been absorbed, but others had not.

Two things stood out in my visit to five of the army's ten infantry battalions. First and foremost the training in each of the battalions was not uniform. Depending on the training background of the junior officers and NCOs, each company sized unit of some 100 to 150 men employed a series of often different tactical doctrines for movement to contact and fire and maneuver when actually in contact. In short, there was a hodgepodge of generally obsolete World War II and Korean War tactics in play. Secondly, the battalion commanders did not really take much interest in training and appeared to be all too preoccupied with their personal business interests. In essence, the corruption and indiscipline of the Lopez Arellano era was still prevalent. To this end the practice of maintaining fictitious soldiers on a battalion's roster, for whom pay could be drawn and the cost of rations issued, was still taking place to a considerable degree and was in essence a second salary for the battalion commander and any other officers who wanted to split the illegal take. Conducive to this situation was the fact that each battalion did its own recruiting and basic training. This meant that higher headquarters in Tegucigalpa had to rely on the word of the battalion commander as to how many soldiers had joined his unit and were still on its rolls; there was virtually no formal accounting. I did not fully realize it at the time, but corruption was all pervasive throughout the middle and higher ranks of the Honduran army and to a degree which would only become known as time went on.

During the 1970s the army's basic infantry weapons had been upgraded and included the 7.62mm Belgian manufactured FAL rifle which was also used by the soldiers of many of the NATO countries, the Swedish 84mm Carl Gustav anti-tank rocket, the U.S. 106mm recoilless rifle and a series of 60mm and 81mm short range mortars. The FAL in the hands of a good rifleman could hit targets at 400 yards range and the Carl Gustav and 106mm recoilless rifle could defeat a T-55 tank with one shot out to a range of 700 and 1,800 yards respectively. In short, the weapons were there in limited quantities, but the small unit training, manpower, and leadership at the battalion level was not. In addition, the infantry was almost always trucked onto the battlefield

The commander of the Honduran army's 1st Armored Regiment, Colonel William Said Speer and the author (right) in 1983. A year later Said was involved in an insitutional coup d-etat carried out by the Honduran military, which saw armed forces' commander Major General Gustavo Alvarez Martinez overthrown and forced into exile. (Honduran army photo)

and then proceeded on foot from its drop off point. There was no tactical airmobile capability of any real note.

The army's mortar-artillery battalions of which there were two consisted of a total of roughly 30 Israeli-manufactured Soltam, 160mm heavy mortars with a range of about four miles. The Israelies were very clever about selling their castoff weapons and equipment to third-world countries with limited budgets and the Hondurans in this case had bought into an "artillery" weapons system which could only be used in a static situation for point defense. Impressive in size, the Soltam was an ungainly and largely immobile piece which was difficult to employ in any form of mobile offense or defense. Clearly what the Honduran army needed was an artillery that could range out to six to ten miles, was mobile in the sense that it could be driven or even airlifted around the battlefield, and could be brought into action within a minute of having received a request for fire. That the U.S. 105mm howitzer could shoot low angle or normal trajectory fires, as well as high angle trajectory fires over mountainous terrain, was going to be a major consideration in re-equipping the army's artillery component.

My last visit for the moment was to the 1st Armored Cavalry Regiment located on the outskirts of Tegucigalpa. Our British NATO ally had gotten to Honduras during the 1970s and provided 16 Scorpion light tanks armed with a 76mm canon, firing a high explosive plastic warhead. Upon impact, this type of warhead adhered itself much like putty to the target's armor plate before exploding and creating a spall-like effect on the other or inner side of the armor plate (e.g. inside a tank turret) in which flakes, chips and splinters of metal would fly around, incapacitating or otherwise killing the enemy vehicle's crewmembers. The Scorpion was the mainstay for many years of the British armored reconnaissance forces in the northern defense sector of West Germany and had only been replaced as the Soviet Union fielded the better pro-tected T-62 and T-72 series of tanks. Now and then a British military attache would come through Honduras to check on the spare parts and ammunition needs of the army's Scorpions, which he vehemently contended were more than a match for the T-54/55 series tanks now flowing into Nicaragua.

Apart from the Scorpions, the cavalry regiment sported some 50 Saladin armored cars, each mounting a 50mm turret mounted cannon and some Israeli RBY reconnaissance vehicles, some of which mounted a 106mm recoilless rifle. It was a force that, if properly supported by artillery and infantry armed with sufficient anti-tank weapons, could probably hold its own against a Sandinista motorized rifle division attempting to traverse the Honduran mountain passes along the two primary avenues of approach into Tegucigalpa: the Danli or eastern approach and the Choluteca-San Lorenzo or southern approach. The regiment also had U.S. M2 .50 caliber machineguns in abundance which would have to serve as both an anti-infantry and anti-helicopter defense against Sandinista air mobile operations. To defend the Choluteca gap, however, would require other measures, which were beyond the capabilities of the armored regiment. My analysis now complete and a notebook chock full of observations, I returned to the MILGP located on a hill overlooking part of Tegucigalpa's international airport to finalize my conclusions and to put together my plan to upgrade the Honduran army.

The security assistance effort inside Honduras revolved around the MILGP which served as a coordinating center for the sales of weapons, vehicles, aircraft, boats, equipment and spare parts, as well as training for the army, air force and navy. While the MILGP worked directly for SOUTHCOM, it was also considered part of the Department of State's "Country Team" inside Honduras. All requests for purchases or that is to say permission to draw down on the monies allocated by State for security assistance had to have the approval of the U.S. ambassador and were sometimes reviewed by other embassy staff personnel and country team elements, such as the Agency for International Development (AID) and the United States Information Service (USIS).

It was understood that the counter-insurgency effort inside Honduras was a synergism where political, diplomatic, economic, and psychological as well as military factors would have to be combined in pursuit of a political objective. How we orchestrated the campaign would make the difference. Lieutenant Colonel Mike Robbins, USAF, was temporarily filling the position as MILGP Commander, while also serving as the Chief, Air Force Section and Commander Robert (Bob) Hopkins, USN, was serving as Chief, Navy Section. Whether one liked it or not, we were all competing for the same pot of monies provided by the Department of State for the purposes of conducting security assistance operations inside Honduras. Mike was working on gearing up the Honduran Air Force (HAF) and its aging, one-dozen Super Mystere B2 fighters and a handful of A-37 fighter bombers to eventually confront the probable future threat of Sandinista-piloted MIG-21 ground attack jet fighters, which, with their twin barrel 23mm automatic cannon, were considered a highly lethal threat to the Honduran air and ground forces. Other reports indicted that the Nicaraguan airfields at Punta Huete, Montelimar, Puerto Cabezas and Bluefields were now being prepared to receive the new aircraft. In addition, the Warsaw Pact's Bulgaria had offered to train some 50 Nicaraguan pilots to fly the MIG-21s, so the threat appeared very real. Nonetheless, the HAF prided itself on being the most technologically advanced air force in the region and very much desired to keep it that way. Bob, in turn, was working on upgrading the Honduran Navy's coastal-patrol capability to better protect the Gulf of Fonseca to the south and the country's Caribbean waters to the north. The Sandinistas appeared to enjoy harassing the Honduran fishing fleet from time to time and this required serious attention. In short, each service had its own special requirements and priorities. We would meet at least once a week to compare notes and keep abreast of what was happening inside Honduras in terms of our respective focuses.

At one of the meetings in July, I presented my observations on the condition of the Honduran army and its shortfalls and what had to be done in terms of getting this force up to par in order to confront a Sandinista invasion. I pointed out that tanks, artillery, armored personnel carriers and other equipment were continuing to arrive at the Nicaraguan ports and that this indicated that the Sandinista armed forces were intending to go well beyond their estimated strength of some 40,000 or about four times that of the Honduran army. Our anticipated security assistance monies had been increased by Congress for use by the Department of State, and for the coming year were said to be in the realm of around $31 million, up from the roughly $9 million of 1981. I stated that, if given priority at that moment in terms of funding for retraining and reequipping the army, I might be able to close the shortfall and have the entire infantry portion of the army retrained and some of the artillery upgraded in about two years. I further explained that what I was proposing was a major change in the army's tactical infantry doctrine and, based on my experiences in Guatemala and at the School of the Americas, this would not come to fruition unless the entire army as an institution was completely re-indoctrinated in the new tactics.

To be effectively implemented, the doctrine had to saturate the Honduran army as a whole. Since the infantry battalions constituted the bulk of the army, this was the place to start and build upon. I also pointed out that the infantry badly needed an airmobile or helicopter airlift capability to increase its mobility in order to shift forces around the battlefield - especially in the mountains. This, of course, would fall under the auspices of the HAF, which controlled all military aviation assets within the country. In this area we would be virtually starting from scratch. In short, if the Honduran army did not become combat ready rather quickly, it could potentially be easily ground down under the juggernaut of a robust Nicaraguan army, which was already blooded in combat from its successful earlier experience against the Somoza regime and expanding rapidly.

Two years to accomplish my program may have seemed like a long time, but it was typically how long the U.S. security assistance system was taking to respond to high priority requests. As a case in point the Logistics Section of the MILGP had orders pending for spare parts and equipment going back as long as almost three years, so Mike and Bob understood my predicament and to a considerable degree sympathized with my position. Nonetheless, they, too, had their own priorities for their respective services. At least, I thought, I had stated my case in no uncertain terms. Having made out a training and equipment implemen-tation plan, I went to see Colonel Jose Bueso Rosa, the Chief of Staff of the Honduran Armed Forces.

Colonel Bueso had a sharp, calculating mind which belied his short, rather stout and otherwise unimpressive stature. More often than not he would be my principal point of contact for dealing with the army since he had the ear of Brigadier General Alvarez, who, of course, made all the final decisions and provided direction to his subordinate services. Bueso listened carefully to my observations on the strengths and weak-nesses of the army, nodding from time to time and digesting all that I had to say. To smooth the more critical aspects of my observations, I had prefaced my observations by telling him how impressive the morale was among the army's soldiers, NCOs and junior officers and that their "can do" attitude was comparable to that of my own army. I did not want this Honduran colonel, a veteran of the 1969 war, to think that an arrogant "Gringo" had come to town to deride his army and then boss him around.

Completing my observations, I then launched into what I thought should be a short term solution for training. I explained that one of the U.S. Army's premier generals, General William E. DePuy, who was running the Training and Doctrine Command (TRADOC) at Fort Monroe, Virginia, was in the process of retraining the entire U.S. Army to fight outnumbered and win. The emphasis was on improved infantry tactics to meet and defeat an opponent through the adroit use of terrain and movement techniques, battlefield mobility, and the most efficient application of all available weapons systems. If he approved, I intended to bring into Honduras a mobile training team (MTT) which would not only retrain each infantry battalion at the squad, platoon and company levels to U.S. standards, but also train one equivalent Honduran army MTT to carry on the training after the U.S. MTT departed. The program would last at least until all ten battalions had gone through the process.

For the first battalion to be trained, the U.S. trainers would conduct the training by themselves with their Honduran MTT counterparts merely observing. Then the Hondurans would directly assist the U.S. MTT in the training of the second battalion. For the third battalion, the Honduran army MTT would be on their own with only one original member of the U.S. MTT remaining in country to observe. By training one battalion every two months the entire program would take about two years to complete. If the Hondurans could form more than one of their own MTTs, the process would go that much faster.

Bueso liked the idea and made a note to see that the army fully supported its implementation. In addition, I suggested that there needed to be a better way to train the new soldier recruits than leaving it up to the individual battalions. Perhaps an army basic recruit training center could provide the uniform, quality training at the individual level that would supplement what the MTTs were doing at the unit level. This would require quality NCOs who could teach the recruit's the new tactics that the MTTs would be emphasizing. The colonel nodded, indicating that he understood my intentions, but said that that would have to wait until he could discuss it with his staff. It crossed my mind that he knew that such a change as this would undermine, if not take away, the "second salary" of many of the army's colonels, causing considerable friction within the upper echelons of the officer corps who enjoyed this form of self-enrichment at government expense.

Bueso's follow-on question was more to the point: "What about the artillery situation?" I explained that this required not only the acquisition of the cannons, trucks, ammunition and all the related supporting equipment, to include fire direction centers and radios, but also the training to go along with it. It was very much dependent on the monies being allocated by the U.S. Congress and how long the logistical pipeline would take to bring everything into play. For the colonel it was a top priority and something he would bring to the attention of General Alvarez, since he knew that Alvarez was well connected to John Negroponte, who, in turn, had demonstrated that he could make things happen within the Washington community in favor of Honduras. Helicopters for airlifting infantry over the mountains were another point of interest and Bueso assured me that the air force would comply with whatever we could provide as a solution.

With Colonel Bueso now behind me and approving my plans, I sent out a flurry of cables through the embassy back to SOUTHCOM requesting the immediate deployment of the initial survey teams required to come into Honduras to make final plans and calculate what would be needed in detail in terms of trainers and supporting equipment. Besides the infantry training MTT, I called for an intelligence training MTT to ensure that the army was prepared to deal with the gathering and processing of enemy battlefield information and a psychological operations MTT to try and improve not only the army's relations with the Honduran people as a whole, but also to be able to exploit PSYOP opportunities or weaknesses presented by the guerrillas inside Honduras. In this case I called for my former comrade-in-arms and Green Beret PSYOPs MTT buddy, Luis Santos. Normally one did not call for a person by name for this type of mission and allowed SOUTHCOM and the U.S. Army Security Assistance Agency at Fort Clayton, Canal Zone (Panama) to coordinate the manning of the MTTs through their own links. Nonetheless, Luis was one of the best Latin American PSYOPs people still on duty with the Army and I was looking for the best! Some weeks later the survey teams began to trickle in-country to kick off my program.

Fortunately, during the intervening weeks while I had been out analyzing the army's battalions and formulating my training/equipment upgrade program, General Wallace Nutting had been watching the situation from his SOUTHCOM headquarters and had even made a visit to John Negroponte in Tegucigalpa. Now more cognizant of the extraordinary military build-up taking place in Nicaragua and keenly aware of what was going on inside Honduras, as well as what it was going to require in general terms of money, arms and equipment to build up the Honduran armed forces, the general was true to his word. At his behest a full blown, nine-man survey team under the direction of Colonel Marc A. Cisneros was deployed into Honduras to conduct a formal, SOUTHCOM-sponsored survey of the Honduran armed forces (HAF) and the army in particular. This survey, called the Force Modernization Study and patterned after what Army Brigadier-General Fred Woerner and his team had done in El Salvador roughly a year earlier, was all encompassing and went far beyond what I had been able to accomplish up to that time. The Cisneros' team spread out amongst the Honduran military and came up with a plan which not only encompassed my own thinking on enhancing mobility and firepower, but also brought into play expertise in logistics, maintenance and technical aspects in the fields of communications and helicopter aviation. The team's work was thorough and called for a security assistance level of some $100 million per year for the next four years! Truly, this was beyond my wildest dreams and more than I could have ever imagined in terms of the detailed technical requirements laid out for enhancing each branch of the Honduran army.

The Study not only energized the MILGP's programs, but created the official basis for Congress to weigh in behind the Department of State with the large amounts of money that would be required to purchase the big ticket items such as the helicopters, artillery pieces and the accompanying training and complex logistical and maintenance effort that would have to be brought into play to support them. The Departments of Defense and State generally accepted the enhancement program as submitted by SOUTHCOM and, with incremental Congressional funding approval, began implementing it. By 1984, including a proposed supplemental, funding for that year totaled some $78.5 million. Security assistance for Honduras was underway at a level which could not have been imagined just two years earlier and would ultimately total about half a billion dollars over the next eight years.

From time to time during my first few months in Honduras and when Mike Robbins was away tending to other business, I acted in the capacity of the MILGP commander. This required me to travel across town to visit the American Embassy and, in particular, consult with Ambassador John Negroponte over various aspects of our security assistance program. On one of these visits, Negroponte gestured for me to sit down in his office while he was speaking on the secure-telephone in an animated manner to the Under-Secretary of State for Latin American Affairs. The conversation, however, appeared to be all one way, top down, with the essence of the ambassador's portions of the conversation revolving around a series of replies: "Of course, Sir! Yes, indeed, very well Sir! We will do that immediately Sir...." I thought to myself, "Even a prestigious ambassador like John Negroponte has to answer to a chain of command, just like in the Army - yes sir, yes sir, three bags full!"

Unfortunately, what I had heard was an indication of a deeper problem within the foreign policy making establishment of the U.S. government. Despite having been in power for more than one year, the Reagan administration still did not have a concrete policy for dealing with the situation in Central America. What was starting to dribble down through the diplomatic and military chains of command to the field were a series of often unconnected programs and policies which could be construed in virtually any manner that one might prefer. For example, within the Embassy in Tegucigalpa one could find those who felt that Washington's policy was that of seeking the direct overthrow of Nicaragua's Sandinista government by force. Others felt that the policy was one of calculated intimidation towards Nicaragua in order to place the Sandinista administration under such stress economically and politically that it would fail, and thus ultimately fall from power. Still others saw the policy as providing a show of force to deter the Sandinistas from military adventurism within the region. And still others entertained the idea that the policy was to lure the Sandinistas into conducting some form of overt act or attack on Honduran territory to provide the United States with an excuse to invade Nicaragua, overthrowing the Sandinista regime by military force to stabilize Central America. If this welter of often conflicting policy approaches were confusing to those "in the trenches" at the Embassy in Tegucigalpa, it was equally so for those dealing in security assistance. The first prerequisite for formulating a successful strategy to deal with the situation in Central America was a firm sense of national direction, and this is what we did not have. As a result, SOUTHCOM found itself operating in a vacuum and for the duration of the war in Central America was never able to promulgate a coordinated regional policy or strategy of any real note.

A week or so later, I was abruptly called to the ambassador's office for a closed door session in which a CIA operative was formally outlining the general thrust of President Ronald Reagan's effort to build and arm an anti-Sandinista resistance force of counter-revolutionaries to penetrate into Nicaragua in order to destabilize the Managua government. Jabbing from time to time at a map spread out on a table, he explained that this was in essence a surrogate guerrilla force, to be covertly equipped, trained and employed at the direction of the *White House* to wage war directly against Nicaragua. While the CIA was the lead government agency in forging the effort, the National Security Council was also to provide direction. In the event that the operation was found out, the cover story to be employed was that the "Contras," as these guerrillas were sometimes referred to in the short form of the Spanish *contrarevolucionario*, were conducting arms interdiction operations along the Honduran-Nicaraguan frontier to stop the infiltration of weapons and ammunition into El Salvador. It was a plausible deception since the press had reported with photos a truck containing a hidden shipment of M-16 rifles which had been captured in late 1981 while attempting to pass from Nicaragua through Honduras and on into El Salvador. The Contras, we were told, were made up of former Somoza National Guard fugitives, mercenaries from various parts of the world, disenchanted Nicaraguan farmers, and Miskito Indians from the Atlantic coastal and Honduran frontier regions.

Fearing that the Indians living along the Coco River would feed and otherwise aid the guerrilla war against Nicaragua, the Sandinistas had deliberately uprooted and relocated the latter group, consisting of some 20,000 people, as part of a larger program to also force them to embrace the Marxist-Leninist politics of the new Nicaragua. Previously, the Miskitos had never been integrated into Nicaragua's heavily influenced Spanish culture and had always opposed attempts by Managua to control them (under the Somozas they enjoyed a semi-autonomous status). Now, those who resisted the Sandinistas saw their villages razed and dozens of people killed outright as a result of the repression. The end result was a tremendous amount of resentment on the part of the Indians against the Sandinista regime. As part of the Contra effort, Miskito guerrilla fighters were now conducting hit-and-run raids against Sandanista troops, while other guerrillas blew up bridges inside the provinces of Chinandega and Nueva Segovia, which effectively cut the vehicular traffic between Managua and Honduras.

According to the CIA agent providing the briefing, the actual mission of the Contras was the destruction of Nicaragua's rural economy through sabotage. This was a significant change from the original strategy of penetrating into Nicaragua to establish a Government of Free Nicaragua, which would then be recognized by Washington as the "legitimate" government of the country so that formal military aid from the United States could be forthcoming. It crossed my mind that we were now sponsoring the same type of operations that the Honduran guerrillas had carried out with the destruction of the Tegucigalpa electrical grid just a short while before. If the Tegucigalpa attack had been counterproductive, would not also the Contra attacks of a similar nature create the same sort of backlash? Already there had been some comments in the press as to human rights abuses by the guerrillas, involving the killing of teachers, coffee pickers and health workers, which undoubtedly would work against them. In any event, Washington's political objectives for the use of the Contras were not all that clear and it appeared to me that these folks were being duped into executing a U.S.-sponsored intimidation policy towards the Sandinistas with no real end in sight. In short, they were to be cannon fodder, sacrificing their lives, and essentially being hung out to dry in the service of fuzzy American political interests. It sounded all too much like Vietnam once again.

Perhaps my being in attendance was to gage my interest in becoming involved in assisting in the coordination of the program, using my MILGP assignment as a cover. If true, my obvious skepticism of the project as a whole and its prospects for success must have caused Negroponte and the CIA to reject me outright, since I was never invited back to attend any further briefings or future meetings concerning the Contra effort. A week or so later Army Colonel Frank Matthews arrived in country to assume the command of the MILGP, releasing me from the necessity of having to deal with the nebulous politics of the U.S. Embassy in Tegucigalpa. While that December it was announced that the Boland Amendment had been put into law by the U.S. Congress, barring any further support of military operations aimed at overthrowing the Sandinista government, the CIA continued to secretly play with fire in Nicaragua.

As part of SOUTHCOM's effort to build up the HAF, it had been recommended by Colonel Cisneros and others that the army needed to participate in large scale, field maneuver operations so as to give the brigade and battalion commanders and their staffs a chance to put into practice what they had learned in their classrooms at the School of the Americas and the Honduran army's own general staff level courses conducted in Tegucigalpa. As a result, during the Fall of 1982, the SOUTHCOM Director of Operations (J-3), Colonel William Comey arrived in Tegucigalpa to discuss with Colonel Bueso the possibility of conducting a combined Honduran-United States military exercise. It was intended that all the services (army, navy and air force) of both nations should participate as part of a SOUTHCOM sponsored exercise.

Bill Comey, a hardnosed infantryman, explained that the army or ground portion of the exercise would take place in the eastern portion of Honduras in the proximity of the Nicaraguan frontier. Essentially, all the troops and equipment were to be trucked into the maneuver area and the forces would then conduct the exercise on foot. Knowing that the U.S. Embassy's policy at that moment was to intimidate the Sandinistas in so far as possible, I suggested that it might be appropriate to include a parachute drop of the Honduran army's entire 2nd Infantry Battalion (airborne), which ought to "scare the willies out of the Sandinistas," who would undoubtedly detect the armada of aircraft participating in the exercise with their own radars located at Esteli to the northwest of Managua. I pointed out that it made no sense to conduct an exercise of this nature if we did not get the maximum psychological value out of it. Bueso liked the idea of the airborne operation, but Comey did not, since it complicated his planning and execution of the joint armies-portion of the exercise and required U.S. Air Force C-130 transport aircraft to participate in ferrying the Honduran paratroopers to a selected drop zone.

Nonetheless, the exercise, known as "Big Pine" took place in February 1983 and went off extremely well, with paratroopers raining down along the Nicaraguan frontier, while the U.S. Navy conducted amphibious operations with various ships and landing craft along the Honduran north coast. The U.S. Air Force was very much present in that it carried out the parachute drops, assorted landings and aerial supply operations, as well as emplacing a sizable radar installation staffed by over fifty Air Force personnel on top of a small mountain just to the south of Tegucigalpa. A total of 1,600 American military personnel participated, as well as some 4,000 Honduran military personnel. Things were beginning to happen in Honduras and it was in the main because of General Paul F. Gorman, who had replaced General Wallace Nutting as CINC, SOUTHCOM.

With U.S. policy towards Nicaragua not being very clear, Paul Gorman took the precaution to prepare as best he could for a possible invasion of Nicaragua. This required that a platform for introducing forces by air into Honduras be developed. Whether the forces would be used for defending Honduras or even offensive operations aimed at Nicaragua was not as important as being prepared for any eventuality. To this end SOUTHCOM took the initiative to establish `, a mini-SOUTHCOM forward operating base and operations and logistics co-ordination center, at the HAF's Pamerola Air Base, located in the vicinity of Comayagua to the northwest of Tegucigalpa. Palmerola's airfield length was extended so it could receive the Air Force's C-141 Starlifter equipment and troop transport aircraft. With its central location on the main north-south road connecting the north coast (Puerto Cortes) with the south coast's east-west Pan American Highway running through the Choluteca Gap, Pamerola (later renamed the Soto Cano Air Force Base) could support and otherwise reinforce much of eastern and southern Honduras as the case might require. In addition, a series of a dozen or so small airstrips were constructed by U.S. Army and National Guard engineers throughout the southeastern portion of Honduras.

This was essentially a clever shell game that General Gorman was playing against the Sandinistas as a cover for a more elaborate construction of an 8,000-foot long airfield much closer to the Nicaraguan border at El Aguacate. In addition, the long range radar site (AN/TPS 43) was activated some eight miles south of Tegucigalpa on top of the Cerro de Mole mountain to provide an early warning of Sandinista aerial operations and aid in the detection of small, Farabundo Marti support aircraft flying over Honduran territory (Choluteca Gap and Gulf of Fonseca) en-route from Nicaragua to El Salvador. An additional smaller, short range, tactical radar (AN/TPS 63), manned by U.S. Marines to further monitor aerial infiltration into El Salvador was installed on top of the mountain which constituted Tiger Island located in the Gulf of Fonseca. To soften the American presence inside Honduras, civic action teams were sponsored by JTF Bravo to build roads, bridges, latrines, schools, health clinics, and to dispense medical and dental treatment in order to build rapport with the local population. While Palmerola was technically still a HAF airbase, it was now also a U.S. airbase which would be enhanced over the years to support any intended operation that President Reagan might have in mind.

After Big Pine had been completed, I flew to San Salvador for a day to see how the situation was going there and to find out if there was anything that we could be doing in the MILGP to help out in the ESAF's war effort against the FMLN guerrillas. In looking at El Salvador's situation it appeared that Honduras could make a significant contribution as part of defending its frontiers and border areas by isolating the Salvadoran insurgency battlefield on land, at sea and in the air in order to cut the FMLN guerrillas off from their base of supply (Nicaragua).

This particularly held true in the area of the Choluteca Gap and the Gulf of Fonseca where infiltration was taking place monthly, if not weekly. That March a Honduran police patrol had a chance encounter and firefight with a FMLN guerrilla unit making its way through the hilly region of the Gap. A captured notebook taken off the body of one of the dead guerrilla leaders contained the compass headings, codes and 125 place names and their coded identifiers - a complete infiltration route or corridor from Nicaragua to El Salvador! While how many guerrilla fighters, supplies, and arms and weapons had actually transited the route to the Salvadoran battlefield to the west and south of Honduras was open to conjecture, the FMLN's intensified operations indicated that they were certainly not lacking in personnel and supplies. What did not make the transit by land generally came by canoes (*cayucos*) or other low profile boats, which were not easily detected by radar, through the Gulf of Fonseca into predetermined drop points along the southeastern coastal region of El Salvador. The third mode of infiltration was by air in which as many as 100 aircraft every three months (about one per day) would come and go, bringing into El Salvador important FMLN personnel and returning to Nicaragua with badly wounded guerrillas for treatment. The situation reminded me somewhat of the Ho Chi Minh Trail in Laos and Cambodia with Managua (the FMLN headquarters) serving as an equivalent "Hanoi," commanding and controlling the war through subordinate headquarters and units on the battlefield.

Immediately upon arriving in San Salvador I had the opportunity to meet Ambassador Edwin Corr whom I had first run across while he was on duty as the U.S. ambassador to Peru in 1981. A former Marine captain in Vietnam during the 1960s, Ed Corr was considered a "trouble shooter" for the Department of State, since he appeared to be assigned to one after the other of the many trouble spots in Latin America (Bolivia was his next assignment after El Salvador). But Ed Corr was not a happy camper. The FMLN at this time were engaged in large-scale conventional operations against the ESAF, while at the same time complementing these activities with sabotage and terrorism in the urban areas and the countryside.

Indeed, it was a stressful time for all concerned, but what irked the ambassador most was that the major power structures in Salvadoran society, principally the military and the economic elite, were very much antidemocratic in their basic attitudes and seemed to be working to undermine the reform programs Napoleon Duarte had brought into play. Ironically and for different reasons, the major plantation owners and the FMLN guerrillas were now aligned *on the same side* in terms of trying to defeat the agrarian reform efforts to distribute land to the landless. The guerrillas did not want the reforms to come to fruition because they would take away a significant part of their just cause and the landed oligarchs did not want the reforms to succeed because they would be losing money, power and prestige (the government was limiting their individual land ownership to a little more than 600 acres at that time). In this regard the latter had brought into play a legion of lawyers to hamstring in every possible way the government's land titling and redistribution programs. In addition, some landowners were distributing their estates among relatives and friends so that the officially allowable acreages would fall below the mandated level of the reform law. It was very frustrating to Corr to have to deal with this day in and day out, when it was so obvious that the programs were critical to the government's claim to legitimacy in order to properly govern the country and defeat the guerrillas.

Ed Corr slammed his fist down on his office table exclaiming: "And I have to go and pound on the president's [Dr. Alvaro Magana] desk every day to plead with him to get control of the death squads so Congress doesn't cut our funding!" He then went on to explain that, besides his problems with Roberto d'Aubuisson, the ESAF's performance on the battlefield had been marred by incredible atrocities perpetrated against the civilian community, and this was playing into the hands of the guerrillas who were hoping that the U.S. Congress would become morally repulsed and cut off all military aid.

A case in point had been the revelation that an ESAF infantry brigade had directed an operation in December 1981 against a supposed FMLN stronghold in the village of Mozote in the northeastern province of Morazan. In reality, the community there was an anti-Communist, Christian lay community with no real interest in the war. The end result of the ESAF's intelligence failure to accurately determine the real nature of the proposed target area and the ensuing military operation resulted in the slaughter of 794 peasants: men, women and children. Only one person, an elderly lady, had survived the holocaust and was able to report what had happened! In another incident earlier that year, the ESAF had indiscriminately mowed down a mixed group of guerrillas and civilians who were being chased by armed helicopters along the Rio Sampul.

Incredible as these and other similar events were, the FMLN did have considerable responsibility for what was happening. There was a tendency on the part of the guerrillas to promise to protect the local villages in the areas under their control in exchange for the people's loyalty to the FMLN cause. The only problem with this was that, when the ESAF showed up in force, the guerrillas dressed in civilian garb would attempt to escape, making no pretense of helping the people. The people in turn would attempt to escape the ESAF by running off with the guerrillas; thus confusion reigned on the battlefield with guerrillas and civilians being mixed together. Unable to distinguish who was who, the end result was that all too often the ESAF soldiers and helicopter gunship pilots would engage anyone observed fleeing the village, including the masses of innocent civilians, under the assumption that they must be guerillas too or they would not be fleeing. Invariably what took place was mass slaughter. It was obvious to me that if John Negroponte thought he had problems, Ed Corr had them in spades. Bidding good bye and good luck to the ambassador, I headed over the ESAF's Joint Intelligence and Operations Center (JIOC). There I ran into Lieutenant-Colonel Manuel Granado, my former XO at the 9th PSYOPs Battalion and later (1975) classmate at the USARSA general staff officers course in the Canal Zone.

Manny Granado was serving as the ESAF's operations advisor and as a result was the principal man who had to help formulate the tactics and strategies to deal with the FMLN's direct battle tactics aimed at defeating the ESAF. At the moment I walked into the JIOC an army infantry battalion was locked in a tense firefight with some FMLN units which had tried to ambush it. Reports were coming in by radio from the battlefield and ESAF staff officers were diligently posting their situation maps with details as to what was going on. Manny looked haggard and worn down, commenting: "It's been like this for weeks now." Despite the maneuvering of various army ground units by truck and helicopter around the battlefield, the war had not been going well. One ESAF battalion after another was coming out of their respective engagements badly mauled, the casualties continuously mounting.

The problem was combat staying power and quality training, and many battalions apparently had neither. They were simply being outfought and frequently outmaneuvered by FMLN guerrilla battalions, which were proving more and more tenacious every day. The success of the guerrillas had enabled them to effectively control major portions of the northern tier of provinces along the Honduran border and FMLN propaganda broadcasts were predicting a military victory within a year. As Manny explained, we were losing the war day by day, week by week, month by month and time was running out! Shocked at what he was telling me, I asked him if SOUTHCOM and Washington were aware of the dire situation that was unfolding inside El Salvador. He assured me that they were now aware of it, but he was uncertain as to what was going to be done. After spending some hours in the JIOC and discussing some ideas on interdiction of FMLN infiltration routes coming out of Nicaragua into El Salvador, I headed back to the relatively tranquil bliss of Honduras.

Upon return from El Salvador and a couple of weeks later, I was at the MILGP coordinating aspects of the various MTTs that were now beginning to arrive in country, when none other than Lieutenant Colonel Nestor Pino of the U.S. Army General Staff's Directorate of Operations (G-3), the Pentagon, strode into my office. I had known Nestor previously in Panama where he had established a reputation as an outstanding leader of an 8th Special Forces Group A-Team during the early 1970s. As part of a special Army Task Force for Central America focused on the insurgency wars taking place inside El Salvdor and Honduras, he was now obviously on some sort of important business.

Nestor came right to the point. The ESAF was having one "hell of a time" trying to defeat the FMLN guerrillas who were all to often decimating the Salvadoran army's infantry battalions in brutal, conventional combats. In addition, the fifty-five U.S. military trainers officially allowed inside El Salvador were just not enough to rapidly train up sufficient ESAF infantry battalions to replace those being mauled on the battlefield. In short, unless something was done immediately to improve the ESAF's performance on the battlefield, we were going to lose the war! Essentially this meant that the FMLN was on the way to imposing its will upon Salvadoran society by destroying the ESAF and conquering the nation outright by force. All the hype about reform and winning the hearts and minds of the people would essentially be meaningless if the ESAF failed. Manny Granado in San Salvador had been correct in his unvarnished estimate of the situation and Washington was taking heed through immediate action. Nestor Pino was the Pentagon's point-man for the action. Helping matters considerably and providing considerable emphasis to Pino's mission was the 27 April declaration by President Reagan that: "The national security of all the Americas is at stake in Central America!"

A day later, Nestor, myself and the Honduran army's G-3 (operations officer), Colonel Wilfredo Sanchez, another veteran of the 1969 war (he had the ignominious experience as a lieutenant of being captured), stood on a small hilltop just to the southeast of Trujillo on the Caribbean coast, surveying what appeared to be some unused farm land. Nestor explained to Colonel Sanchez that what the Pentagon wanted to do was to establish an infantry training center to prepare for combat as rapidly as possible one complete ESAF infantry battalion after another. These were not ordinary battalions but double the standard 700-man size, totaling some 1,500 men each. The idea was that they could take heavy casualties and still prevail against the smaller-sized FMLN units. It was not a new concept and was historically what the U.S. Army had done during World War I, albeit on a larger scale (20,000 man infantry divisions had been pitted against the German machineguns on the Western Front with the idea that, even if the enemy mowed down thousands of doughboys, thousands more would prevail and eventually overrun the German positions).

Each ESAF battalion would be flown into the Trujillo airport, whose airstrip would be reconditioned to accept USAF C-130 aircraft, and then trucked to the training center a few miles away. Upon completion of the training, each battalion would immediately be flown back to San Salvador and committed directly into battle. Wilfredo Sanchez understood quite clearly that the loss of El Salvador to the FMLN would tend to place considerable pressure on Honduras, which might, in turn, find its own national security situation compromised, facing hostile forces on two fronts. Unfortunately, there was no time to debate the issue and a decision was needed… now! The farmland and its adjacent hills were ideal for what Nestor Pino had in mind, but he needed to coordinate and bring into place the trainers and their equipment to begin instruction, and this would take some weeks. Sanchez waved his arm in a great semicircle, declaring "It's all yours!" In one fell swoop it appeared that Nestor Pino had solved the ESAF's training problem. But it would not be all that easy.

While Sanchez's decision generally met with approval in Honduran military circles and especially General Alvarez, due to the national security concerns mentioned above, there was still a tremendous residue of bitter feelings on the part of the Honduran army against the ESAF. Politics now came into play and, as part of the agreement to allow ESAF infantry to train on Honduran soil, General Alvarez demanded that the 125 U.S. Army Special Forces military trainers assigned to conduct the mission at Trujillo first train a Honduran infantry battalion. With little choice in the matter and realizing that it would give the training cadre a chance to work out its program, the Pentagon agreed.

Unfortunately, the first Honduran unit selected to undergo training that June at what was now called the Regional Military Training Center (RMTC) was the 5th Infantry Battalion - one that had just recently completed training under the tutelage of one of my Green Beret MTTs! I argued against this as a total waste of time, but Colonel Bueso maintained that it was a "point of honor" for the first Honduran battalion trained to outshine the future, incoming Salvadoran battalions. Nevertheless, the 5th Battalion completed its training in record time and the RMTC churned out enough sufficiently well-trained Salvadoran army battalions to go head-to-head with the FMLN so that by mid-1984 the crisis on the Salvadoran battlefield was essentially over. Coincidental with the RMTC initiating its training, another interesting event took place in July 1983 in the eastern Honduran Department (province) of Olancho.

While the various Honduran Communist insurgent organizations were not only operating clandestinely in country, they were also training a number of their members in Cuba and Nicaragua to participate in what they called "columns" or 100-man commandos. One such group had been carefully prepared and organized inside Nicaragua for insertion into Honduras. The mission of this group of about one hundred guerrillas was to foment an uprising and otherwise spark a revolution inside their homeland to overthrow the government. Remembering that "the population is to the guerrilla as the water is to fish," they intended to conceal their revolutionary operations by blending into the local towns and countryside. With all arrangements apparently made, the column began its infiltration into Honduras.

One of the first problems encountered by this column, led by Jose Maria Reyes Matta, was that they had not packed enough food to last the 200 or more miles they would have to march over mountainous terrain in order to penetrate into Honduras. Intending to live off the land, they had found the mountains not only slow going on foot, but also lacking in natural sustenance. Just the crossing of the Coco and Patuca rivers had exhausted the men and the end result was that, as they passed into Olancho, they had virtually run out of food. Their operation was now in dire jeopardy. To resolve the problem some of the guerrillas who were native to the area were dispatched to forage for food among their relatives and neighbors. Under most circumstances making contact with one's family and friends should have provided an adequate solution and a happy ending. Unfortunately for the guerrillas, they had been overtaken by events: Honduras now had a democratically elected government as a result of a generally free and open election, there were political parties and unions functioning, a free press operated openly, an agrarian reform movement was in process, and the military was seemingly out of power and now serving the country. In short, the government was well on the way to winning the hearts and minds of the people. All these factors weighed in against the guerrillas and, when combined with the fact that a civil defense committee or rural militia had been formed in the Olancho area to be on the lookout for possible insurgents, this caused their fortunes to decline rapidly.

The first alert that there was something afoot in Olancho was provided by the people to their local police. Apparently unimpressed by the guerrillas' explanations that they were about to be "saved" from government repression and further insurgent exhortations to join the revolution, family members and erstwhile friends had immediately passed the word to local authorities. The police, in turn, passed the information on to their Tegucigalpa intelligence center. In turn, that center alerted the army which then deployed its fully trained, special operations commando force into the region to find and destroy or capture the insurgents. This force was commanded by Major Ricardo Luque Portilla, one of the Honduran army's foremost special operations officers. The account of the counter-insurgency operation which I was provided with came first hand from one of its participants, Lieutenant Oscar Arturo Alvarez Guerrero, a former ROTC graduate of Texas A&M University, whose uncle was General Gustavo Alvarez.

Upon arrival in the Olancho area and knowing that the insurgents were still up in the mountains, Major Luque sent a twenty-one man reconnaissance force on patrol to attempt to find out where the guerrilla base camp was. With assault rifles and grenade launchers at the ready, Alvarez's men gradually made their way into the high, rugged mountains immediately to the east of the town of Catacamas. Finding the guerrillas in the jungle of this part of Honduras was not easy, since they moved only at day and then rested at night. Presuming that the guerrillas would undoubtedly camp out near some sort of small stream or river, the patrol eventually found and followed a foot trail leading along a stream to the insurgent base camp located on a small knoll. Now reinforced by more of Luque's men, the patrol waited until the guerrillas began to cook their evening meal. The idea was to allow as many of them, including the guards, to gather around the cooking fire and only then attack, taking them unaware.

Using the light of the fire as a guide, Alvarez and his men stealthily crept up on the camp to about point-blank range. Upon the signal to attack, a searing fusillade of automatic weapons fire inundated the guerrilla campsite, killing about a third of the guerrillas and enabling the small commando force, outnumbered by about four to one, to wound and capture another third. The combined surprise and shock effect of the incoming fires caused the remaining third of the guerrilla force to panic and scatter back out into the jungle. Those who were able to flee were never heard from again. It was virtually a textbook example of how to run a surprise assault.

Despite this success, in July 1984 another group of guerrillas, this time a 19-member group of Lorenzo Zelaya guerrillas was reported as having entered from Nicaragua into the Department of El Paraiso immediately to the south of Olancho and east of Tegucigalpa. Detected and then engaged, most of the 19 were captured in yet another unsuccessful effort to establish a viable revolutionary insurgent network inside Honduras. In sum, the people were siding with the government, and the guerrillas now found themselves more often than not tilting at windmills in their attempts to create a viable revolution. While the army's special operations forces were seeing action during the Spring of 1983, things had not been dull for elements of the army's 1st Armored Cavalry Regiment (actually the size of a U.S. Army armored cavalry squadron).

Around 2 AM of the morning of 29 April 1983 the Salvadoran FMLN guerrillas, numbering several hundred men, conducted a surprise night attack on the Salvadoran end of the Amatillo International Bridge separating Honduras from El Salvador on the western boundary of the Choluteca Gap. The bridge carried much of El Salvador's trade with Panama, Costa Rica, and Honduras, and was thus a prime target for the insurgents' strategy of debilitating El Salvador economically. The first volleys of rifle and machinegun fire cut down the sentinels guarding the bridge, decimated the Salvadoran customs officials, and wiped out the dozen-man police security detachment sleeping in their wooden billets. The commander of the police detachment was captured, tortured and shot.

While this was taking place, other guerrillas looted and burned the nine cars and commercial trucks waiting to be processed through customs and cross the bridge at sunrise. The occupants, caught by surprise and unable to fight back, died in their cabs and seats. The remainder of the local population, keeping low and under cover from the streams of bullets spattering about the bridge and customs houses, clustered in their adobe huts trying to avoid antagonizing the guerrillas. Some were not so lucky: eight houses were burned out with Molotov cocktails (bottles of a flaming mix of oil and gasoline). A few terrified people made their way down the embankments of the Goascoran River, which formed the border at this point, and crossed the semi-dry streambed to safety on the Honduran side of the bridge. The screams of women and children were distinctly audible to the Honduran customs personnel who attempted to observe the obvious carnage taking place in the dim moonlight some 400 yards away.

Although the incident was reported, some three hours later, at about 5 AM the Hondurans manning their border outpost came under intense assault rifle and machinegun fire as some twenty guerrillas began working their way along each side of the bridge toward them. A third group was detected as it began to set demolition charges along the underpinnings of the bridge. The Hondurans returned fire with rifles and pistols, hitting and killing or wounding two of the guerrilla sappers. Nonetheless, after the guerrillas had withdrawn from the bridge and roughly an hour later, a demolition charge exploded and took down a full span of the bridge, effectively rendering it useless.

At about 6:20 AM an army cavalry force under the command of Captain Carlos Andino and located about forty miles away, guarding the approaches into Honduras from Nicaragua on the Pan American Highway, was alerted to go to the rescue (better late than never!). Charging west along the highway in two RBYs with 106mm recoilless rifles, three RBY machinegun carriers and three ¼-ton jeeps mounting M2 .50 caliber machineguns, the cavalry reached the outskirts of the bridge by 7 AM. After a short reconnaissance to size up the situation Andino engaged the FMLN who had deployed a 100-man force down into the river bed to storm the Honduran customs houses. The cavalry's machineguns and 106mm recoilless cannons raked the guerrillas who were thrown back in disarray, losing some 60 personnel. The FMLN guerrillas, having accomplished their mission of bridge destruction, now retreated back into the hills of eastern El Salvador. While the action showed that Honduran frontier communications needed a great deal of improvement in order to enable the security forces to react in a timely manner, it also showed that the FMLN guerrillas were not adverse to attacking Honduran government personnel if it served their interests.

Between August 1983 and February 1984 JTF Bravo carried out another large maneuver exercise, called Big Pine II, which was considerably more extensive than the first. Besides some 5,000 American military personnel, two U.S. Navy aircraft carrier task forces and the U.S.S. New Jersey were also involved, and a practice amphibious assault landing was conducted by the Marine Corps along the Caribbean coast. The Hondurans pitched in with several infantry battalions and another parachute drop by the 2nd Airborne Battalion in the vicinity of Jamastran, which was later converted into an airfield near the Nicaraguan border.

While one purpose of the exercise was to begin to prepare the battalion commanders and their staffs in battlefield maneuver, the other was to indicate that Washington was deadly serious about protecting Honduras from a Sandinista invasion. But the impact on Nicaragua was even greater. That October 1983, the United States had carried out an invasion of the Caribbean island of Grenada by air and sea (Operation Urgent Fury) to overthrow a pro-Castro regime. This, of course, appeared to increase the possibility of military action against Nicaragua. Would the Sandinista regime be next? It was not out of the realm of the possible and the Sandinistas took the implied threat very seriously. But Big Pine II had much more going on besides the obvious, media-reported news and photography.

Marc Cisneros had reported in his 1982 Survey to SOUTHCOM that Honduras was very badly in need of some form of artillery. While this was all good and well, the problem was that the security assistance pipeline could not respond in a timely manner to this type of request. In fact it was reported that with other U.S. Army logistical priorities already in place, the first artillery pieces of any caliber would not be available for some years! And here is where General Paul Gorman's political connections within the Washington community came in handy.

In order to immediately procure a full battalion's worth of eighteen 105mm howitzers, their towing vehicles and all the other essential equipment associated with an artillery table of organization, as well as the training for the Honduran army, the general talked the Joint Chiefs of Staff into having an entire artillery battalion from the 101st Airborne Division deployed to the vicinity of Puerto Castilla (Trujillo) on the Honduran Caribbean coast. It was to bring down all its guns and equipment. Besides dropping off its equipment 100 percent, the battalion would also train an equivalent Honduran artillery battalion, which would then assume full ownership of the American guns and equipment.

Had anybody else suggested drawing down on one of America's key, strategic airborne assault units, they would have been cashiered from the service for "stupidity." The general's solution, coming from the highly respected Gorman, was perceived as "brilliant." It certainly did the trick and on 1 November 1983 the Honduran 1st Artillery Battalion came into being with 18 relatively new 105mm, state of the art howitzers, which could be slung from helicopters and moved around the country. It was a quantum jump in firepower for the Honduran army, and it was all Paul Gorman's doing.

Overlapping some of the Big Pine II joint training exercises, the CIA-sponsored Contras intensified their activities inside Nicaragua. Likewise air, land and sea raids took place along the Nicaraguan Caribbean coast and shipping from the Netherlands, Liberia, Panama and the Soviet Union was hit by cleverly laid mines. Other attacks in the form of raids struck five ports and naval facilities on both the Caribbean and Pacific coasts (Puerto Sandino, Corinto, Potosi, San Juan del Sur and San Juan del Norte). If the surrogate guerrilla forces sponsored by Washington were not the equivalent of an act of war, then surely the mining and amphibious raids must have been. While the incriminating details could not be proven, the continued acts targeting Nicaragua provoked a blanket Congressional shut-off of any aid to the Contras; it was a decision which would have considerable repercussions within the Reagan administration as the years wore on.

While I had been unsuccessful in getting Colonel Bueso Rosa to convince General Alvarez to establish a national army basic training center, General Gorman finally convinced the latter that that was exactly what Honduras needed. Previously the army had used press gangs as a recruiting technique by sweeping through major cities and towns to pick up young men at the plazas and entertainment centers. In 1982 a new constitution had decreed that all able-bodied men between the ages of eighteen and thirty were liable for eighteen months of compulsory military service, so manpower was no longer a problem. Given that UH-1H helicopter training was now ongoing, the RMTC was training one Honduran infantry battalion for every Salvadoran battalion trained, and we had just given the army its first real artillery battalion, Alvarez could not refuse Gorman's recommendation. I called for a special NCO infantry training MTT to train up the cadre that the new basic training center would need as tactics instructors. Once again the Army's Green Berets came to the fore and provided a team that put together a cadre of twenty-four Honduran army sergeants trained in Bill DePuy's infantry tactics. With the cadets at the Francisco Morazon Military Academy also being trained in the new tactics, the needed doctrinal saturation effect I had wanted to achieve throughout the army was now becoming a reality.

In the morning of 31 March 1984 about ten weeks before I was to leave Honduras to go to Washington for a new assignment at the Pentagon, I routinely called over to now Brigadier-General Bueso Rosa's office. An unfamiliar voice answered the phone and stated that the general was not only not in, but he was no longer on duty; then the phone was abruptly hung up - a *golpe* had taken place! In our situation, a coup d'etat of any sort, even an inter-institutional one within the military as this one appeared to be, was a serious thing. I immediately called over to Major Jerry Clark the Army Attache and Defense Intelligence Agency representative on duty at the Embassy in Tegucigalpa. His response to my question as to what was going on was: "We haven't the faintest idea about what's going on! They took us by surprise."

The "they" that Clark was referring to were Brigadier-General Walter Lopez, and Colonels William Said Speer, Leonel Riera Lunati and a host of others from the Third and Fourth Promotions of the Francisco Morazan national military academy. This group was thoroughly disgruntled over the apparently high-handed approach of Gustavo Alvarez Martinez who had arranged to have himself promoted during the previous year first to the rank of major general and then, in turn, to have selected comrades in arms from the Second Promotion of the military academy to be promoted to brigadier general.

The intense jealously that existed between the various military academy graduating classes, known as "promotions" (*promociones*) knew no bounds. Because promotions, assignments, and financial gain of the incumbent military faction, or in this case the graduating class in control of the Honduran military at the moment, were at stake, jealous internal in-fighting was now tearing the highest levels of the institution apart. At issue here was who would control and continue to profit from the national military pension fund (*Instituto de Prevision Military - IPM*). This fund had been created in 1972 out of monies allocated to the Honduran military as part of its budget. It soon became known as a "slush fund" for high-ranking officers who profited from the IPM's investments in their own family businesses or who channeled funds to their own projects. As a result the upper echelons of the military were now involved in agro-industry, banking, stock brokerage, real estate, radio stations, insurance, credit card schemes, automobile rentals, real estate, and funeral homes, among dozens of other commercial enterprises, none of which had anything to do with national defense. This income in the scores of millions of dollars from these businesses supplemented to a large degree other earnings from the military's control of the merchant marine, immigration services, police, automobile registrations, border check points, and customs offices at seaports and airports.

But Alvarez Martinez had gone even further by setting up the Association for the Progress of Honduras (APROH), which extorted to a considerable degree contributions from wealthy Honduran businessmen under the guise of furthering the latter's business and national security interests. In short, the general was operating outside the norms of the military, which required that the armed forces commander consult the Superior Council of the Armed Forces (CONSUFA), which was the committee-style, governing authority of the armed forces. This group of 25 to 30 senior officers from the army, navy and air force and national police were supposed to make all the important decisions affecting their respective institutions and decide on the selection or dismissal of the top

Ambassador John Negroponte decorates the author for service in Honduras, 6 June 1984. Negroponte skillfully maneuvered the U.S. ship of state through Honduras's treacherous political waters, contributing significantly to the success of the American foreign policy in the region. (U.S. Government photo)

leadership for each service. Alvarez had pointedly ignored CONSUFA, attempting to move away from this collegial decision-making forum to embrace a vertical command structure, which would centralize power under his control at the very top of the military structure. Reinforcing Alvarez's power was the fact that under the 1982 Honduran constitution, the president of the country had no legal role in the selection or dismissal of the armed forces commander; only the CONSUFA did. In the end it was the general's often arrogant and high-handed, if not insulting treatment of subordinates, who were not part of his promotion group, that finally led to his overthrow and forced exile to the U.S.A.

The coup plotters selected Brigadier-General Walter Lopez Reyes of the Honduran air force as the new armed forces chief and then presented their decision to President Suazo Cordova as a fait accompli. As the nephew of Oswaldo Lopez Arrellano and a hero of the 1969 war against El Salvador, Walter Lopez was seen as "old guard" and willing to maintain the authority of the military in the face of the constitutional government. While the coup d'état did take the Embassy (ambassador, CIA, and military attaches) and myself completely by surprise, it did not change the modus operandi of the United States or its relationship with Honduras. Joint and combined training exercises took place, the RMTC continued to train up Honduran and Salvadoran infantry battalions, and the Contras sustained their operations against Nicaragua. To insure that the status quo of the American-Honduran military relationship would remain on an even keel, General Gorman quickly stepped up to bat to deal with the potential crisis. In this regard he established an understanding with General Lopez in which the former explained to the latter that they needed each other in order in order to protect Honduras and accomplish American interests in the region. To this end Lopez pledged continued close cooperation with the United States.

As things settled down in mid-June 1984 and I prepared to go to Washington, D.C., en-route to another assignment in Latin America, in El Salvador Jose Napoleon Duarte was inaugurated on 1 June as the first feely elected president in 52 years. In closing out my portion of the security assistance effort in the battle for Central America, an Army infantry officer, Lieutenant Colonel Lawrence Salmon took my place at the MILGP. Over the remainder of the 1980s, he, in turn, would be replaced by other lieutenant colonels who would continue the thrust of the security assistance initiatives already in place, enhancing them as the opportunities and funding permitted.

How the battle for Central America would ultimately turn out came as a surprise and was the result of factors and events relating to the turbulent politics of the region. Nonetheless, as matters stood by the Summer of 1984, a number of things had been accomplished in Honduras by the U.S. security assistance effort: the Communist insurgency had been stopped dead in its tracks, protecting the survival of the fledgling democratic regime in power; the Honduran army was well on its way to becoming re-equipped and re-trained; SOUTHCOM had forged an advanced staging area which could be used for either the defense of Honduras or as a platform for a formal invasion of Nicaragua; and Ronald Reagan's undeclared war and surrogate, Contra guerrilla forces were placing the Sandinista regime in Nicaragua under ever increasing pressure.

*   *   *

The security assistance effort in Honduras was enhanced over the remainder of the 1980s as a direct result of increased funding and an intensified interest in maintaining a strong U.S. position in Central America. The Honduran army's principal infantry weapon, the Belgian FAL, was replaced by the U.S. Army's infantry assault rifle, the M-16. The infantry battalions were increased from 11 to 16 and further organized into brigades (three or four battalions per brigade) to better integrate artillery fire support and to facilitate their command and control in battle. In addition, another battalion (18 howitzers) of 105mm artillery was created, giving the Honduran army a total of 36 pieces. Four 155mm towed artillery pieces were also provided as a battery to give the army an extra, longer range punch and 30 M-167 Vulcan automatic air defense cannons were procured to enhance the army's air defense of its infantry battalions against the Sandinista helicopter threat. The army took on a new look with a camouflaged combat uniform, new-style helmets, a completely new series of tactical field radios, and an upgraded educational program, which provided each new recruit with the opportunity to learn to read and write.

The air force also went through a major upgrade. Twenty-four UH-1 helicopters and fully trained crews were ultimately placed at its disposal to better support the army and provide it with a battlefield mobility unlike it had ever had before. By the early 1990s the HAF had four Hughes 500 attack helicopters in its inventory. In addition, it also received enhanced capabilities in the form of ten F-5E and Tiger fighter/ground attack aircraft to reinforce its now aging Super Mystere B-2s. Even it's A-37 fighter-bomber attack squadron was increased to 13 aircraft, giving the HAF a total of over 25 combat aircraft; far superior to anything the Sandinista air force could claim as an equivalent. In turn, the Honduran navy was not left out, increasing its coastal patrol capabilities in terms of armed swift boats and other surface craft, while forming a supporting 600-man marine infantry strike force.

JTF Bravo continued its training exercises throughout the remainder of the 1980s, beginning with Big Pine III and Universal Trek in February and May 1985 respectively. These exercises featured a massive amphibious landing on the northeastern coast of Honduras and involved 7,000 U.S. troops and 5,000 Honduran troops, as well as 39 U.S. Navy warships. An even bigger exercise, involving 3,000 helicopter assault troops from the 101st Airborne Division at Fort Campbell, Kentucky, and a Marine amphibious assault force of some 1,800 men from Camp Lejune took place as Operation Solid Shield in May 1987, which simulated the repulsion of a Nicaraguan invasion of Honduras. The White House was ratcheting up the pressure on the Sandinistas to the degree that Managua's Daniel Ortega, a former guerrilla-revolutionary leader against Somoza and then president of Nicaragua, accused Ronald Reagan of planning an invasion of his country. During those years some 5,000 National Guard engineers from Alabama, Arizona, California, Missouri and North Dakota were rotated through Honduras to assist in the construction of roads and airfields in eastern Honduras, leading some pundits to describe the country as the "USS Honduras."

In November 1985 another democratic presidential election took place and Jose Azcona of the Liberal Party replaced Suazo Cordova on January 27, 1986, marking the first time in Honduras in over forty years that one civilian government peacefully succeeded another. If U.S. military aid averaged about $40 million after 1984 (the Honduran military actually received some $70 million that year) through the end of the decade, Washington's economic aid to the country was at least double, if not triple, and would exceed a billion dollars alone. Land reform continued apace, albeit very slowly, and over 32,000 legal titles were eventually issued to poor farmers who previously had lived in fear of having their lands confiscated by the unscrupulous, large land owners. The U.S.-sponsored Peace Corps increased its activities inside Honduras through its some 350 volunteers who fanned out over the country to promote rural development, better grass-roots political organization and improved farming and sanitation techniques.

While the Honduran military's capabilities to defend its borders increased considerably during the 1980s, the institution was continuously plagued by various forms of corruption at the highest levels, which invariably undermined the ability of its top leadership to perform in a fully professional manner. With the encouragement of the American Embassy in Tegucigalpa, CONSUFA replaced the armed forces commander General Walter Lopez in 1986 with Captain (the equivalent rank of colonel) Humberto Regalado, the commander of the Honduran navy. I had known Humberto ("Frenchy") Regalado when he was a student at USARSA in 1975. He had once confided to me that, as a naval officer in the army-dominated Honduran armed forces, his career "would go nowhere." Now the fickle finger of historical fate had destined him to lead his nation's armed forces. Nonetheless, he was known to U.S. intelligence as a corrupt officer who enjoyed skimming payoffs from fishermen, as well as proceeds from the flagging of civilian ships. This was all in conjunction with other kickbacks from construction projects and the proceeds from budgeted food support funds for non-existent naval personnel. Another serious problem for the White House during those years was that the Honduran military was also involved in drug-trafficking.

About the time Regalado was accused openly of participating in the drug trade, his half-brother Rigoberto, then the Honduran ambassador to Panama, was arrested in the Miami airport for smuggling cocaine (twenty-five pounds) into the United States. Indeed, even Bueso Rosa, formerly the Armed Forces Chief of Staff, was captured, tried and convicted in a late-1984 assassination conspiracy against then President Suazo Cordova. The conspiracy involved some $20 million in confiscated cocaine in south Florida which was to be used to finance the planned takeover of the Honduran government. Whatever the links, Honduras was becoming more and more a major transshipment point for the Medellin Cartel's and other trafficker's cocaine trade from Colombia into the U.S. market. In March 1988, the *New York Times* exposed Honduran citizen Juan Matta as a drug kingpin with close ties to the Honduran military, which was further linked to the Colombian Cali cartel by its military attache in Bogota, Colonel William Said, the former commander of the 1st Armored Regiment. In short, there was a Honduran military mafia which was fast developing a reputation for unbridled corruption and was linked to five distinct cartel-groups inside Honduras (Bay Islands, Atlantic coast, Tocoa ["Little Cali], Granjero [farmers], and lawyers' cartels). Operating through a series of clandestine airfields, lobster boats and containerized shipping, thousands of pounds of cocaine and other drugs were being passed through Honduras by these cartels. The result of all these activities was an incremental boom in construction, real estate, tourism, commerce and sports; all funded from the profits and money-laundering that was taking place.

Unfortunately, corruption and illegal self-enrichment had become part and parcel of the Honduran military's value system and would continue as such over the years and well into the twenty-first century. The year 2002 found the *Miami Herald* reporting that ten retired military leaders, including the former armed forces commanding general, Mario Hung Pacheco, were being sought by the Honduran Attorney General for fraud, violation of their constitutional duties and embezzling over half a million dollars in military funds. But dishonesty was not only found in the Honduran camp.

By early 1984 the Contra funds were running out and the Reagan administration turned to Congress to obtain more funding. The funds might have been forthcoming had not the CIA's participation in mining the Nicaraguan ports (a blatant act of war) not come to light. The mining provoked a Congressional shut-off of any "covert" aid to the Contras. At this time, rather than serving as a foreign policy advisor and arbitrator for the president concerning the positions of the various agencies, the NSC staff actually became not only a policy-making but also a policy-executing agency. Not helping matters was President Ronald Reagan himself who indicated to Robert McFarlane, his national security advisor, that he wanted to persuade the Iranian government to use its presumed influence with Shiite Hezbollah terrorists to free the American hostages being held in Lebanon, while at the same time keep the Contra operations in play against the Sandinistas. How this was done was of little concern to Reagan, as long as it did get done. In late 1984 Lieutenant Colonel Oliver North, a Marine Corps staff member on the NSC, moved to fill the void left by the Congressional restrictions, obtaining funding by surreptitious means. To this end he arranged for one thousand TOW antitank missiles to be shipped to Iran in exchange for influence and money, which was to be secretly funneled into bank accounts supporting Contra operations.

In essence, President Reagan had ordered the arms sales and the diversion of funds and then gave them over to North to bring each of the two ends to fruition. To the Director of the CIA, William Casey, was given the task of coordinating and carrying out the training, support and conduct of the Contra operations against Nicaragua. Everything was intended to conceal the role of the U. S. government and also the role of the president. By first diverting the Army's TOW antitank missiles to the CIA, which then shipped them as a sale to Iran, the Oliver North operation jacked up the prices of the weapons and then siphoned off the profits to private bank accounts to help fund the Contras. In reality the transfer of a portion of the profits from the Iran arms sales to the Contras was illegal in that it was inconsistent with and directly violated the Congressional Boland Amendment. In short, Oliver North and Vice-Admiral John Poindexter (North's immediate supervisor) were attempting an end-run around Congress's intent by running their own secret, covert war, carrying out their own secret diplomacy, and formulating and executing their own secret foreign policy initiatives. In so doing, they were digging their own graves, which ultimately resulted in the Iran-Contra scandal and summarily ended their careers.

Simply put, Ronald Reagan had lost control of the NSC. His failure to exercise his presidential responsibility in specifying in detail the roles and responsibilities of the NSC staff, supervising their activities, clearly laying out his foreign policy objectives for Central America, and keeping Congress informed would taint not only himself, but also his administration. It was little wonder that in the summer of 1982 General Wallace Nutting and Ambassador John Negroponte did not have a clear understanding as to where the United States was trying to go in terms of Honduras and the battle for Central America and what they should be doing about it.

During the early to mid-1980s Nicaragua's victorious Sandinistas, coming to power with an estimated 90 percent popularity rating, intended to build a Cuban-style socialism in an atmosphere of prosperity. The idea was to destroy the Somoza regime and its economic power base, to replace the old regime's brutality and inequality of treatment of Nicaraguans with a fairer, more humane, and less corrupt system, and to reactivate the war-damaged economy. At the time of the revolution an estimated 52 percent of the population was illiterate, malnutrition plagued about 75 percent of the nation's children and the infant mortality rate was one of the highest in the region. There was a dire need for reform and all this was to be accomplished within the context of the Sandinista's Marxist-Leninist doctrine.

Considering that Nicaragua was potentially one of the richest countries in Central America, with abundant arable land, considerable hydroelectric reserves, and significant timber and mineral resources, the FSLN guerrilla leaders had reason to be optimistic. Initially around two million acres from former Somoza family estates were turned over to landless peasant workers, who either formed private plots or cooperatives with their new holdings. While roughly a thousand state farms were created as part of the government's central planning process, the large landholders who had supported the anti-Somoza revolution were generally not bothered and their estates remained for the most part in tact. To assist the Nicaraguan economy, which had been cut off from its American markets via Washington's trade embargo, the Soviet Union provided some $4 billion in economic aid and trade. In addition, Fidel Castro provided some two-thousand teachers from Cuba to assist in educating and indoctrinating the masses. The end result of this effort would be a doubling of the number of schools and the reduction of illiteracy from over 50 percent down to about 12 percent. Half a million peasants became literate and education was made free from preschool through the university level. Hundreds of Cuban para-medical personnel were assigned to Nicaragua and assisted in improving the health of the rural workers and their families in the countryside. Measles, diptheria, and polio, diseases that once took a heavy toll among children, were virtually eliminated. As a result, infant mortality fell about 50 percent. For the first time many families received electricity, potable drinking water and adequate food. To demonstrate the popularity of the revolution, in 1984 the Sandinista's Daniel Ortega successfully ran for president.

As the U.S.-sponsored Contra effort became more intense in its effort to wreck the Nicaraguan economy and undermine the government, the Sandinistas found that they would have to reorganize themselves to defend their country. Fidel Castro sent General Arnaldo Ochoa, fresh from a successful campaign in Angola, to advise the EPS (Sandinista Popular Army) as to what it should do. Ochoa broke down the army into independent counter-guerrilla battalions, retraining them to conduct their own ambush and hit-and-run warfare, exploiting their own helicopter mobility (12 HINDs and 35 HIPs) against the Contras. A universal conscription law went into effect, requiring all men aged 18 to 40 to register for military service. Over time Ochoa would pit some 50,000 Sandinista troops against the Contra's 15,000.

Although outnumbered, the Contras continued their attacks, inflicting considerable damage on the Nicaraguan economy and reducing coffee production (the main export crop) by as much as a third. The attacks also cut down on the production of corn and beans for domestic consumption, making increased imports of these commodities necessary. Economic cooperatives, state farms, sawmills, tobacco drying facilities, bridges and power lines and trucks all became Contra targets. As time went on the war created an impossible budgetary problem for the Sandinistas, with defense expenditures mounting to almost half of the gross national budget. Frustrated that the Contras were able to raid out of secure base areas from inside Honduras, the EPS, now around 80,000 men (four times the size of the Honduran and about twice the size of the Salvadoran armies) conducted hot pursuit operations into Honduras in 1986 and again in 1987 in an effort to inflict a series of decisive blows against the Contras. While tactically somewhat successful, the EPS operations amounted to nothing more than a strategic, self-inflicted wound.

When the U.S. Congress heard of the EPS incursions into Honduras, the evolving Iran-Contra Scandal was ignored for the moment and in 1986 $100 million was voted in support of Contra operations. The fighting between the Contras and the EPS was often brutal with the civilian population suffering incredible hardships. Assassinations, rapes, outright murders, armed robberies, kidnappings, intimidation, property seizures, and even cattle rustling had become a part of everyday life. Landmines killed and maimed both the combatants and the innocent by the score, if not hundreds.

By the end of 1986 inflation inside Nicaragua had passed 1,000 percent and was skyrocketing, eventually reaching 33,000 percent in 1988. This and the loss of production due to the devastation of cultivated areas, the killing of cattle, the sinking of fishing boats and the destruction of electric power generation plants, caused thousands of people to leave productive work for the more remunerative black market operations that increasingly took place in the urban areas. Nicaraguans now found themselves enmeshed in a "survival economy" with no end in sight. The only reason why the country did not collapse was the fact that it was receiving some $600 million in foreign assistance a year from the Soviet Union and its Warsaw Pact countries. But it was inside El Salvador that the battle for Central America would reach its climax.

The FMLN guerrillas embarked upon a 5-point strategy during the rest of the 1980s to win their war in El Salvador. In each case the American-sponsored security assistance effort responded to the strategy in play. First and foremost the FMLN continuously attacked the basic tenants of the reform process involving free elections and the provision of land to the poor (agrarian reform). Threatening the people directly with death ("vote in the morning and die in the afternoon") if they participated in the free and open democratic processes, the guerrillas attempted to disrupt each and every election. Their failure in these efforts was noted in the fact that the government ran five successful elections: constitutional assembly (1982), presidential election (1984), legislative and municipal elections (1985), municipal elections (1988), and again, a presidential election (1989). In direct defiance of the FMLN threats, the people generally turned out in mass, often over a million voters, to mark their individual ballots.

In terms of the agrarian reform, the guerrillas threatened with death any person who accepted land from the government or supported the agrarian reform process. Despite the guerrillas' threats and the landed elite's own somewhat successful attempts to circumvent the intent of the land-transfer process through coercive and legal means, about a quarter of the rural population or over a million people benefited from the process. In short, the Duarte government had seized the "moral high ground," establishing its own credibility with the people, which it and the follow-on governments would not relinquish. Establishing this legitimacy was in itself a major turning point in the war and undermined to a large degree the FMLN's just cause of the earlier 1978-80 period.

A second and very important element in the FMLN strategy was to break El Salvador's economy. There was a logic behind this strategy that suggested that the closing down of the economy would cause the population to revolt against any government in power. To this end the guerrillas targeted the nation's electrical power grid (junction boxes and transformers), systems of communication (buses, trucks and trains), and bridges with various forms of sabotage and ambush operations. In addition, the agricultural base of the country was directly attacked, reducing the production of cotton, coffee and sugar by as much as a third to a half in some years. With about half of the economy shut down and 50 percent unemployment nationwide, it looked as though the guerrillas might achieve their goal.

Nonetheless, guerrilla frustration mounted over the lackadaisical and non-committal attitude on the part of the people during the middle and latter half of the 1980s and the FMLN made the decision to punish Salvadorans by depriving them of food, water, transport, light and sanitation. Through the use of assassinations, kidnappings and general terrorism the guerrillas also planned to constantly harass and intimidate the population and the government. At the same time the guerrillas, in their desperation, tried to force the people to give them money and food, and when the people did not have it or could not give it, to make the people work for them.

The war now became a tremendous hardship, if not living hell, for the people as they struggled for survival and it was only the $4 billion in economic aid from the United States over the remainder of the decade that enabled the country to rebuild its badly damaged economic infrastructure enough to carry on. By 1986 alone some 900 reconstruction projects were under way, focusing on bridges, roads, water and electrical services, and schools. In 1986 a government sponsored medical vaccination program reached out to some 400 thousand children; the FMLN had nothing to offer along this line. In addition, enhanced helicopter mobility enabled the ESAF to better protect the key lines of communication and move electrical repair teams to key points of the damaged infrastructure. The government could build, but the guerrillas could only destroy; a contrast which was not lost in the eyes of the population.

A third element of the FMLN strategy focused on breaking the government's control over the population. In the rural areas this involved coercive threats, backed up by bombings and raids, against the municipal infrastructure of the nation. A dozen or more mayors were assassinated and many others wounded with the result that, of some 262 municipalities, roughly a hundred did not have serving mayors. During 1989 alone, some 214 mayors received death threats, causing around 80 to resign their positions. Often the municipal administrative offices were trashed or blown up, destroying and damaging precious documents (records of marriage, taxes and death etc), which were critical to the administrative stability and psychological well-being of the population. In the urban areas the presiding judges were frequently threatened with death if they ruled against the FMLN in a legal case. The guerrillas demanded that the local populations incorporate into the FMLN revolutionary effort. There were to be no neutrals, and everyone was considered a "fighter." This meant that youths as young as eight to ten years old were press-ganged into joining the guerrilla ranks.

A final aspect of this part of the strategy was the FMLN decision to deliberately use booby traps in the form of anti-personnel mines on the trails leading from one town to another. Allegedly designed to inhibit the movement of the ESAF's ground forces, the mines were indiscriminant in their effects, killing and maiming hundreds of innocent children who habitually used the trails to go to school and visit family members and friends. In response to the guerrilla strategy, the government created some 220 civilian self-defense patrols at the rural village level which were to be reinforced by ESAF rapid response units. Also implemented was a civic action campaign in Chalatenango as part of the counter-insurgency effort. With death squad activity now greatly reduced and the image of the ESAF positively rebuilt to a large degree, the Duarte administration began a psychological operations (PSYOP) campaign to exploit the FMLN's use of anti-personnel mines. Billboards with photos of groups of maimed children lined the major road networks, the captions reading: "This is how the FMLN treats your children!" The PSYOP effort in this regard was so effective that by the end of 1988 more of the population by far perceived the FMLN guerrillas as the primary human rights violators in the country. In short, the FMLN were becoming over time their own worst enemy.

As mentioned before, the FMLN attempted to defeat the ESAF in open battle and undoubtedly would have done so had it not been for the big-battalion training effort conducted in the United States and at the RMTC in Honduras. The guerrillas had built their forces up to some 15,000 fighters who initially inflicted grievous losses on the ESAF. Nonetheless, the Salvadoran army never gave up and untiringly returned to the fight time and time again. During 1985 the improved fighting capabilities of the ESAF and its ability to endure heavy losses began to prove itself. The some 15,000 guerrilla fighters estimated to be in action on the battlefield a year earlier had been reduced to about 6,000 by the end of a year. The FMLN, now convinced that they could not defeat the ESAF, made the decision to pursue the military part of their strategy as a long, drawn-out, protracted war.

Interestingly enough in 1986, a number of the FMLN's more nationalistic *commandantes* or battalion commanders came to the conclusion that the guerrillas had actually accomplished their goals of causing the government to institute the basic reforms which were desired as part of the insurgency's "just cause" and that it was pointless to pursue the war. Because the key Marxist-Leninist guerrilla leaders did not want to accept the reforms in play and insisted instead on pursuing the war to achieve power via a total overthrow of the government, some of the more nationalistic guerrilla leaders now opted to leave the war. This dissention within the ranks dismayed the Marxist-Leninist leadership of the FSLN and caused them to become even more steadfast in their belief that only by a violent overthrow of the Duarte administration could their own goals be achieved. More and more the earlier just cause at the beginning of the 1980s was being subverted by an overriding FMLN interest in achieving political power through brute force.

A last element in the FMLN's strategy was the effort to influence the United States Congress to withdraw all funding and military support of any kind on behalf of the ESAF. This strategy in itself might have been decisive if the international left and other anti-war religious groups had succeeded in convincing a majority in Congress that the San Salvador government was amoral in its prosecution of the war (death squads and atrocities during the early 1980s) and was therefore not redeemable. To confront this possibility, Napoleon Duarte appeared before Congress during the mid-1980s to plead his case for continued support. His success in this endeavor and Ronald Reagan's own unflagging support for the reform efforts inside El Salvador saved the situation, guaranteeing that the ESAF would be able to hold its own and that the government's reforms would ultimately prevail in the end. A key statistic working in favor of Duarte was the fact that death-squad assassinations were reported as having dropped to 22 a month by 1986 and 1987, down from an estimated 800 per month for the earlier part of the decade.

Despite this decisive setback the FMLN made one last major attempt to rally the population to its side in December 1989 with an all-out attack against the five largest cities in El Salvador. Against San Salvador the guerrillas adroitly maneuvered some four thousand fighters from out of the nearby hills and volcano slopes, who penetrated into a portion of the city. Arriving with extra assault rifles and ammunition in hand for the expected ground swell of popular support on their behalf and anti-government fighters to join their ranks, the guerrillas were confounded by a population that not only rejected their overtures to overthrow the government but also fled in front of their advances (some 35,000 panic-stricken refugees escaping pell-mell into other ESAF protected parts of the city). It was a sobering if not defining experience for the hard-core FMLN *comandantes*, many of whom had fought for their "cause" throughout most of the 1980s. In short, the reform efforts fostered by Duarte and then continued by the follow-on, democratically elected president, Alfredo Christiani, had been more convincing to the general mass of the people than all the machinations and strategies that the FMLN guerrillas had brought into play. Ballots had won out over bullets!

While the battle for Central America was on-going during the latter part of the 1980s, another dynamic was brought into play from an unexpected quarter. During the summer of 1987 Oscar Arias, then president of Costa Rica, offered an alternate solution to the head-to-head conflicts taking place in the region. He was very much concerned that the hardening of the Reagan policy towards Nicaragua would ultimately lead to American military intervention in that part of Central America. To forestall further escalation of the conflict and to achieve a peaceful resolution that would promote regional stability and security, his plan looked to resolving the conflicts through dialogue, by which Costa Rica, Honduras, El Salvador, Nicaragua and Guatemala would commit themselves to a cease-fire and regional reconciliation. Democratization and free elections, respect for human rights, cessation of assistance to irregular forces or insurrectionist movements, and the respect for each country's sovereignty and territorial integrity by not permitting organizations or groups to use their respective territories to destabilize the other governments within the region were all part and parcel of the plan.

In the short term, a full commitment to the plan would mean the termination of the Washington-sponsored Contra campaign against Nicaragua, the FMLN's Nicaragua-supported guerrilla campaign against El Salvador, and the resolution of the various wars through the political process of free and open elections with the people determining who would lead their respective nations. On 7 August 1987, at Esquipulas, Guatemala, all the serving presidents in Central America signed up to the plan, which then became a fully subscribed accord. The Reagan administration did not like the accord since it served as an alternative to its operations supporting the armed opposition to the Sandinista government. Ironically the White House's coercive pressures against the Sandinista regime did have the unanticipated effect of stimulating the cooperative effort led by Oscar Arias, which eventually led to the peaceful resolution of the battle for Central America and accomplished all the principal U.S. objectives for the region. One very important outcome of the Arias peace plan was that it launched the process which led to the 1990 elections in Nicaragua.

Inside Nicaragua, the Sandinista president Daniel Ortega seized upon the Arias peace plan as a solution to his problem of how to escape from Ronald Reagan's confrontational policies which had not only essentially bankrupted Nicaragua but also kept it in a continuous state of crisis and under considerable pressure from the Contra incursions. To this end he called for a general election for the 24th of February, 1990. In his mind he presumed that with the 90 percent popularity rating and acceptance that the FSLN guerrilla revolution had achieved in coming to power in 1979, in conjunction with the various economic, educational and medical reforms achieved during the 1980s, the winning of the election by the Sandinistas was a foregone conclusion. Nonetheless, the actual winning of the election by Violeta Chamorro (the widow of the slain newspaper editor, Joaquin Chamorro) and her coalition of 14 non-Communist parties called "UNO" (National Union Opposition) by a 55 to 41 percent margin came as a complete surprise and stunned the Sandinistas. There were many reasons for the surprise turnabout in the Sandinistas' political fortunes and most of these were of their own doing.

In general the people had voted against the Sandinistas because of their corruption and mismanagement of the economy. Over the decade of the 1980s Managua's central planning programs produced an overall 50 percent drop in national production. Land reform had taken place but land titles had been withheld from the new peasant-farmers. Price controls instituted to deal with food shortages and inflation (33,000 percent in 1988) as part of an austerity plan merely exacerbated the situation and by 1989 real wages were found to be 10 percent less than in 1981. Per capita income remained at about $300 per year through most of the decade. The Contra campaigns caused the Sandinistas to devote about half of their national budget to defense mobilization and the maintenance of an army of some 80,000 men. The forced enlistments of young men to fight the Contras and the resulting battlefield casualties and deaths caused many Nicaraguan families to turn against the government. Scores of thousands of rural farmers and their families also turned against the Sandinisatas when they were uprooted from their traditional homes and lands along the Honduran border and relocated into the interior as part of a government effort to create a desolate, no man's land as an obstacle to Contra incursions.

In addition, the Sandinistas, in their single-minded efforts to promote Marxist-Leninist ideology, tended to deprecate and otherwise ridicule the customs, traditions and religious tenants of the people at large. Their unmistakable contempt and disdain for the traditional ways of ordinary people and their continuing restrictions on strikes, freedom of expression, assembly and association, as well as intimidation by government-sponsored gangs, called "turbas," further polarized public opinion. The consequences of all these activities merely convinced the majority that the Sandinistas were not the open-minded liberals that their revolutionary propaganda had proclaimed. While the people suffered considerably throughout the 1980s, it was noted that the Sandinista leadership now lived in relative luxury in their former Somoza family-owned homes and drove high-priced Mercedes Benz automobiles, indicating in the Orwellian sense that while all party members were equal, some were "more equal" than others. In the end the economic crisis and Sandinista policies stigmatized the original, earlier pro-revolutionary enthusiasm on the part of the people and substituted it with a general apathy and bitterness which brought forth its discontent in no uncertain terms at the ballot box backlash in the election of 1990.

Inside El Salvador by 1990, it was clear that the army could not defeat the guerrillas and the FMLN could not impose a military takeover of the country by force. In short a seeming stalemate had ensued. While the guerrillas demonstrated that they could often outmaneuver the army's ground forces, the ESAF's roughly 60 assault and transport helicopters, supporting some 24 infantry battalions and a force of some 40,000 men, could always mount a successful counter-attack against any point of attack or raid that the FMLN was able to perpetrate, thus blunting the guerrilla's effectiveness. In 1990 this caused the Commanding General of the FMLN, Shafik Handal, to reconsider his options in light of the fact that the Sandinistas had lost power in Nicaragua, now isolating the FMLN more than ever; the Soviet Union was in the process of disintegrating, resulting in a cutting off of any further aid via Nicaragua and demoralizing the Marxist-Leninist movements throughout Central America; and the Salvadoran people continued to reject the FMLN guerrillas' military operations even when they appeared relatively successful.

For all of the 1980s Handal and his Marxist-Leninist cohorts had dismissed representative democracy as a sham: a form of corrupt, bureaucratic device invented by local elites to further their interests in excluding the masses from any form of governmental decision making and insuring their dominance over the latter. His decision to embrace the peace accord and, in turn, the democratic process inside El Salvador meant that the FMLN had seriously underestimated the power of a defended democratic process. They would now have to change from guerrilla warriors into peaceful social democrats and pursue their objectives through a democratic process for better or worse. With the FMLN accepting the peace accord and signing a peace pact in January

1992, the civil war in Central America was for all intents and purposes at an end, only in Guatemala would the negotiations drag out until the mid-1990s.

The United States was able to accomplish all of its security assistance objectives in the battle for Central America. The Marxist-Leninist Sandinista revolutionary government in Nicaragua was turned out of power and its army neutralized as a threat to the region; the Farabundo Marti (FMLN) guerrillas in El Salvador put down their arms and committed themselves to the reform processes in play; and the insurgencies inside Honduras, seeing themselves overtaken by events and peacefully induced reforms and democratic practices, gave up their revolutionary intentions. This did not mean that the breaking out of peace and the implementation of democratic processes and structural reforms brought great joy to the local populations. Indeed, by the beginning of the twenty-first century, dominating cultural value systems tended to undermine the U.S.-promoted reform processes in virtually every country in the region. While Washington believed that it could transform what was a violent and unjust series of societies into more liberal and democratic ones, the truth remains that human character, history, culture and social structure are often unrepentant and highly resistant to change from outside influences.

In Nicaragua, ineptness, inefficiency and blatant corruption on the part of the follow-on, democratically-elected governments have contributed to 70 percent of the country living in poverty and about half the population once again illiterate, with another half-million poverty stricken Nicaraguans having migrated into neighboring Costa Rica and other countries to look for work. In short unemployment, hunger and lack of medical care plague the large majority of the country's society.

Inside El Salvador, despite the fact that the economy has grown every year since the war ended in 1992, land scarcity remains the greatest fundamental issue confronting its people. With an elite group of about a hundred families still controlling most of the nation's wealth, over 40 percent of the people are jobless or severely underemployed, and about a quarter of the population remains illiterate. In short, the extremes of wealth and poverty are as great as ever; an ever-present enigma of widespread poverty amid potential wealth. Well over a million Salvadorans, who fled the war and poverty, now dwell legally or illegally in the United States and send lifesaving remittances to their families left behind. To a degree this has ameliorated the tensions that still exist. In the free and open democratic elections that have taken place, the ARENA party has dominated the political scene. Nonetheless, Shafik Handal's FMLN political party and its affiliates have improved their social-democratic performances at the municipal level to the point that they have moved from a 22 percent popularity rating in 1992 up to a 42 percent rating some ten years later; a turn in political events which indicates that, had Handal and the insurgent leadership embraced the Duarte reform efforts of the early-to-mid-1980s, the FMLN might have done even better, potentially winning national elections at the onset of the twenty-first century.

During 1999 in neighboring Honduras, President Carlos Flores Facusse, the constitutional commander-in-chief of the armed forces, named a civilian lawyer as the new minister of defense, placing the military for the first time in modern Honduran history completely under a civilian chain of command and rule. No longer is democracy just a façade for relatively autonomous military rule. Nonetheless, the country remained the poorest nation in the region with almost 80 percent of the population still living in poverty (Latin America as a whole has a 44 percent poverty rate). Contributing to the situation was the fact that Honduras has no real civil service, which means that incoming governments replace all serving previous officials with their own clients. In short, appointments are still made according to a corrupt spoils system similar to that of the former caudillo-style, dictator system of the previous nineteenth and twentieth centuries and politicians continue more often than not to serve their own personal interests rather than those of their constituents.

Investigations into the counter-insurgency campaign conducted by the army and the police (identified as "Battalion 3-16") during the 1980s revealed that of some 184 persons captured and never heard from again 105 were Hondurans, 39 Nicaraguans, 28 Salvadorans, 5 Costa Ricans, 4 Guatemalans and one each from the United States, Ecuador and Venezuela. Honduran courts eventually declared that the government would have to pay indemnification payments to a dozen of the surviving families. While General Gustavo Alvarez, the former chief of the Honduran armed forces, did go into exile to Miami after he was ousted from power in the 1984, he returned to Honduras in early 1989 as a Bible-toting, "reformed-Christian missionary." For his efforts, Cinchonero insurgent gunmen summarily shot him down dead on a Tegucigalpa street. It was merely a guerrilla retribution in what had been fought out as a vicious underground war. With the exception of JTF Bravo, Washington's interest in Honduras waned considerably after the end of the Cold War battle for Central America. Nonetheless, the Soto Cano-based unit continued to provide timely assistance in Washington's counter-narcotics efforts, and considerable humanitarian aid and relief for the region well into the twenty-first century.

Even Fidel Castro's Cuba saw the proverbial "handwriting on the wall" with the dissolution of the Soviet Union in the early 1990s and gave up all pretenses of attempting to foment revolution in a democratically aligned Central America. Cuba was now an anachronism of the Cold War. Indeed, as Central America slid once more back into its more traditional historical role as a Latin American backwater region of "banana republics," one might conclude as the French have often observed: *Le plus c'est change, le plus c'est la meme chose.*

CHAPTER 4

DRUG WARS IN THE ANDES
1985-87

Albeit the war in Central America was a major focus for U.S. foreign policy, things were happening in South America that also attracted Washington's attention in the summer of 1985. After having worked the previous year with Army General Staff's Directorate of Operations at the Pentagon and then further having received an orientation from the Defense Intelligence Agency (DIA), I was looking forward to my new assignment as a military attache in the Andean country of Bolivia. The military attache concept was not new since the French had conceived of it some two-hundred years earlier as a way by which the great powers of Europe could "spy" on each other via formally recognized military personnel who were granted diplomatic status and assigned to each of the various countries.

In my case, as the Army-Navy Attache, I was simply to find out what the leaders of the Bolivian army and navy were doing and thinking. The naval designator for the position came about because the Bolivian "navy" only had two merchant marine ships plying the Atlantic, a handful of motorboats operating on its rivers and Lake Titicaca situated on the high Andean plateau, and a couple of pontoon-equipped Cessna-type seaplanes, hardly worthy of assigning a fulltime Navy officer to the American Embassy in La Paz. The army on the other hand was the largest military service in Bolivia and had the equivalent of a reinforced division, with infantry, armor, engineer, airborne, commando and ranger units scattered throughout the country. The air force, having a series of C-130 transports, T-33 fighters, and UH-1 helicopters, was the third military service of interest and was deemed by DIA to warrant two Air Force attaches, a colonel or senior member of the Defense Attache Office (DAO) and a major as an assistant. Most U.S. military attaches serve as integral parts of the American embassy to which they are assigned and, in addition to reporting to the DIA, they serve as additional sets of eyes and ears for the American ambassador and the rest of the "country team," the Department of State's (DOS) descriptor for its respective embassies.

Every American ambassador serving in a foreign country has three basic functions: the first is to personally represent the President of the United States and the DOS by developing insofar as possible cordial relations with the host country's government, leaders, and people and explaining what are Washington's policies that involve that country; the second is to report to Washington as to what is going on inside the country and what its leaders (and even the political opposition) are thinking in terms of policies and intentions; and lastly, the ambassador must *solve problems* regarding the United States and his or her country of assignment. In terms of its traditional relationship to the United States, Bolivia would normally have been just another backwater country in the Western Hemisphere, except for one problem - international drug trafficking. This one issue, involving the production and transshipment of cocaine as an illegal drug into the United States and its relationship to the region as a whole, would propel Bolivia into the front ranks of conspicuous problems to be addressed by Washington, involving the U.S. military in one of its more unusual campaigns of the Cold War period.

Bolivia, the sixth largest country in South America in terms of area (some 424,000 square miles or about the size of California and Texas combined), is bounded on all sides by other nations: Brazil to the north and east, Argentina and Paraguay to the south, and Peru and Chile to the west. The country's forbidding geography centers on the Andean mountain ranges in the west, which surpass 12,000 feet in some places and impede the economic and political integration of the nation. This is offset by the sparsely populated, flat, savannah-like Amazon rain forest to the east of the Andes and the dry Chaco region to the south. By far of greater importance to the reader for the purposes of this chapter are the lower, eastern slopes of the Andes mountains which provide a transition of sorts in the form of tropical, lowland valleys and relatively fertile growing and farming regions known as the Chapare and Yapacani areas around Santa Cruz and the Yungas region to points northwest. These

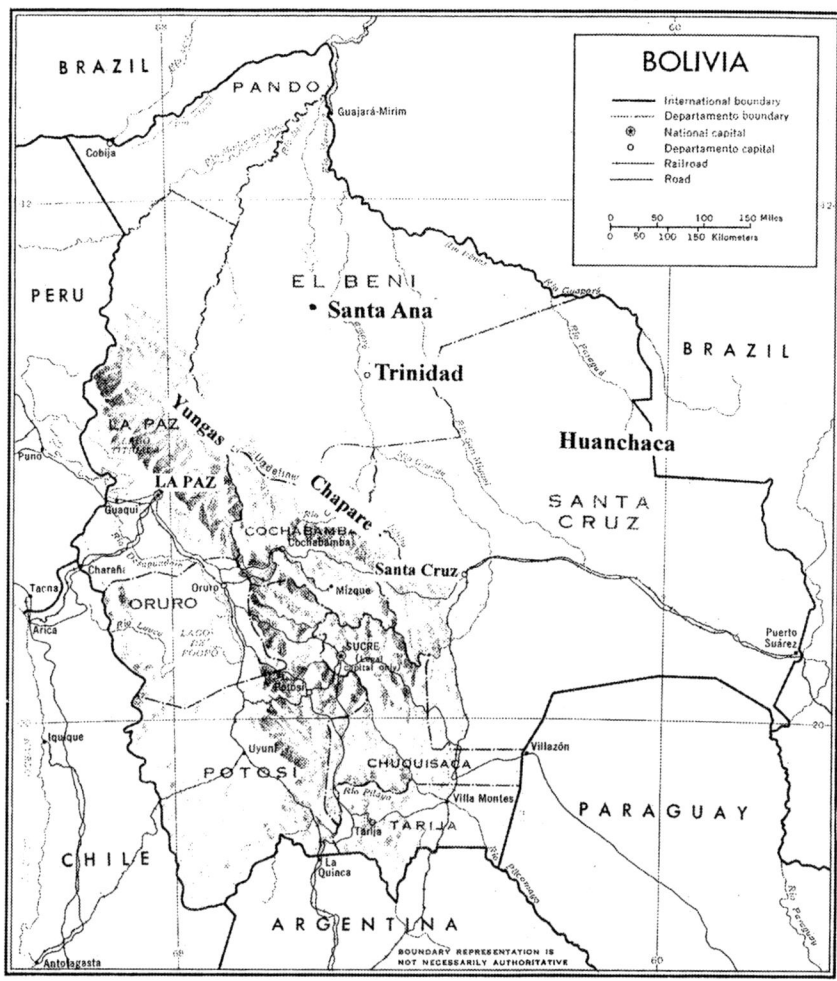

descend eastward and out into what is called the *llanos* or lowlands of the Amazon Basin.

The country's population of about seven million people is divided into two distinct societies: one Spanish-white mixed with Indians (mestizo), and the other pure Indian. Of the two general divisions, the indigenous Indians, consisting in the main of Aymara and Quechua groups, make up roughly two-thirds of the total population. More than half of the population is crowded into three cities: La Paz, Cochabamba, and Santa Cruz. Otherwise more than one-third of the population lives in communities of 250 people or less.

But it was the discovery of tin at the end of the nineteenth century that brought the country into contact with the international market system, diversifying it from its hitherto previous dependence on mining gold and silver. Nonetheless, it was the tin-barons or a tiny minority of economic elites (the Aramayos, Patinos and Hochschilds etc.) and their political cronies that dominated the country. While things went well for the tin-barons, especially during World War II when the Allies primarily depended on Bolivian tin to support their war effort, the situation changed dramatically in the aftermath of the war as the highly competitive world markets discovered another lucrative source of tin in South East Asia. Malaysia, with its highly economical techniques of tin-ore strip mining, quickly surpassed the Bolivian tin-mining industry, which used a far more expensive deep-mining operation, requiring extensive tunneling. As a result, by the early 1950s, Bolivian tin could not compete as a profitable enterprise with the Malaysian market; for all intents and purposes Malaysia had put Bolivia out of business! This set the stage for a major evolution in the nation's politics.

Generally speaking, Bolivia was considered politically unstable, if not almost ungovernable, and had an infamous history for more than a century of coups, counter-coups, and changes of government, averaging about one per year. As World War II came to a close, class-based competition within the country evolved into the formation of political parties and led to an alliance between Dr. Victor Paz Estenssoro's National Revolutionary Movement (MNR party) and the Bolivian Workers' Central (COB labor union party) and other indigenous Indian groups. Paz and his supporters, including middle-class intellectuals, small businessmen, and junior military officers, felt that Bolivia's traditional, semi-feudal rulers - large landholders, senior military officers, and mine owners - were inept and corrupt and had left Bolivia the poorest and most backward country in South America (life expectancy was 33 years and two of every three children died by age ten from undernourishment). With workers excluded from the political process, their demands for better working conditions ignored, and their organizations frequently suppressed, it was perfectly logical that labor would support the MNR.

When Paz's MNR challenged the dominance of the tin-based oligarchy, winning a landslide electoral victory in 1951, the ruling military government prevented the party from assuming power. As a result, with Paz initially in exile, Hernan Siles Suazo and a party of armed Indians and workers overthrew the military government and Paz was then called back from exile and installed as the legitimate president. This victory of the people swept away the old political order. It was a complete social revolution, as the government took over the tin mines, created a state mining corporation (COMIBOL) to run them, and then redistributed land from the landed oligarch's extensive haciendas to needy Indians. This comprehensive land reform ultimately enabled some 200,000 peasant families in the Andes for the first time in Bolivian history to own land and become wage-earning farmers. In addition to property rights, there was universal suffrage for all those over twenty-one years of age regardless of sex or literacy, which ended the Indian's condition of semi-servitude and provided them with a sense of dignity and pride. After being reelected in 1960 and again in 1964 for a third four-year term, Paz found himself overthrown after several months in power by a resurgent military, led by his vice president and air force General Rene Barrientos. Nonetheless, Barrientos' death in a helicopter accident several years later, in turn, led to still another coup by air force General Hugo Banzer, whose repressive regime would last eight years.

Despite the fact that Banzer's government had ratified an anti-drug convention in 1976 to control the legal manufacture and distribution of coca leaf products, limit their use to medical purposes, and to suppress illicit trafficking by the end of the decade, Hugo Banzer's extended family was itself heavily involved in narcotrafficking. His government now provided state-controlled bank loans to the early developing cocaine industry. Money ostensibly borrowed for agricultural ventures was directed to construct a drug production apparatus, which was further linked to drug trafficking cartels principally operating out of Colombia. If the quantity of acres of coca leaves being grown can be said to be an indicator of drug trafficking activities, then the virtual doubling of coca acreage from 6,000 acres to over 12,000 acres during the Banzer regime's six years (1972-1978) indicates the true nature of the situation.

Fed up with the incompetence and corruption of the Banzer government, involving rampant clienteleism and a vast system of patronage in support of a complex series of civil and military cliques, a series of labor strikes led to the president stepping down and the calling of new elections, all controlled and rigged by the Bolivian military over the next few years. It was a tumultuous period with five interim presidents unsuccessfully attempting to serve out terms of office. Not happy with the results of the June 1980 election, the army, led by General Luis Garcia Meza, overthrew the presiding, congressionally-appointed interim president, Lydia Gueiler, in July. Now in power Meza presided over one of the most brutal regimes in Bolivian history, lasting a little more than a year.

It was during the 1980-81 dictatorship of Garcia Meza that the Bolivian government was singled out for its conspicuous connections to the drug trade. After he had overthrown Lydia Gueiler with the financial aid of the principal narcotrafficker in Bolivia, Issac Chavarria, Garcia Meza then made Chavarria the Minister of Government, directly linking himself to narco-politics and the drug trafficking effort. With Chavarria also linked to the Colombian Cali and Medellin drug cartels, there was now formed a virtual symbiosis of the narcotraffickers and state government working together to foster, protect and engage in the illegal, international drug-trade effort. In a machiavellian manner the regime placated the U.S. Drug Enforcement Administration (DEA) office at the La Paz Embassy by persecuting competing drug traffickers, all the while protecting its own trafficking interests and markets. Disturbingly at the same time, DEA-sponsored coca bush eradication and crop substitution efforts were gradually suspended at the direction of the La Paz government, as they more and more came into conflict with Garcia Meza's interests. Over time, even objecting DEA agents in Bolivia were declared *persona non grata* by the government. When Washington officially suspended much of its $127 million in assistance and aid programs as part of a policy which refused to recognize the Meza regime, the American ambassador, Marvin Weisman, was also summarily ordered out of the country! At this time Washington declared Bolivia a pariah nation and worked to isolate the country by cutting off all forms of international financial support (International Monetary Fund, World Bank etc.).

During this period a tightly-knit, family-tied Bolivian agro-industrial elite of several dozen families operating out of the Beni and Santa Cruz regions and led by cattle rancher Roberto Suarez promoted and coordinated most of the narcotrafficking operations; all the while supported by the unqualified state backing and patronage of Garcia Meza and his cronies. Colonel Luis Arce Gomez, was Suarez's cousin, as well as serving as Meza's minister of interior. This is not to say that the impact of narcotrafficking on Bolivia was negative. Hospitals, roads, schools, and even low income housing and other basic services were for the first time made available to some segments of the local population in the Cochabamba, Santa Cruz and Beni Departments (provinces) as part of a natural, as well as deliberate, infrastructure derived from the profits of the drug trade. That the national government did not have the resources to compete with the traffickers was not lost on the otherwise poor population who inevitably appreciated the efforts of the drug lords on their behalf.

Yet, like so many other similar dictatorships, the Bolivian military found its own institution pulling against itself with petty jealousies, and internal feuding and intrigues becoming dominant as competing groups and interests, both civilian and military, vied for the spoils of the drug trade. In short, the military institution had converted itself into little more than a collection of predatory warlords, parceling out pieces of the state and the national patrimony among themselves. When Bolivia's overall isolation contributed to a decline in its economy, pressures grew for a change of government. Officers within the institution responded with one of Bolivia's infamous *golpes* (coups) which eventually succeeded in placing General Celso Torrelio in power as the new president in late 1981 (Garcia Meza and Arce Gomez fleeing to Argentina) . Torrelio in turn attempted to end Bolivia's international isolation by favorably influencing Washington through announced intentions of reintroducing the democratic process and combating the cocaine drug trade. The DOS responded in kind by dispatching Edwin Corr, then the serving U.S. ambassador in El Salvador in late 1983, to Bolivia to assist in the reinstitution of formal democracy and assert Bolivian-U.S. control over cocaine production and trade there.

Ed Corr did succeed in prodding the Bolivian political system forward and in fostering a transition to democratic rule with Dr Victor Paz Estenssoro elected as president in 1985. It was a top Washington priority to strengthen the new democratic initiative now in place and to sustain it for as long as possible so as to provide continuity for future U.S. policy initiatives. To secure better cooperation, Washington promised Paz a drug control program ($30 million) and an aid package ($58 million), provided that the latter eradicated some 8,000 acres of illegal coca bushes by 1986. In addition, $4 million was allocated to form, train and equip a 300-man Rural Area Mobile Police Unit (*Unidad Movil Policial Para Areas Rurales - UMOPAR*) to patrol the coca growing zones.

The United States Agency for International Development (USAID), part of the country team in La Paz, was provided with about $2 million which was to be used to stimulate a crop substitution program, whereby coca farmers were to pull up their coca bushes and replace them with other AID-supplied crops, such as potatoes, oranges, apples etc. Unfortunately for AID its project ground to a halt when it was found out that the targeted coca growing areas in the Chapare region were effected by erosion, excessive moisture due to seasonal flooding, rapid loss of fertility due to leaching, soil acidity, and the lack of organic matter. In short, the area was apparently conducive to no other agriculturally lucrative crops except coca, which thrived in this moist, tropical climate. Because the coca farmers were able to improve considerably their standard of living (earning over $5,000 per year) compared to the rest of the majority of the population (earning around $600 per year), they had no incentive to curtail their production of what were perceived as the sacred and traditional coca leaves. With the farmers viewing coca production as both socially acceptable and financially fruitful, between 1982 and 1985 the actual number of total acres under cultivation doubled and then tripled to around 75,000. Coca had become the cash crop of choice, since the plant could be harvested three-to-four times a year, providing the family involved with a continuous flow of income.

While the coca production situation was becoming worse, the democratic process was moving forward. The hotly contested election of August 1985 found the former military dictator of the 1970s, Hugo Banzer, pitted against the venerable Dr Victor Paz Estenssoro. As I arrived in Bolivia in the final stages of the hard-fought electoral campaign, Ed Corr was genuinely happy to see me, having made my acquaintance on previous assignments in Peru and El Salvador. When he found out I had learned to ride horses at the Peruvian Cavalry School some years earlier in Lima, he was ecstatic and exclaimed: "Banzer will probably win the election! You can go horseback riding with him and find out what he is thinking…, and then report back to me."

This was obviously a mission statement, if not a plan of sorts, but, as so often happens in politics, there are surprise winners and losers in national elections and this was one of those occasions. Dr. Paz won the election when the Bolivian Congress interceded on his behalf and he was sworn into office 6 August at 78 years of age. General Banzer appeared to fade away into retirement, but not before he and Paz had formed their "Pact for Democracy" in mid-October, which committed their MNR (Paz) and ADN (Banzer) parties to work within the Bolivian congress to put into effect certain economic reforms and strengthen the new president's power to deal with emergency situations, especially those involving labor issues. With the election now concluded and the democratic process sustained with one democratically elected incumbent replaced by another, Ambassador Corr left Bolivia and was replaced by Ambassador Edward Rowell. My equestrian future in the service of Uncle Sam had ended before it had even begun.

The economic situation the new Bolivian president inherited was a disaster. With inflation running well over 26,000 percent (It took a bushel basket of Bolivian pesos to purchase a loaf of bread!), the national debt was around $3.7 billion and well beyond the capability of the government itself to service. To make matters worse, that October the bottom fell out of the international tin market and the London Metals Exchange terminated all trading in tin, Bolivia's principal foreign exchange earner. With the Andean mining industry no longer a viable option for work, scores of thousands of former miners now headed for their one best option to find work - the coca fields. Nonetheless, Paz undertook an austerity plan which reduced inflation to 11 percent in little more than a year and drastically cut state spending, which also included the cutting of state payrolls and the termination of the state's subsidizing of the mining community, further causing ever more miners to turn to growing coca as a means of survival.

In addition, as part of an effort to restore international capital investment, the economy was liberalized to the degree that the bloated and inefficient state was disengaged and the private sector was placed in charge of the engine of economic growth; free competitive capitalism and the market economy had come to Bolivia! All this came as a complete, but happy surprise for the Country Team, which had expected Dr. Paz to remain true to his more traditional, government focused, socialistic philosophy. To enhance the process, Paz allowed a tax amnesty on all repatriated capital, relaxed disclosure requirements from the Central Bank, and prohibited official investigation into the origin of outside wealth brought into the country. This latter policy was designed to stimulate the economy by bringing into play those narcotrafficker profits and other private financial assets remaining outside the country. In effect, this "don't ask - don't tell" policy raised short term bank deposits from $28 million to $228 million over the next two years.

While the La Paz government's economic re-structuring plan was all good and well, by mid-1985 Bolivia had become the world's second-most-important source of coca leaves (40 percent, behind Peru's 60 percent) and the third largest producer of cocaine hydrochloride (HCl) or cocaine (behind Colombia and Peru respectively), estimated at around 92 tons. Ambassador Ed Rowell intended to work closely with Dr. Paz's government to overcome both Bolivia's economic crisis and flourishing drug trade. Overcoming the economic crisis would enhance the democratic process by stabilizing the country and curtailing the drug trade would work towards accomplishing President Ronald Reagan's goal of stopping illegal drugs, particularly cocaine, from entering the United States.

Aware that some 40 percent of the U.S. national population between the ages of 18 and 25 were using drugs, another ten percent (20 million people) of the adult population age 26 or older were also using drugs, and that the hospitals nation-wide were saturated with emergency room cases dealing with cocaine-related drug overdoses, the president had declared "war" on drugs in early January 1982. Nancy Reagan, the president's wife said: "Just say no!" As such, *all* U.S. government agencies were expected to assist, each in their own way, in addressing the drug issue, which was seen as a social scourge and a blot on America. This policy was implemented by the Department of State, which included in its Bolivian-based Country Team a component of the DEA and its own Narcotics Action Unit (NAU).

The DEA's principal strategy was to attack the problem at its source, the Bolivian peasant and coca farmers in the Chapare region at the foot of the Andes, and one way or another to get them to pull up (eradicate) their coca plants or bushes. Since the U.S. Congress had mandated in 1983 that Bolivia would have to eradicate something over 8,000 acres of coca bushes for the next several years or lose its multi-million dollar aid package, it was imperative for the DEA to achieve success or see its program closed down. Nonetheless, after two years effort it was obvious that the program was going nowhere for as many or more coca bushes were being planted for every one cut or pulled up and destroyed. Often the eradicated bushes would disappear for awhile and then be rediscovered in other coca plots nearby, along with new seedlings.

The several hundred-man, DEA-sponsored UMOPAR was attempting to force the issue by directly confronting the some 250,000 coca farmers and their family members. Finding itself outnumbered by roughly a thousand to one, the UMOPAR could make no real headway and program was found to be failing miserably. An informal Country Team study indicated that it was costing the Washington about $1,000 for every coca bush actually eradicated! In addition, by the latter part of 1985 inside the continental United States, the cocaine client admissions to hospitals across the nation were found to have doubled since the advent of the Reagan administration! These were startling figures for an administration which had supposedly declared "war" on drugs several years earlier. As the weeks went by the Country Team in La Paz became more and more frustrated.

At one meeting I attended in October 1985, Ed Rowell announced that a successful anti-drug and coca eradication program in Bolivia was essential and that we were now operating under a Washington-mandated "national security imperative." The entire Country Team was tasked with the mission to come up with ideas on how to quash the coca-cocaine production then taking place inside Bolivia. This was indeed a significant shift in the interest and intensity of the U.S. policy for Bolivia, but as the weeks went by and November came on, there were no new ideas being brought forth outside of the counter-drug approaches already in play.

A frustrated Jeffery Biggs, the Deputy Chief of Mission (DCM), chairing one of the meetings asked in desperation, "Isn't there someone in this room who can give us a solution?" I felt sorry for Jeff Biggs. Like most people at the American Embassy in La Paz, including myself, fighting drugs in Bolivia had not been part of our official bailiwick or even mission. Approaching him after the meeting, I volunteered to study the problem, provided that I could have complete and open access to all sections and components of the Embassy that might be able to shed some light on the problem. Cooperation was the key. If I could make a reasonably accurate analysis of the situation, then I might be able to provide one or more courses of action as viable solutions. He agreed.

The next couple of weeks were spent interviewing people in DEA, NAU, AID and a host of other Embassy personnel. As I gathered information concerning the issue, I came to the conclusion that the current anti-drug policy then in play for eradication was propelling the Embassy into a head-on collision course with over a quarter of a million Bolivian peasant farmers. In short, this policy was placing the Washington in the incompatible position of possibly fostering a civil war in the coca growing regions, centered in the main on the Chapare region, which might well spread to the rest of the country, undermining the fragile democratic process in play, as well as the U.S. anti-drug policy objectives. Simply put, the coca bushes now grown in the vast subtropical regions of the Chapare, Yungas and Apolo, which involved some 15,000 square miles or an area about the size of Vermont and formed a gigantic swath along the lower fringes of the Andes, constituted the core of the growing problem.

Not only had coca leaves (*Erythroxylum* being the scientific term for the plant) been cultivated for some two thousand years, but coca farming was now estimated to be providing virtually each and every peasant family with a two-acre plot in the Chapare with an income of up to $7,000 per year - at least ten times what the average Bolivian was earning! "Coca," as the leaves were called, were part and parcel of the Andian Indians' culture and mystique going back to pre-Incan times, being chewed at weddings, birth celebrations and other social events. When chewed with lime juice it served to suppress hunger, thirst and fatigue. Whether used as a mild stimulant to combat cold and fatigue, as an appetite suppressant to dull hunger pangs, or as a sign of social acceptance and friendship, it was from the point of view of the Indians a symbol of cultural identity and loyalty and therefore an essential if not vital mainstay or factor in their livelihood and life-style. During the colonial period, Spanish overseers had accepted and even encouraged the use of coca leaves by the Indians working in the Potosi silver mines, since they served as a food substitute and represented a cost savings ("free lunches"). In short, coca, as the cash crop of choice, was not only a highly lucrative enterprise, improving the standard of living of everyone who was involved in its production, but it also was considered socially acceptable by the coca farmer's society.

My study also indicated that the coca industry was actually quite complex. In the Chapare region alone there were some 5,000 crude laboratories for processing the coca leaves into a form of paste. In essence, the freshly picked leaves were bundled and transported to a "laboratory" where the leaves were deposited on a plastic sheet in a maturation pit and then mixed and crushed with kerosene and diluted sulfuric acid, called by the DEA "precursor chemicals." Through the process of stomping with bare feet in the pit, the leaves were converted into a paste-like substance. At this point alcohol was then added to the paste to bring the alkaloids to the surface, allowing the remaining syrup to be siphoned off and left to solidify into what was called cocaine sulfate paste or *base.*

The base at this stage was generally sold at the farmer's doorstep to paste buyers who, as brokers or middlemen, would then take it to a higher level laboratory complex where it was passed through a final stage wherein it was washed in either ether or acetone solutions and then further dried under the intense heat from high-wattage lamps to produce chlorohydrate of cocaine or HCl. Successful completion of this final step in the process meant that the drug could then be transshipped to other parts of the hemisphere for further shipment into the United States. With three-to-four harvests per year, coca farming was a year-round enterprise. Essentially, Bolivia had now moved from an economy of tin to an economy of coca and the question for me was: where was the most vulnerable point in the narcotrafficking process *inside* Bolivia that could be reasonably attacked to produce decisive results, and not cause a civil war?

Talking over the problem with some of the people in DEA convinced me it was at the final phase in production or the formal laboratory process where the coca paste was finally converted into refined cocaine that a vulnerability could be found. This was a highly technical process requiring sophisticated equipment in the form of high-powered drying lamps, large amounts of chemicals stored in 55-gallon steel drums, and an electrical power generation capability, involving up to 6,000-watt generators. This level of production at fixed and relatively isolated refining centers also required a dozen or more highly trained pharmaceutical personnel who were familiar with how to mix the ether and acetone solutions with the paste in the right combinations to produce a quality product. This final phase required a major logistical effort in terms of procuring equipment, supplies and personnel. In addition, the laboratory had to be located in a fairly secure area to permit either airplanes, seaplanes or boats to pick up the packaged cocaine and move it onward into the marketing chain. This meant that an airfield or a boat landing site, or maybe both, would have to be nearby. The DEA information available indicated that laboratories were almost without exception located in the more remote areas of Bolivia, especially the Beni, Pando and Santa Cruz departments - an area about the size of France and serviced by about 200 distinct aircraft. To my way of thinking these sites were undoubtedly difficult to completely camouflage and would surely have some form of telltale signature or distinctive signs that a comprehensive aerial reconnaissance could identify.

There were other aspects to the laboratory situation which were also very interesting. To bring airplanes and boats into a cocaine production site required considerable coordination, usually by radio. Certain intelligence sources maintained that up to six drug trafficker flights were going from Bolivia to Colombia every day, which meant that a considerable amount of radio-signals traffic was taking place almost around the clock. It struck me that RDF or radio-direction-finding techniques and radar ought to be able to detect the flow of aerial traffic and even pinpoint the approximate location of a laboratory or even a drug trafficker coordination center. In addition, there was Bolivia's eastern and northern border with Brazil, consisting of over 600 miles of rivers and another two-thousand miles of interior rivers which laced the Beni, Pando and Santa Cruz regions. These all constituted lines of communication which could be engaged in the air and on the rivers; the aerial link being the most notable, since that was how the traffickers appeared to move their refined cocaine product out of Bolivia.

But DEA's information on the laboratories in particular was meager and often suspect. Even though some 200 traffickers had been identified, no one could say for sure how many or exactly when and where the laboratories were operating. Estimated figures in the form of "educated guesses" ranged from around a dozen to as many as two-hundred or more laboratories operating from time to time. We definitely needed help in clarifying this key point. My conclusion about all this was that the narcotraffickers were generally operating with relative impunity. In short, there were several key centers of gravity which we could target: the coca farmers and their fields, the cocaine laboratory production system, and the lines of communication on the ground, along the rivers, and in the air, which the traffickers relied upon to both feed their laboratories and fly the finished cocaine out of Bolivia.

In early November I presented my findings to Ambassador Rowell. In the main he was interested in my strategy for dealing with the above situation in order to quash the traffickers' operations. I pointed out that the purpose of my strategy concept was to bring about the collapse of the coca market inside Bolivia using an indirect approach. Since coca farmers had to make at least $30 per hundredweight of coca leaves as a minimum profit, any depression of their market below that amount would mean that they were now involved in an unprofitable business. If this situation could be brought about and sustained, there would be sufficient leverage placed on the farmers to cause them to desist from growing coca crops, forcing them to switch to some form of alternate crop substitutes sponsored by AID (AID was also offering to pay $1,000 for each acre of coca plants that were eradicated). In brief, we would be making an indirect attack on the farmers and their coca crops as a key center of gravity without them ever really knowing it. As such, massive interdiction of trafficker lines of communication and laboratory busting were to be the keystones of the strategy.

The strategy concept called for a triad of interdiction operations which, if addressed intensively on a sustained basis year-round, would produce decisive results. In this highly militant approach an airmobile task force, consisting of UMOPAR-transported police in U.S.-piloted helicopters, was to directly attack the traffickers' HCl laboratory systems, destroying their supplies and equipment and capturing in so far as possible any and all personnel encountered on site. In addition, the laboratory systems, located in the Beni, Pando and Santa Cruz Departments, were to be sealed off from cargos of coca paste and precursor processing supplies flowing in via selected rivers and roads from the Chapare and Yungas regions. This would require the involvement of a series of mobile riverine forces (UMOPAR elements transported in US-supplied, 16-foot swift boats) and vehicle roadblocks at critical choke points.

The last or third component of the strategy involved a national aircraft flight registration program, which would be surreptitiously monitored by U.S. aerial detection and intelligence gathering platforms and radars (Air Force E2-C AWACS) which would pinpoint and then assist the Bolivian Air Force's (BAF) T-33 planes to intercept the narcotrafficker aircraft flying into and out of the suspected laboratory sites. Suspect aircraft which refused to land for inspection at designated airports were to be shot down by the BAF as legitimate, criminal targets. The use of dusk to dawn curfews and close inspection of mandatory flight plans and aircraft documents would further insure control of Bolivia's air space and inhibit the use of the estimated 500 small airstrips scattered throughout the region. In short, participation by the notoriously corrupt Bolivian military was to be kept at a minimum to reduce the possibility of bribes (traffickers paid in the range of $1,000 for each series of shipments ignored by governmental authorities), and the interdiction activities would be carried out by Bolivia's DEA-advised UMOPAR wherever possible. Thus, the U.S. would play both a guiding and supporting role, while Bolivia's police and judiciary would deal directly with the traffickers to enforce the law of the land.

Ed Rowell realized that there was not a moment to lose. The strategy would not only have to be coordinated with Washington, but also with President Paz. In addition, if we were to take advantage of the following summer's dry season of some 90 to 120 days (July - October) to initiate operations (the airmobile assaults), we would have to do considerable intelligence gathering, operational planning, and obtain the necessary helicopters, boats, radar-equipped aircraft, as well as train the forces involved. I suggested that, as a minimum, we would probably need about four months of intense intelligence preparation of the "battlefield" to give the operations planners and executors sufficient targeting data to work with. At the latest this should commence by 1 March 1986. In addition, I wanted to see the participating UMOPAR personnel trained secretly during the month of May at the Army's Fort Sherman jungle operations training center in Panama by a joint DEA and Army Special Forces MTT (and Navy-Marine elements as required) and then clandestinely inserted back into Bolivia sometime in June to achieve the maximum amount of initial surprise against the traffickers.

The cover and deception plan for all this was to be the "Fuerzas Unidas 1986" joint Bolivian-American military training exercise that was scheduled to begin in late April and run on into early May or longer. Conducted under the auspices of SOUTHCOM, the exercise had been scheduled well over a year in advance and had been announced in the local press and, as such, would not particularly alert the traffickers that something was up. It was obvious to us that SOUTHCOM, headquartered in Panama, would need to become involved in virtually all aspects of the Embassy's counter-drug offensive in Bolivia. To this end the actual implementation of the strategy would entail to a large degree the militarizing of the drug war. In the Embassy's anti-drug, strategy-concept cable transmitted to Washington in early December, a psychological operations (PSYOP) concept was also included to enhance the anti-narcotics educational programs already in play and sensitize in so far as possible the mass of the Bolivian population to the seriousness of having illegal coca production and narcotics trafficking taking place inside their country.

In early January Ed Rowell arranged to have a meeting with Victor Paz at the latter's presidential offices in downtown La Paz. Accompanying the ambassador in uniform, I could see that I was to be the symbol of the "big stick," while Rowell himself would "speak softly," as was his diplomatic way. During the several months since the national election, the ambassador had developed an excellent rapport with the Bolivian president and had won his confidence as a genuine supporter of the democratic and reform processes in play. Paz himself was indebted to Washington for supporting his fledgling government after the1952 revolution (Between 1953 and 1961, the U.S. gave Bolivia $178.8 million in grant aid and in 1957 supplied nearly 40 percent of its national budget.). In early 1986 Paz was once again engaged in another struggle; this time to see who would run Bolivia: the elected constitutional government or the narcotraffickers.

Sitting at one end of a long conference table headed by the Bolivian president, Ambassador Rowell discussed in general the outline of our proposed drug interdiction "blitzkrieg" to overwhelm, saturate and paralyze the drug-laboratory system. Besides myself, also present was Dr. Paz's military aid, whose confidentiality was questionable. It was therefore wise for Ed Rowell to be circumspect in what he had to say to the president. In short, it was explained that Washington would like to quash drug trafficking inside Bolivia with a series of UMOPAR-led, U.S. military-supported operations which would eliminate narcotraf-ficking, all the while avoiding alienating the relatively innocent Bolivian civil population working in the coca fields.

Since 1952, no Bolivian government had been able to survive against strong and united *campesino* (Indian) opposition and Paz appeared to appreciate our concern about not confronting directly the farmers in the Chapare region. For the anti-drug operations to succeed, it would require a formal, but limited U.S. military presence inside Bolivia and also require the support of the Bolivian military. Nevertheless, only president Paz could approve a foreign intervention of this nature into his country. After listening carefully to what Ambassador Rowell had to say and thinking it over for a minute or so, the Bolivian president turned to him and said: "Mr. Ambassador, you can do anything you want to do!"

Still venerated as a hero of the 1952 revolution, which had brought the masses their basic economic, human and political rights, including an Andian land reform involving private property ownership, Dr Paz was laying all his cards on the table and risking his presidency by al-lowing a foreign intervention into Bolivia. He further stated that drug trafficking was a threat to his society (at this time school teachers were being reported as having abandoned their classrooms to work in the coca fields) and undermining the moral foundation of Bolivia, and he wanted to put a stop to it any way he could. In this vein he also sug-gested that the actual plan intended to be executed be kept a secret until the moment it was executed. He knew all too well that trafficker familial ties, as well as other political linkages to his government, the military, and corrupt politicians inside the Bolivian Congress, ruled out any further revelations of the concept's details. While Paz did not make an issue of it, Bolivia was a constitutional democracy and the presence of foreign military forces of any kind on national soil required the ap-

The author (left rear) accompanies General John Galvin (CINC, SOUTHCOM) and Ambassador Edward Rowell (wearing glasses) after having just visited with Bolivian President Victor Paz Estenssoro in La Paz, Bolivia, February 1986. (U.S. Government photo)

proval of the Bolivian Chamber of Deputies. In the end it was Paz's job to control the political situation, and he did just that.

Carte blanche! The Bolivian president had given the United States of America full authority to do whatever was necessary to defeat the drug traffickers inside his country. It was nothing short of amazing and I could not recall from my knowledge of modern Latin American politics a similar occurrence having taken place. A solid base for U.S. intervention into Bolivia had now been laid by Ambassador Rowell and now it was only a matter of time for the Washington community to begin its implementation. Some weeks later, General John Galvin, the Commander-in-Chief (CINC), SOUTHCOM, paid us a visit in La Paz to learn first hand what we were thinking about in terms of our "war" in the Andes. The visit appeared to be a good omen, since it was his command with its responsibilities for all of Latin America south of Mexico that would undoubtedly be involved in supporting our strategy. Unfortunately, at that time the general was very much focused on the Central American war effort and the last thing he wanted was a distraction to the south which would siphon off his limited assets, then supporting operations in El Salvador, Honduras and Nicaragua. This consideration aside, the drug war was being conducted by the United States worldwide and included the Western Hemisphere as well as Europe, the Middle East, and Asia. And for this reason we did have a point!

To coordinate and oversee its intended world-wide anti-drug effort, the White House had created the Office of National Drug Control Policy (ONDCP). It was here that all the decisions and activities regarding the war on drugs outside the United States were ultimately approved, funded and implemented. Nonetheless, as February came on there did not appear to be any other formal acknowledgement of our cable or any interest in it at all on the part of Washington in terms of meeting our time constraints. As March came and went, I mentioned to Ed Rowell that time was running out if we were to conduct a well-coordinated, intelligence-driven attack on the laboratories. If nothing else the special training required for the UMOPAR needed to be coordinated with the Department of Defense (DOD) and the DEA, and the trainers and supporting helicopters procured as well. One would have thought, given the urgency of the "national security imperative" we were operating under, that the ONDCP as the lead agency in Washington for fighting drugs regionally would have at least sent an official down to La Paz to conduct a liaison visit to find out what was going on in detail inside Bolivia, discuss the merits of our plan, and otherwise determine what the agency could do to implement the Embassy's strategy on behalf of the U.S. national security interest. April came and went and May came on - still nothing.

During this time the government of Dr. Paz did formally charge in its Congress the nefarious Garcia Meza, as well as fifty-five of his former colleagues, with various crimes, involving sedition, armed uprising, treason, murder, fraud and drug trafficking. With good anti-narcotics laws now finally in play and traffickers being taken into custody from time to time, it was definitely a good sign and was interpreted by us to mean that the Paz government was in full accord with the U.S. anti-drug policy and coming on strong. In Washington, President Reagan formally declared on 11 April that drug trafficking constituted a national security threat to the United States and issued his National Security Decision Directive (NSDD) 221 to that effect. At about this same time President Paz, in a note to Ed Rowell reaffirmed his previous carte blanche, verbal authorization and formally *invited* the U.S. to support the Bolivian anti-drug effort. All this was good and well, but it was not until June that the anti-drug tempo actually began to change dramatically.

Towards the end of June, as Ambassador Rowell was leaving the front entrance of the Embassy, he was accosted by a member of the international news media who inquired as to when the "helicopters" were due to arrive in Bolivia. A startled Ed Rowell did an about face, reentered the Embassy, and proceeded to his fifth floor office where he could speak by secure telephone to one of the DOS undersecretaries responsible for Latin America. Indeed, there was something up and he was informed that a 160-person Army, airmobile task force called "Task Force Janus" was due to arrive within two weeks to begin operations against the narcotrafficker laboratories!

Surprise that it was, it appeared to be better than nothing. Task Force Janus included six high performance UH-60 (Black Hawk) helicopters, which would arrive in country on Air Force C-5A cargo transports at the Santa Cruz international airport to support what was called "Operation Blast Furnace." So the die had been cast. There was to be no intelligence preparation of the battlefield, no special training of UMOPAR personnel out of country, no clandestine insertion to gain the element of surprise, and no aerial interception of narco-aircraft! Both myself and the DEA agents with whom I had been working closely with were absolutely dismayed. Nonetheless, despite this setback involving inadequate preliminary preparation, the operation pressed ahead.

The U.S. Army's UH-60 Blackhawk helicopter was the workhorse of Washington's 1986 counter-narcotics campaign during Operation Blast Furnace, ferrying Bolivian ant-drug police and their DEA advisors into narcotrafficker production sites. (U.S. Army photo)

SOUTHCOM had been directed by the Pentagon-based Joint Chiefs of Staff (JCS) in late June to execute a series of helicopter raids against the drug laboratories in Bolivia. With only a couple of weeks to gear up for the operation, General Galvin had turned to his U.S. Army South component and its 193rd Infantry Brigade under the command of Major-General James R. Taylor to organize and initially run the show. While the 193rd was charged with the defense of the Panama Canal, it was now being tasked to do something entirely different. I had worked for Jim Taylor as his operations officer seven years earlier when he was a colonel and commanding the 5th Mechanized Infantry Division's Support Command at Fort Polk, Louisiana, and had found him to be an energetic and consummate professional in every sense of the word. By 1986 Taylor was now recognized as a stellar officer among the general officer corps of the Army and it was little wonder that Galvin had selected him to run the operation. As Taylor told me quite pointedly: "It's very strange that they put a major-general in charge of a company-sized force [captains command companies], but this operation must not fail!"

Over the next few days a series of distinct intelligence collection, target development, planning and operations, communications, and logistical staff groups poured into La Paz to plan up and then begin the execution of Blast Furnace. Maintenance, supply, transportation, aero-medical evacuation, medical, and fuel and equipment handling capabilities all had to be integrated into the planning and execution to insure that the operation would run smoothly and commence on time. While initially operating out of the Embassy with the support of the U.S. Military Group under the command of Colonel Robert Brown, the actual command and control of Blast Furnace would take place from a forward operating base in the Beni. In this case, due to the short time frame involved, the town of Trinidad, which had an airport capable of receiving C-130 transport aircraft, had been selected as the forward and principal operating base for Janus.

Two weeks later on 14 July and almost on cue the C-5A transports began landing and disgorging their Black Hawk helicopters, equipment and personnel at the Santa Cruz airport. Any pretense at surprise was now lost and scores of small narcotrafficker aircraft and an estimated 800 persons fled Bolivia in panic to neighboring countries at all points of the compass. Nonetheless, with this obvious initial impact having taken place, it remained to be seen as to how this would play out in terms of the success of the operation. General Taylor's task force went to work and, as soon as the Black Hawks were assembled, it headed for Trinidad, located in the heart of the drug-laboratory region. Here a tactical operations center and maintenance/refuel-rearm point, protected by a forty-man Army infantry platoon, was established off to one side of the airport. Air Force aerial bulk fuel systems (3,000 gallon C-130 "Blader Bird" aircraft) landed at Trinidad and then transferred aviation gas into 500-gallon rubber blivits to support the UH-60's high fuel consumption, which was often as much as 2,000 gallons per day. When it was found that improper fuel-transfer equipment had been sent to Bolivia, General Taylor, himself, jerry-rigged fuel nozzle couplings and hose hookups to correct the situation.

Intelligence inputs on the initial narco-laboratory targets to be attacked were now integrated into the daily airmobile strike plans, which were then executed by the Black Hawks and their DEA-accompanied UMOPAR assault forces. A rapid reconnaissance of the zone of operations reduced the two-hundred or more suspected targets to some fifty, which were then attacked at the rate of about one or two per day. To ensure security the UMOPAR personnel participating in the various missions were only notified of a pending strike an hour or so before the helicopters took off to attack the target of interest. During one of the first strikes conducted by some 30 UMOPAR anti-drug personnel (also called "Leopards"), who were accompanied by several DEA advisors and an official government prosecutor, a cocaine processing lab known as "El Zoro" was encountered. In addition to two airstrips, hangars, laboratories and dormitories, the site even sported a recreation area and a children's park. It was estimated that as many as 75 people lived and worked there. While no one was present at the site when the raid started, two lab employees returned to El Zoro in their Cessna aircraft and one was captured by the Leopards.

Eventually twenty-two other laboratories were discovered over the next several months, but no cocaine was seized and no important arrests were made. Most facilities that were located were found to have been abandoned, and a few, such as El Zoro, just within days of the UMOPAR arriving. While the helicopters could range out to about 200 miles in a radius around Trinidad, this did not cover the entire zone of potential targets and more distant temporary operating bases further away from Trinidad were sometimes established to further extend the strike force's range of operations. This all took time and meant that lucrative targets might not be reached quite as rapidly as one might have liked. Ironically, the largest laboratory discovered during the period of Blast Furnace was not due to the efforts of Task Force Janus at all, but due to the great misfortune of one of Bolivia's highly esteemed and leading botanists, Dr. Noel Kempff.

Some weeks after Blast Furnace had begun, Noel Kempff was leading a small group of fellow botanists into the Beni's Huanchaca rainforest, located about 250 miles southeast of Trinidad near the Brazilian border, where they stumbled onto a major drug-laboratory complex. Hidden inside Bolivia's national botanical preserve, the facility was stocked with approximately one-thousand 55-gallon drums of precursor chemicals, including ether, acetone and hydrochloride acid, and was awaiting the delivery of a huge batch of coca paste to be further refined into cocaine. Ironically, while listed as *Target 157* by Task Force Janus because of an agent report, the site had not yet been reconnoitered and verified for possible attack. As Kempff's followers proceeded along a well-worked trail leading into the forest, eagerly noting the numerous varieties of plant life, they ran into some narco-gunmen. The gunmen had become suspicious as to why an unannounced Cessna aircraft had landed at their grass airstrip just a short distance from the laboratory site. Uzi sub-machineguns cut Kempff and most of his group down, killing all but one who managed to escape.

As the news spread as to what had happened at Huanchaca, the Bolivian air force's leaders reacted by attempting an aerial counterattack against the laboratory but to no avail. The target could neither be located nor could the actual attack aircraft be assembled, armed and fueled on the short notice necessary to be effective. In the meantime thousands of people, principally in the Santa Cruz Department, conducted massive protest marches against the drug traffickers over the murder of their beloved Dr. Kempff. This massive, spontaneous outpouring of antagonism against the traffickers had never been seen before in Bolivia. Nonetheless, because of the experimental nature of Blast Furnace, no thought had been given in Washington to the possibility of having a PSYOPs team on hand to support the operation and, in this case, to exploit the sympathies of the highly aroused Bolivians against the nacotraffickers. After a few weeks the passions of the people subsided and life went on as normal.

Eventually Task Force Janus did mount an operation against Target 157 inside the Huanchaca botanical preserve. The invading UMOPAR strike force, airlifted to the site in their Black Hawk helicopters, encountered the thousand drums of chemicals and most of the lab's processing equipment. The narco-gunmen or guards and those drug processing personnel at the site had vanished. At this point in time the facility and its chemical contents became a matter of considerable debate reaching to the level of the Bolivian Ministry of Interior. What should have been a simple demolition effort to destroy the precursors in the remote outback of Bolivia now became a heated issue fueled by the fear that a massive fireball created by the burning chemicals might get out of control and adversely affect the area's ecology forever.

By the time a SOUTHCOM explosive ordinance disposal (EOD) demolition team had returned to the site to check on the condition of its demolitions already in place, half of the thousand barrels of chemicals had already been removed by the traffickers, presumably into neighboring Brazil. Although the EOD team leader had assured Ambassador Rowell that a safe, self-contained destruction of the chemicals could have been accomplished (placing the drums end-to-end and then setting them on fire in increments), the remaining five-hundred drums at the site were never destroyed and they, too, eventually disappeared! Some six years later in April of 1992, the former Minister of the Interior, Fernando Bartholemy, was officially cited in a Bolivian legislative commission report, which stated that he had protected and covered for the drug traffickers, including those involved in the Huanchaca laboratory matter and the death of Noel Kempff.

As the original Country Team strategy had envisioned, Operation Blast Furnace did bring about a collapse of the narcotrafficking system inside Bolivia. With the temporary shutdown of most, if not all of the drug laboratories, the coca farmers and crude paste makers had no buyers, driving the price of coca leaves to as low as $14 per hundredweight or well below the breakeven point of the required minimum of $30 needed to sustain the coca growers. Initially, the coca farmers placed no special blame on anyone in particular - what had happened with Blast Furnace had been "an act of God." As a result, while some farmers decided to wait and see what would happen, other farmers from at least five coca-growing villages sought assistance from AID for developing alternate crops.

While this was all good and well from Washington's point of view, the fact that the interdiction campaign had not been sustained from the dry season, ending for the most part in October 1986, through the rainy season (November - March) and on into the next dry season of 1987 meant that the narcotraffickers could rapidly reconstitute their operations and linkages to the coca-farming community. And they did, negating AID's efforts to implement a viable and lasting crop substitution program. As it was, with the all too brief notice given for the execution of Blast Furnace, AID did not have enough resources on hand to satisfy all the various requests from the temporarily destitute farmers.

At the beginning of 1987, the price of 100 pounds of coca leaves gradually rose once again above the required minimum profit level of $30 and even back to levels running between $60 and $88 or about what they had been prior to Blast Furnace. This indicated that the drug trafficking system inside Bolivia had fully recovered. By early 1987, it was further estimated that some 80,000 acres of coca were being farmed, producing around 92 tons of cocaine every year. As the summer of 1987 came on and my two-year tour of duty as an attache came to an end, it was also noted by DEA intelligence that the coca farmers were being mobilized into unions to better resist any future antidrug operations. Groups, such as the *Federacion Especial Campesina del Tropico Cochabambino* (Special Peasant Federation of the Cochabamba Tropics), began a deliberate campaign to lobby the Bolivian congress over concerns for their "traditional" coca-growing interests, which they claimed were being thwarted by the U.S.-sponsored anti-drug policy and the UMOPAR's continuing drug interdiction operations. With the coca farmers now aroused and better organized than ever before as a virtual "coca lobby," the Country Team in La Paz found itself no better off than before. Even Victor Paz, himself, became a target of the drug traffickers who placed a $400,000 bounty on his head.

The immediate lesson learned from the ONDCP's Operation Blast Furnace was that, while generally successful in the short term in temporarily shutting down the coca leaf-cocaine production system, unless the drug traffickers were attacked continuously, using a sustained, year-round interdiction format with no letup during both the dry and rainy seasons, they would reconstitute their operations and decisive results would be difficult if not impossible to achieve. While not fully appreciated by us at the time, there were other dynamics in play outside of Bolivia, involving the drug wars in the Andes, and these would turn the narcotraffickers into wily and highly resilient enemies, who would remain very difficult to subdue well into the twenty-first century.

* * *

— B O L I V I A —

During the remainder of the 1980s the La Paz Embassy steadily pursued the drug war in Bolivia. Nonetheless, despite some successes which saw the price of coca leaf drop to around $20 per hundredweight during the Spring of 1988, the effort was generally uneven, producing no decisive results. One of the major problems that the Embassy faced inside Bolivia was the matter of narco-related corruption, which constantly plagued the anti-drug effort. It had become so bad in the armed forces that it was necessary for president Victor Paz to relieve both the commander and chief of staff of the Bolivian navy for illegally utilizing government boats and seaplanes in support of transshipping paste and cocaine on behalf of the traffickers. Even the commanders and senior leaders of the UMOPAR were often found to be taking narco-bribes in exchange for information as to when and where operations were going to take place and had to be replaced on a continual basis.

Only in September of 1990 was there a dramatic change, due in the main to the efforts of a recently assigned DEA official, Donald Ferrarone. After studying the situation in Bolivia, he had independently come to the same conclusion as I had: that only a year-round, intelligence driven operation, attacking the traffickers at their advanced laboratory sites and cutting their road, riverine and aerial lines of communication would enable the Bolivian and U.S. governments to shut the drug production system down. Outspoken and hard-driving, Don Ferrarone now provided a new element to the war on drugs - his own personal leadership. In addition to Ferrarone arriving on station in 1990, SOUTHCOM had also undergone some changes in command with General Maxwell Thurman becoming the new CINC. Thurman had presided over the successful U.S. invasion of Panama in December 1989 and was chomping at the bit to take a crack at the drug war in the Andes. In addition, with the civil war in Central America now coming to a close, SOUTHCOM could now begin to refocus much of its intelligence gathering assets to fight the narcotraffickers throughout the region.

That September Ferrarone's DEA-UMOPAR operations in the Santa Cruz area netted not only one of Bolivia's top 35 drug traffickers, Carmelo "Meco" Dominguez, but also almost all the senior members of his organization, including pilots, chemists, money managers, and paste buyers, as well as records, safe houses, front businesses and nine aircraft. This effectively dismantled a complete narcotrafficking organization! In another surprise raid some 600 UMOPAR and 33 DEA agents, arriving in helicopters and riverine swift boats, attacked the drug trafficker safe-haven and town of Santa Ana de Yacuma. Here 54 persons were arrested, 15 cocaine base and HCl laboratories were destroyed and 42 aircraft were seized. The seized aircraft were estimated to be about half of the narcotrafficker air fleet then operating inside Bolivia! In addition, some 15 drug trafficker properties, including ranches, were seized. The raid effectively disrupted trafficking operations in west-central Bolivia and frightened six major Bolivian traffickers into surrendering to Bolivian authorities.

While other similar successes took place, it was only in early 1991, and only after much pressure from the Country Team, that a hesitant Bolivian Congress and government agreed to permit formal Army Special Forces training and anti-drug operations under American control. The Bolivian government's position was that interdiction, prevention and alternate development were the real goals of its anti-drug strategy and not merely eradication through the use of coercive military force. Nonetheless, the $33 million in promised U.S. military aid from Washington was now conditioned on the participation of all the Bolivian armed forces in the drug war. These operations were to focus only on cocaine processing and trafficking routes outside the coca growing regions. While the Green Berets trained the UMOPAR, Navy SEALs trained the Bolivian navy's riverine strike force and accompanying marine infantry company, and Army aviators trained the BAF's 12-helicopter, anti-drug air wing. In addition, two Bolivian Ranger battalions were trained in counter-narcotics operations and an engineer battalion was prepared to conduct civic action construction missions on behalf of the population.

Washington also weighed in with other much needed support. While an aviation radar detection system was installed by SOUTH-COM at Santa Cruz and Trinidad, the Bolivian navy's anti-drug strike force (called the "Blue Devils") was enhanced with the addition of five riverine support vessels for operations and logistics, 20 high-speed patrol boats and 10 Zodiac, inflatable rubber assault boats. The BAF's total aircraft dedicated to drug interdiction missions was brought up to two C-130 Hercules aerial transports and 22 UH-1 helicopters. In all, this was a formidable force to be arrayed against the traffickers. Equally important were SOUTHCOM's intelligence assets which provided aerial reconnaissance and signal intelligence, which, when combined with the human intelligence reports available to DEA, enabled the UMOPAR to conduct one successful operation after another.

As successes mounted and the price of coca leaves per hundred-weight fell to below $15, the Bolivian trafficking organizations began to falter in their resolve to stay the course. As a result, a number of the purchasing organizations in the Chapare disbanded or merged with other trafficking networks for protection. Over a period of only about two years Ferrarone's campaign had taken down the majority of the 35 known drug trafficking groups, leaving only an estimated ten still operating intermittently. To keep the paste and refined cocaine flowing, Colombian drug cartel representatives from Cali and Medellin intervened in the production effort inside Bolivia. Flying into the Beni and Santa Cruz Departments, they took charge wherever they deemed it necessary, displacing Bolivian functionaries and becoming more and more directly involved in both the purchasing and processing of the coca leaves.

There was a significant difference in the way the Colombians operated. Whereas in the past the Bolivian buyers would often extend credit to the coca leaf producers and paste makers, the Colombians operated strictly on a cash basis. This made it difficult for the Bolivian farmers and others who were attempting to set up coca processing/farming businesses or were trying to recover from losses due to UMOPAR operations. While the Colombians could ensure the continued operation of their marketing systems to some degree, they were very much like fish out of water and, being unable to blend into the Bolivian social fabric, were relatively easy to identify and target. Nonetheless, the Cali and Medellin traffickers brought into play some production techniques which enabled the coca growers to take their coca leaves and process them so that the cocaine products or coca paste could be suspended in a liquid mixture called *agua rica* ("rich water"). This now meant that cocaine in a liquid state could be stored indefinitely in large quantities in plastic jugs at an intermediate stage of production without spoiling, preserving the producer's investment until such time as a buyer thought it was safe enough to stop by to make the pickup and render payment. This extended the shelf-life of the basic cocaine product and enabled the lower end of the production system to survive the vagaries of the UMOPAR's strike operations on the coca market.

One of the objectives that the U.S. wanted to accomplish inside Bolivia was influencing the coca farmers to switch to alternate crops. Despite the plethora of potential crops which could be exploited for this purpose, it appeared to AID at this time that only soybeans had any long term promise of competing with coca as a crop substitute. Soybeans, being a hearty crop and one of the few which could also thrive in the Chapare, sold well on the international market and appeared to be the ideal and only solution as an alternate crop. Unfortunately, the Department of Agriculture (DOA), fearing undue competition with the U.S. soybean farmers, quashed the initiative. Ignored was the fact that both Argentina and Brazil exported soybeans into the world market in far larger quantities than Bolivia could ever hope to produce. The Embassy in La Paz and the Genneral Accounting Office in Washington argued against the DOA, contending that one could not hope to take effective action to destroy Bolivian coca production, leaving 300,000 or more producers jobless, unless some adequate substitutes in the form of employment, income and foreign exchange were generated on their behalf. It was further argued that Bolivian soybean exports would only equal about 3 percent of the world market (the U.S. accounted for 38 percent and Brazil another 30 percent). Despite this analysis and Washington's own position that drug trafficking in Bolivia was a threat to national security, the DOA refused to change its position; thus quashing this lucrative alternative crop initiative and indicating that it was a far more powerful force than the ONDCP within the Washington bureaucracy. As it was, there were already some three thousand private and independent soybean producing farmers in Bolivia's Santa

Cruz Department, indicating that it was, indeed, a feasible crop and could very well have been the answer to Washington's alternative crop substitution problem.

By 1993, so successful had been Don Ferrarone as the epitome of a successful DEA country director, he was now transferred to another posting in South East Asia where he would continue to wage the drug war on behalf of the United States, fighting the international traffickers in the infamous "golden triangle" of Burma, Laos and Thailand. While there was no doubt as to his successes in setting back the narcotraffickers inside Bolivia, the mid-1990s found the U.S. anti-drug program in Bolivia continuing to make some progress, but still generally meandering along in terms of a decisive end result. It was now estimated that in the Chapare alone coca leaf production was enabling the traffickers to acquire an estimated 195 tons of cocaine per year. The coca growing federations had rebounded under the direction of astute labor leader and agitator Evo Morales, who even was able to get himself elected to the Bolivian Congress; a position under Bolivian law that gave him immunity from criminal prosecution. Ironically, as fate would have it, another dynamic was thrown into the drug war in Bolivia in the form of former military dictator General Hugo Banzer.

In 1997 Banzer ran for the Bolivian presidency in an open democratic election. Putting together a mega-coalition, involving four other major parties and his own ADN, Banzer garnered 80 percent of the seats in the La Paz Congress, which enabled him to legislate virtually by decree. Possibly trying to redeem his tarnished image of the 1970s, the new president declared himself in favor of meeting Washington's annual coca eradication target of around 16,000 acres for Bolivia. Nonetheless, what appeared to truly animate Banzer and drive his anti-drug policy forward far more than anything else was the alleged death of a beloved family member due to an overdose of cocaine. This event literally caused the 73-year old president to turn with a fury and vengeance against his erstwhile narco-allies of his previous administration.

As a result there was a frenzy of activity to eliminate coca growing in the Chapare and four of the army's most reliable infantry regiments were moved directly into the region to begin eradication in earnest. That Banzer had been a ruthless dictator in previous years now inspired considerable fear in the coca farmers who were now confronted with an implacable government policy of "zero tolerance" towards what had been known as the "sacred leaf." With their lives on the line for failing to cooperate, the farmers' formerly highly effective regional unions and alliances now began to disintegrate in the face of Banzer's wrath.

During this unrelenting campaign waged in the main by the Bolivian army, the BAF, and the UMOPAR, dozens of resisting coca farmers were killed and another 1,200 went to jail. Between 1997 and 2002 or over the five-year period of Banzer's administration, the attack on this key center of gravity found 148,000 acres (1 acre potentially = 7 pounds of refined cocaine per coca crop) of high grade coca plants pulled up and otherwise eradicated, causing the illegal production of cocaine inside Bolivia to drop from 234 tons to less than 8 tons annually (30,000 acres of legal coca for medicinal purposes was still authorized in the Yungas)! This was a severe blow to the narcotraffickers and delighted both the American Embassy in La Paz and Washington alike. Nonetheless, there was a cost in all this.

The months of on and off civil violence and road blockages in reaction to the government's focus on the Chapare reduced overall economic activity in Bolivia by nearly half. Net losses to the Chapare farmers participating in alternative development crops exceeded $1.25 million and the production and marketing infrastructure created by AID was sometimes destroyed by protesting coca growers. Even hard-won market linkages with Argentine and Chilean buyers were also severely tested by the inability of the Chapare-based, alternative crop producers to always comply with their delivery contracts. As the 2002 election came on and Banzer passed away, the issue of growing coca remained. Illegal coca traditionally had represented some $400 million in earnings annually for the local economy and, with 60 percent of the Indian population living in a state of poverty, it remained very difficult to find a suitable income alternative.

Undaunted and otherwise at a loss as to what to do to survive, numerous coca farmers began to hide their coca cultivations among the AID sponsored, alternative banana crops now being introduced into the region. But this was not all. The 2002 national election found the populist leftist Evo Morales, the former coca farmer and labor activist leader now turned politician, running for the presidency and only falling short of election by some 43,000 votes! Albeit the apparent end of a long anti-drug campaign inside Bolivia, lasting around 17 years and costing the American taxpayer around $1.3 billion, the end was not yet in sight for the U.S. anti-drug effort in the Andes. Taking advantage of a broad groundswell of anti-government opposition over the catalytic issue of Bolivia exporting part of its natural gas resources through its old nineteenth century enemy, Chile, Evo Morales rallied his constituency in an alliance with a variety of indigenous Indian groups to help foment a series of national strikes in 2004 and 2005. These ultimately brought down the governments of President Gonzalo Sanchez de Lozada and Carlos Mesa. Having once lost their livelihood in the tin mines, the coca farmers were adamant about it happening again; thus challenging the American investments in military- supported counter-narcotics and developmental aid programs for the future. Morales exploited his political success and coca-related national sentiment to successfully run for president in 2005, taking office in early 2006. Whe war on drugs had come full circle in Bolivia.

— PERU —

From the early-1980s and on into the 1990s, Peru was the world's largest single source of coca leaves, providing for about two-thirds of the total cocaine produced or some 500 tons. A country of a little over 21 million people, 75 percent of the population was underemployed or not employed at all. Mere survival was for many the only hope or aspiration in life. For half the population it was more important for their children to be working to support their family rather than spend time in school. About the size of Alaska, Peru is characterized by a high Andean mountain chain running through the country from north to south. While its western Pacific Ocean coastal region consists of arid, desert-like plains abutting the mountains to the east, on the other or eastern side of the Andes lie the tropical zones and jungles of the headwaters of the Amazon river complex.

It was this Amazonian tropical region, known as the Upper Huallaga Valley (UHV), which borders on Brazil further to the east and Colombia and Ecuador to the north and produces around 60 percent of Peru's coca leaves, that became a principal anti-drug focus of the United

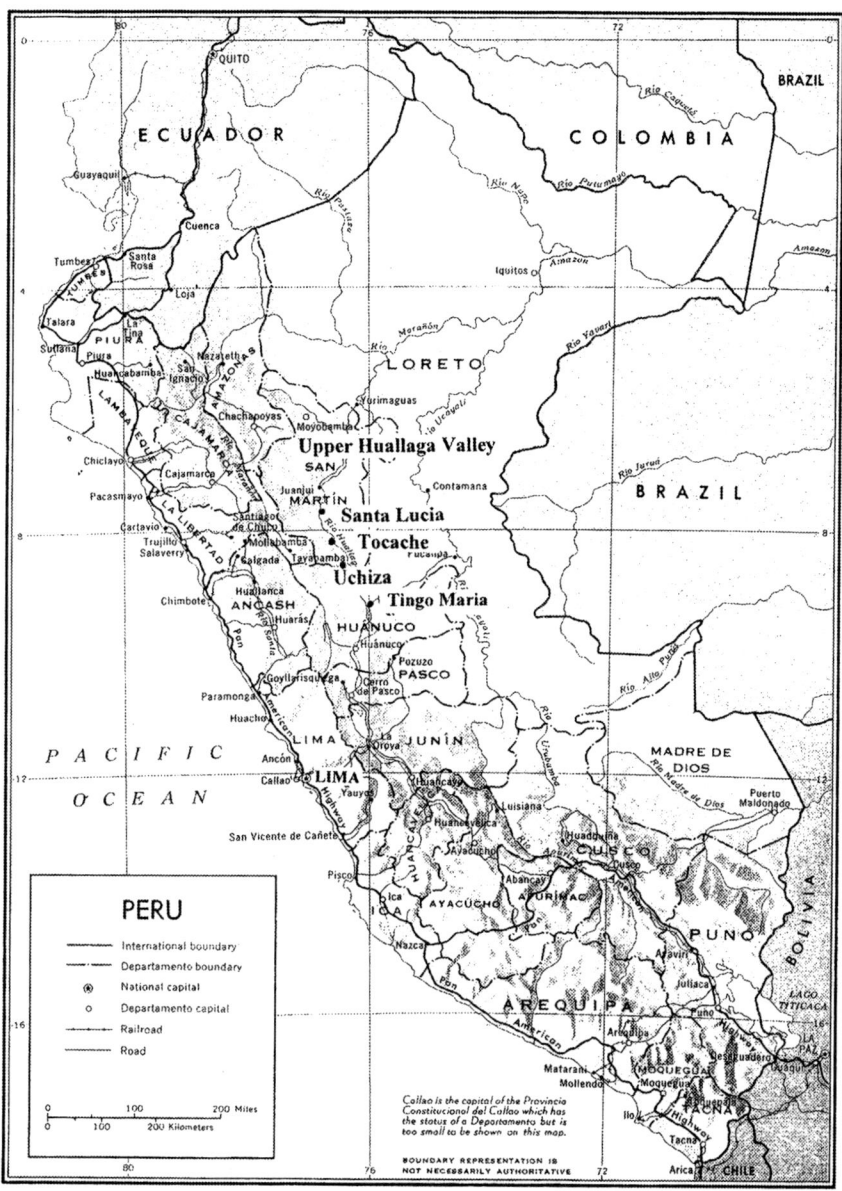

States. Over time, the high but very fertile, Andean valleys to the south, such as those formed by the Urubamba and Ene Rivers in the vicinity of Ayacucho and Cuzco were also recognized as important parts of the international cocaine trade. In short, coca was growing in fourteen of Peru's 24 departments (provinces).

Much like their ethnic brethren in Bolivia, the Indians of Peru also revered the coca leaf as a sustainer of life, as well as an enhancer of their own economic well being. Nevertheless, it was the narcotraffickers, operating mainly out of Colombia to exploit the lucrative high demand market in North America and Europe, involving billions of dollars in profits, who saw the great potential of Peru. And it was the remote UHV, with its 8,000 square miles and over 100,000 inhabitants, that enabled the Colombians and their cartel-linked buyers to purchase coca leaves for conversion first into paste and then ultimately into the high quality, refined cocaine so demanded by the consumer markets of the world.

Between the UHV and the Andean valleys to the south, business boomed and the poor Indian *campesinos,* numbering up to a million in the various coca-growing regions, for the first time in their lives began to subsist reasonably well with their now readily exportable coca crops. Earnings ran from around $1,500 up to $10,000 for each two-to-four-acre plot. Wage laborers, picking leaves or making paste could earn as much as $5 per day or about double the official minimum wage. To counter the ever escalating quantities of coca leaf being grown in the UHV, by 1982 the Peruvian government, assisted by AID financial support, began the Special Project for the Upper Huallaga. This project had as its objective the weaning away of the farmers from their illegal coca to embrace legitimate, alternate crop substitutes.

Yet, almost from the onset of the serious American and Peruvian efforts to stem the drug trade in Peru, there was a serious complication that had ubiquitously come into play. Towards the end of a previous tour of duty in late 1981, during which time I was serving as an Army-sponsored exchange officer to the Peruvian army's Lima-based academic center at Chorrillos, I had awakened one morning to find dead dogs strung up on various lamp posts throughout the city. What was going on? What did this mean? Some days later there was a mysterious car bombing of the outer security wall of Ambassador Ed Corr's residence.

What myself and Peruvians in general had encountered and would ultimately learn over time was that these were the opening "shots" from a deadly, rural-based, Maoist-oriented, Communist insurgency called the *Sendero Luminoso* (SL or "Shining Path"), which had been preparing for 17 years, or since the 1960s, to launch a revolutionary effort to overthrow the national government and take over the entire country. The Shining Path then unleashed a reign of terror throughout most of Peru which increased in such strength and ferocity over the next couple of years that it became a destabilizing force far beyond the ability of the local police forces to cope. The SL operated on two principal fronts, one that was revolutionary and focused initially on the high Andean regions around Ayacucho and another that was very much a commercial enterprise and centered on the coca growing regions of Peru.

The roots of the SL phenomenon were eventually traced to the Ayacucho Department of the early 1960s where a dissident, high-Andean intellectual elite and a group of young, energetic and impressionable men and women of Quechua Indian and mestizo origins had joined together under the leadership of a Huamanga University professor by the name of Doctor Abimael Guzman. As the militant cadres and agitators for the revolution, they had been exposed to Guzman's interpretation of Marxist analytical concepts of human exploitation as an explanation of the Peruvian reality; whereby, they were told, they had become the "children of the deceived." In addition, they learned that the Spanish language and culture had been deceitfully imposed upon their Indian ancestors by the Spanish-Iberian conquest as part of a strategy of domination and monopoly control by an oligarchy centered on Lima.

There was a certain logic and historical correctness to what Guzman had to say (even the military's Center for Higher Military Studies - CAEM at Chorrillos had concluded that rural conditions in Peru were so archaic and unjust that it was only a matter of time before an insurgency would eventually take place) and it was received by fertile minds, who also believed in a Quechuan utopia of people living in absolute peace and harmony, without exploitation, greed, graft, corruption, or the dominating structure of the state, political parties, classes or even democracy. Guzman further taught this as a dogma and said that anything that smacked of the trappings of the old state or semifeudal colonial order was "contaminated," since it was not legitimate in its protection of the people's interests. Contamination included among other things the national governing structure, elected mayors, unions, cooperatives (symbols of exploitation and corruption), other parties of the left and right, and all non-governmental entities such as churches and businesses.

Peru's concepts of liberty and equality were scorned as falsehoods and myths when confronted with the reality of the human misery and degradation which was the visible, everyday lot of the poor in Peru. Indians were derisively viewed as those who could, even at best in the urban areas, work only in the most subordinate of roles as peons, day laborers, and maids. That the highly-touted agrarian reform program of the 1969 military government of General Juan Velasco had provided land to some 360,000 farm families but at the same time had not improved the Indians' political influence at the national level of government was considered as one part of this reality. Corruption, combined with an unresponsive and uncaring Lima government and its indifferent administrators, who presided over the ever deepening rural poverty in the Andes, was a fact of life in Ayacucho and this contributed to a loss of considerable legitimacy on the part of the government, not only in the eyes of the university students, but also the campesinos in general. In short, the western-oriented and urbanized criollo classes in Lima were perceived by Guzman's followers as looking down upon Indians in general and denying the latter the educational and employment opportunities that should have been theirs. All this added fuel to the smoldering revolutionary fire that would eventually break out as a "people's war" to sear Peruvian society to its roots. With a perceived "just cause" in play, the catalytic situation only required a leader with a "solution."

Doctor Abimael Guzman, known as "Doctor *Puka Inti*" (Incan for the "Red Sun") and head of his Peruvian Communist Party (PCP) did offer a solution. To escape from their perceived conditions of virtual feudal slavery, Guzman told his followers it was now necessary to engage in a revolutionary war which would both educate and cleanse Peru's society and eliminate the dominating, illegitimate state structure and government. This was to be a "popular war" or revolution as advocated by Mao Tse Dung (China's successful Communist revolutionary leader), and would last as long as necessary to first secure the highlands or periphery as a base of operations and second to surround and overrun Lima proper, the governing center, as part of a massive, popular uprising.

While the SL did not solicit help in any militant form from other leftist groups inside the country, the *Tupac Amaru* Revolutionary Movement (MRTA) inside Lima competed with the former as a second and parallel insurrectionary movement, appealing to any and all disaffected people throughout Peru and promising a revolutionary government along the lines of Fidel Castro's Cuba. While the MRTA busied itself by attacking symbols of "imperialism," such as the Kentucky Fried Chicken and Pizza Hut restaurants, Mormon churches, and radio and television stations, as well as some government offices inside Lima, the SL went to work in Peru's outback.

With the need for a reliable source of funding to finance its efforts, the SL began in 1983 to extend its operations into the coca growing regions of all parts of Peru, contesting and frequently ousting from many areas the competing MRTA guerrillas. In the UHV the SL effected a type of protectorate relationship in support of the coca farmers in exchange for a form of "tax." By this means the SL was able to gain control of up to 90 percent of the UHV. In so doing it ruled by the law of the gun, helping the coca farmers to keep from being swindled or underpaid by the narcotrafficker buyers and the other purchasing and shipping organizations which formed the infrastructure for the drug trade. Here too, the buyers and traffickers also paid their share of "taxes" or fees as a price for not being molested by the SL and allowed to ply their trade.

In exchange for exacting taxes, the SL guerrillas also provided the "service" of protecting both the coca growers and traffickers from the distrusted and bothersome government officials, coca eradicators, and police and military forces. Anyone who did not accept the SL's extortion racket, paid with their lives. Nonetheless, as the only organization in the UHV that openly defended the coca growers' rights to production, the SL did gain a certain amount of legitimacy in the eyes of the campesino farmers. As a result they were able to form loose coalitions and interest groups called Fronts For the Defense of the People's Interest (FEDIPs), consisting of both legal and illegal, local coca growers and farmers.

Washington wanted to go directly to what it perceived was the source of the coca production problem in Peru - the coca farms, which generated several or more coca-leaf crops every year. This supply-side strategy could best be carried out, or so it seemed in the early 1980s, through a process of completely eradicating the coca bushes. Parallel to this effort was the Peruvian army and anti-drug police forces' dual missions of defeating both the SL guerrillas and the narcotraffickers. Ironically, these two missions would work at cross purposes.

The army maintained that its number one priority in the UHV was actually the elimination of the SL insurgency, and not the destruction of coca bushes. It therefore made the deliberate effort to befriend the coca growers whose support was seen as critical for defeating the guerilla movement. In this case campesino support was perceived as essential for isolating the SL from its sources of funding, logistical support and valuable information about the government's counter-insurgency operations. If isolation was not always possible, at least information could be obtained from the coca farmers to assist reconnaissance patrols to better target SL guerrilla units roaming the UHV. Peruvian General Alberto Arciniega made the point quite clearly: "There are 150,000 peasant coca farmers in the zone. Each one of them is a potential guerrilla. Eradicate his field and the next day he'll be one!"

To offset and work around the army in the UHV, the DEA, with permission from the Fernando Belaunde government, created its own rural, mobile strike force called the "DIPOD" or Directorate of Anti-Drug Police. This was made up of members of the Peruvian National Police (PNP) and was similar to the Bolivian UMOPAR and often referred to by that name. Unfortunately, this force was frequently ignored, left undefended and sometimes even actually prevented from carrying out some of its own counter-drug operations by the army. In November 1984, 23 coca eradicators and government police inspectors were murdered by the SL. A few months later in January 1985, fifteen farm laborers including women and children were also killed by the SL. It appeared that these events were related and carried out by the guerrillas as retribution against those farmers who had become involved in Washington's (AID) alternate crop projects. By mid-1985 there was a serious concern on the part of AID that some of the Peruvian civilian officials were losing enthusiasm and initiative for their work and becoming more concerned about personal safety.

At the same time, it was found that the army and DIPOD personnel in the UHV were becoming ever more susceptible to corruption in the form of drug trafficker bribes. The peasant coca farmers themselves did not particularly like or trust the soldiers and police and became more and more irate as the latter roamed around their plantations, disrupting an otherwise relatively tranquil accommodation and business relationship that had developed with both the SL and the traffickers. Financially speaking, it was estimated that a two-acre plot of coca was earning a level of income at least twice that of a similar plot of coffee and up to twenty times that of a similar plot of rice. As a result of the above situations, both the army and police missions in the UHV were seen as abject failures by Washington. Despite the DEA's offer to pay each farmer $300 per two acres of coca plants destroyed, the average farmer was now receiving between $4,000 and $20,000 for a year's worth of coca leaves. Things came to a head in April and May of 1986 when militant coca farmers and their FEDIPs cut the roads into the UHV and for several days even laid siege to one of AID's offices at the town of Aucayacu, about twenty miles north of Tingo Maria. The following June an estimated 3,000 farmers surrounded and proceeded to stone a detachment of DIPOD police, burning two of the government's eradication trucks. Simply put: things were not going well in the UHV.

Despite President Ronald Reagan's NSDD 221 formal announcement of the war on drugs, the UHV airports of Tocache and Uchiza were noted as receiving between two and five trafficker aircraft each day, landing and picking up between 800 and 2,500 pounds of coca paste per planeload for onward shipment to laboratories inside Colombia. Paying $600 to $750 per pound of paste and some $8,000 per landing and takeoff, both the farmers and the traffickers respectively paid their "war taxes" to the SL. These were small transaction costs compared to the hundreds of thousands, if not millions of dollars which were being made from each shipment to the international drug markets in North America and Europe. If the police got in the way of these transactions, as happened in late May 1987 at Uchiza, the SL merely wiped out the village detachment and burned its office. Later that year when the DEA and DIPOD counter-attacked in force with some 1,200 police and helicopters to wipe out 40 laboratories and capture 14 aircraft, along with thousands of pounds of coca paste and cocaine base, the net result was that the overall flow of drugs was not particularly stemmed and Washington estimated that Peru was still producing some 370 tons of refined cocaine for the international market. While other estimates ran as high as 500 tons, the only thing one could be sure of was that there was an incredible amount of cocaine product coming out of Peru.

Exasperated with the course of events and taking a leaf from Operation Blast Furnace, Washington and Lima decided to formally establish an airmobile operating base in the middle of the UHV. Located in 1988 on the west bank of the Huallaga River in a relatively remote area without a road network connecting it to any of the major towns, "Santa Lucia" had the purpose of supporting 500 DIPOD police and a dozen or more UH-1 and five Bell helicopters flown by U.S.-hired contract pilots, which were to seek out and destroy narco-laboratories within a two-hundred mile radius. The airmobile operations did drive the farmers and traffickers outside the operational range of Santa Lucia, but trafficking continued apace. It was noted that some traffickers were so confident of their operations that their couriers carried lots of up to $20 million to be laundered in the six-dozen exchange houses found in Lima and other towns throughout Peru. The amount of narco-dollars entering the Peruvian economy was now said to be somewhere between $400 million and $1.2 billion per year. Inside the United States, the Senate Judiciary Committee reported that some 2.4 million Americans were cocaine addicts (one out of every hundred citizens) and another ten percent (24 million) were indulging in some form of cocaine product or other illegal narcotics. In addition, during the period of a year an estimated 400,000 "crack babies" (crack being a derivative of cocaine) had been reportedly born in hospitals throughout the nation.

In April 1990 the Santa Lucia base itself came under attack from an estimated two-hundred well-armed guerrillas using rockets, mortars and machineguns. One Green Beret trainer on duty with the DIPOD quipped: "Between the G-forces [guerrillas] and the D-armies [drug traffickers] and sometimes even hostile host forces, it's very hard to keep up with who's trying to blow you away!" Around this time, Alan Garcia, now president of Peru, found it necessary to dismiss some 1,700 corrupt officers, including over one-hundred police generals and colonels. One police colonel in the Lima area, earning a monthly salary of $500, was reported to have said that he had the opportunity to earn up to $70,000 a year in the UHV by merely looking the other way when drug trafficking was taking place. Since the low-paying, police pension plans were being all but eroded away by the inflationary financing (over

3,000 percent) of the Garcia administration, it was little wonder that it was difficult to resist temptations in the form of dollar bribes then being offered by the myriad of traffickers and their agents.

At about the time the discredited Garcia regime was replaced through elections in June 1990 by the Alberto Fujimori government, General Maxwell Thurman, CINC, SOUTHCOM, began to intensify the tempo of operations in the UHV. Thurman had concluded that the eradication campaign was stagnating and that other alternatives needed to be brought into play to achieve decisive results. Taking a cue from Napoleon's famous dictum: "If you can dominate your enemy's line of communication, you will dominate the battlefield," Thurman now waged his war inside Peru.

With the "battlefield" being the UHV and the Peruvian highland valleys to the south and the "line of communication" being the aerial links out of Peru into Colombia, SOUTHCOM began to maneuver four ground-based radars around the Iquitos and Andoas regions of northern Peru, as well as a series of E2C AWACs and U.S. Custom's P3 search aircraft to help identify and hand off suspected narcotrafficking aircraft to the Peruvian air force's (FAP) A-37 and Tucano interceptors. With 70 to 90 trafficker flights per month entering and exiting Peru's airspace there were plenty of targets. Over an eight month period (October 1990 to May 1991), the FAP successfully intercepted 55 trafficker aircraft. Unfortunately, one of the planes shot down a month later on 9 July 1991 was an unregistered commercial aircraft with 17 people aboard; none survived.

In response to the radar-supported aerial interdiction program, the traffickers now began to schedule their flights at night. Very typically narco-aircraft would leave Colombia around 3 to 5 PM enroute to Peru. Communicating by radio to a ground station in Colombia and one in Peru, they would receive final approval and routing instructions for the often up to six-hour flight ahead. Sometimes even guiding on SOUTHCOM's own radar beams, they would try to land between 10 PM and 2 AM at the destination airfield where the aircraft loaded between 1,000 and 2,000 pounds of cocaine base or HCl, refueled, and then took off for the return flight to Colombia before sunrise. Compounding the aerial interdiction problem was the fact that the Peruvian civil aeronautics agency and the FAP only controlled 58 of the

396 airports. In addition, there were reported to be some 2,000 grass airstrips potentially available to the traffickers throughout the country. Besides the grass airstrips, there were also thousands of miles of rivers on which to land hydrofoil or seaplane aircraft.

This meant that, even with the best of all-source intelligence in play, the drug war in Peru was much like a gigantic shell game with the traffickers more frequently than not able to outmaneuver their American and Peruvian adversaries. Despite Fujimori's specific orders to have the FAP take control of the airfields in April of 1991, it was reported in July that trafficker aircraft routinely continued to use even the government controlled airports in the UHV with little or no restraint on the part of the military or the police. Even more important was the fact that the FAP had little or no night fighting capability and was reduced to attempting to make its intercepts only during periods of daylight. As a result, trafficking continued unabated, despite narco-aircraft being shot down virtually every week.

But it was Alberto Fugimori, very much concerned about the on-going SL insurgency, who set the tone for counter-drug operations in Peru, declaring to President George H.W. Bush at an anti-drug summit in San Antonio, Texas, in February 1992: "We want the coca growers to be our allies, not our enemies!" Returning to Peru and citing bureaucratic inefficiency and a lack of cooperation and corruption as hindering the nation's progress, in early April the Peruvian president proceeded to abolish the national legislature and judiciary and suspended the national constitution. He would now rule by decree as a new-born populist and caudillo-style dictator with the support of the military, commercial business elites, and the people in general. His act, albeit castigated by the international community as a setback to democracy, was well received by Peruvians in general who found themselves facing an intransigent SL insurgency which had murdered an estimated 21,000 people, a stagnant economy with 7,650 percent inflation, and a government heretofore unable to resolve any of the society's socio-economic and security problems. Despite the declaration of a "state of emergency," which essentially suspended constitutional guarantees and placed the country on a war footing, with rule by decree, direct military control, curfews, and an all-out war declared against the SL guerrillas, the situation in terms of the insurgency began to deteriorate badly.

With a reported strength of around 100,000 persons, which included guerrilla fighters and supporters and a war chest of some $30 million garnered from its "war taxes," Abimael Guzman was extending his attacks nationwide. Car bombings in Lima alone killed and wounded hundreds of people and damaged some 400 hotels, banks, government buildings, offices, shops, and homes, forcing the government to cancel its annual Peruvian Independence Day celebrations. The dynamiting of electrical power pylons and stations by the guerrillas came with such frequency that major portions of the capital were left without electricity on a daily basis. The total cost to the government and its people was now estimated at around $500 million. In short, brimming with confidence that he was now choking off Lima's food, water and electricity, the SL's Red Sun was now embarking upon the last phase of his campaign to isolate and then strangle the capital as a prelude to his anticipated great national uprising to overthrow the government. Nonetheless, the SL had made some mistakes which would seriously compromise the success of their campaign to conquer Peru.

By discrediting the government and Peruvian societal values, the SL had hoped from the onset of its guerrilla war to be able to substitute its own standards of law and morality in order to govern the areas they controlled. In the Andean highlands cattle thieves, disloyal husbands, dishonest merchants, corrupt government officials, and those who drank alcohol and caroused were subject to stern guerrilla justice and retribution, which frequently meant death for the perpetrator. In some cases where a major land lord was killed or forced to flee his plantation, the guerrillas then redistributed the property among the nearby villagers and cancelled any outstanding debts that remained. While there was a guarded, positive response on the part of the peasant communities to these actions and the stern prescriptions of revolutionary morality, the SL demanded in return an autarkic society based on economic self-sufficiency with little or no administrative, commercial, and political links to the national government and its infrastructure.

Nonetheless, not fully cognizant of all the complexities of traditional agrarian communities, the farm-to-market system, and the deep hatred of any domination felt by the campesinos, the SL all too often tried to forcibly reorganize the communities into unrealistic economic and social arrangements, such as communes. These included shutting off access to local markets and imposing improper planting techniques on the peasant farmers for their local food crops. Indeed, the entire market economy system of the highlands, as well as the rest of Peru, was declared decadent and a trapping of the oppressive Lima regime; and therefore not to be tolerated within the SL's new concept of how Peruvian society should function. As a result, through the use of vicious, selective terror against uncooperative farmers, wealthy peasants, hostile cooperatives, numerous town mayors and other individuals, the SL made as many enemies as friends. Only the indiscriminate and heavy-handed, "take no prisoner" tactics of the Peruvian national security forces, involving the army and the police, worked in a countervailing manner to maintain some peasant sympathy on the side of the SL.

Still, the long term effect of the SL's policies was to gradually turn what had been a cooperative population against the Shining Path revolution and all that it stood for. Exploiting this now adverse situation against the SL, the army began to form village self-defense forces (called *rondas*), made up of both men and women armed with shotguns, to help protect the peasant farmers and their families against SL incursions and harassment. If nothing else, for the short term, this stalemated the SL's guerrilla operations throughout Peru and complicated to a large degree the revolution's efforts to rally the people to its cause.

While Guzman had organized his revolution into six regional commands, supported by networks of cells and guerrilla units, which provided intelligence, logistics and operational support for the SL's revolutionary strategy, it was his move into Lima proper to directly command and control the overthrow of the seat of government from a forward position that contributed to his downfall. Operating from a safe house in the Los Sauces neighborhood, he coordinated and controlled his guerrilla forces through the use of computers, telephones, and a system of couriers. Nonetheless, a special government police commando and anti-terrorist unit (DINCOTE) was able, through tip-offs from local citizens not in sympathy with the revolution, to locate the SL leader's safe house. After observing the site and tapping its telephones for some days, the police moved in on 12 September 1992, capturing not only Guzman himself, but also dozens of computers and some 200 diskettes and files, which laid out in considerable detail both the organization and location of most of the SL's units throughout Peru.

With this intelligence coup, the police and army rolled up some 1,200 guerrillas during the next several weeks. Over the next year or so, an additional 2,386 guerrillas, mostly from the SL, were killed or captured and imprisoned. Abimael Guzman himself was convicted of causing the deaths of some 25,000 persons and sentenced to life imprisonment by a military court. Once the Red Sun's trial and imprisonment had been publicized, another 5,516 guerrillas surrendered, taking advantage of Fujimori's offer of virtual amnesty with full citizenship as a reward. This was a major blow to SL ambitions and while there was some vicious fighting between the army and still unrepentant guerrilla cadres it all but brought about the decisive defeat of the revolution. Only some SL remnants out in the outback of the UHV, now rebels without a cause, were able to hang on over the years, exploiting their war taxes from the traffickers and coca farmers in order to survive more in the style of bandits than actual guerrillas.

While Fujimori's campaign against the SL had proceeded without letup, Washington had not given up on the war on drugs in the UHV. Beginning in 1991 a mysterious plant fungus appeared to come from out of nowhere to attack the coca bushes throughout the region. The fungus (Fusarium Oxysisparum) had apparently been experimented with by the CIA and DEA in Hawaii at a secret laboratory and then introduced clandestinely into the UHV. While the fungus also attacked bananas, yucca and other citrus crops growing in the area as part of the AID's alternate crop programs, it was highly effective as an insidious anti-drug strategy in terms of achieving decisive results in the northern part of Peru. It could not have come at a more appropriate time, since Peru was being rated as producing up to 640 tons of cocaine HCl and cocaine base.

In addition to the fungus-based strategy, Army Green Beret and Navy SEAL trainers, equipped with satellite-linked tracking and communications equipment, stepped up their respective campaigns on land and along the rivers of the Amazon headwaters to intercept freighters, motorboats and dugout canoes, as well as personnel on foot, infiltrating agua rica, base, and even refined cocaine to points north. By 1996, between the fungus eating away at the coca crops and the FAP shooting down narco-aircraft, 25-pound bundles of coca leaves in the UHV were now selling at an all-time low of $2 compared to $127 some years earlier, and a pound of coca paste had gone from around $600 in price down to around $115. As a result, the ensuing crisis over the drop in leaf and paste prices caused a number of coca farmers to begin switching to palm hearts, AID's new alternative crop, which was earning some $1,500 per acre, per year.

By the end of the 1990s, despite the coca growers attempts to expand their crops into the immense Loreto Department to points north and east to escape the ubiquitous presence of the coca fungus, it was found that actual acreage in Peru still under cultivation had fallen from around 370,000 acres to a low of 86,000. Much of this was now found in the scattered coca plots of southern Peru's highlands and valley regions of the Apurimac and Ene Rivers where, once again, the SL guerrillas were attempting a comeback on a small scale. With narco-transshipment aircraft still being shot down by the FAP, the longer distances to fly, and the resultant dangers and costs incurred for growing coca, the Colombian drug cartels and their leaders made a deliberate decision to encourage yet another shift in the coca growing areas, this time directly into Colombia itself.

— C O L O M B I A —

Colombia, which anchors South America's north Andean mountain chain on the Caribbean Sea, has been known as a "narcotrafficker's paradise." It is also a country of paradoxes, which highly complicates Washington's war on drugs in that part of the hemisphere. While considered to be one of Latin America's oldest democracies with a population of about 31 million, it also has one of the bloodiest histories, involving endemic societal violence and sporting one of the highest murder rates in the world or upwards of 30,000 deaths from homicide each year. This is to say that on an average, over a given period of any two years, as many Colombians die as a result of violent deaths as the American military lost in combat during its ten-years war in Vietnam. Highly educated elites have traditionally ruled the country to the benefit of the urban areas, but also to the detriment of the rural outback. Disparities in income, living standards, and access to health care and education are endemic to the latter.

As a result, beginning in the 1960s, those who felt themselves frustrated and marginalized sought to redress Colombia's socio-economic and political injustices by forming armed insurgency movements, which began to challenge the government for the allegiance and control of the population. At the same time and conducive to narcotrafficking was the up to 70 percent of the rural sector which was reported as living in a general state of poverty, along with about a third of the urban population. This was despite the fact that the Colombian economy was rated far larger, healthier and more diversified and productive than most others in the region.

To offset their dismal economic situation, some 300,000 Colombians gravitated toward direct or indirect employment in the cocaine trade during the 1980s. This employment ranged all the way from coca growers, paste makers, security guards, radio operators, lawyers, accountants, pilots, mechanics, chemists, chemical engineers, and laboratory workers to the big time traffickers or "narcobarons," as the directors of the major drug cartels were often called.

In the coca fields of the Guaviare Department it is hot and humid, with some 110 inches of rain annually. Under these conditions, and with appropriate fertilizing, coca bushes can be stripped of their leaves every 35 days or about ten times a year. It is not that the *Ipadu* leaves are part and parcel of the Indians' tradition. They are not and there has never been any form of culture or tradition concerning coca inside Colombia. Simply put, and much like Bolivia and Peru, the coca bush is the most lucrative crop in an outback where there are no roads, no markets, no electricity and no clean water. There is, however, something special about Colombia which makes it particularly conducive to being the hub for most narcotrafficking operations taking place in the Americas and especially for the cocaine trade being targeted on the continental United States.

While various factors have contributed to Colombia's unique position in fomenting the international trafficking of cocaine, it is contended by various experts on the subject that it is both the ease of production and the reduction of risk for the traffickers that has distinguished it from all the other countries in the Western Hemisphere. One of these factors involves the weakness of the state, its institutions and values. Over the years, as the Colombian government became less accom-

modating and less responsive to the people it was supposed to serve, corruption in both the public and private sectors abounded. In time a wide gap between written law (dejure) and socially acceptable behavior (defacto) developed. This contemptuous attitude towards the law on the part of much of the population generally found its expression in the phrase: *Yo obedezco pero no cumplo*! ("I obey but I do not comply!"). This is to say people obeyed the law to the degree that it was convenient, but otherwise ignored it. In short, for those working in the government, one offered a deal to their friends and applied the law to their enemies.

In daily life this dichotomy was often played out in the contraband tradition of numerous underground economies which went back centuries, flaunting the law in order to flourish. This informal economy's accelerated development during the twentieth century reflected and reinforced a traditional lack of respect for state laws and regulations dating back into Spanish colonial times. People had simply become accustomed to living and operating in what North Americans would consider an illegal or quasi-legal manner. Along with this a long history of smuggling and contraband activities had taken place. In short, dishonesty was accepted as the norm in the struggle for survival. Whether it was manufactured products entering and leaving the country, livestock, coffee, emeralds, gold artifacts, or other items for which one sought to avoid export-import controls and tariffs, Colombians excelled at not only smuggling but also at the laundering of the proceeds from this often lucrative activity. To this end much of one's social status was based to a large degree on how wealthy you became. It was generally unimportant how the wealth was obtained and people did not ask too many questions in this regard.

Another key factor bearing on why narcotrafficking particularly flourished inside Colombia is that the government lost control over much of the nation's territory of some 455,355 square miles, a size equivalent to California and Texas combined. This was due in part to the various Communist-inspired insurgencies which were contesting the government's legitimacy and right to rule, and in part due to the sheer magnitude and large expanse of the national territory itself which fronted on both the Caribbean Sea and the Pacific Ocean. The geography of the country finds the western third subdivided into a series of rugged Andean mountain chains, ridges, hills and intervening valleys and rivers, running on a generally north-to-south axis, which naturally divide the country into relatively isolated zones and make communications and therefore control all that much more difficult. The remaining two-thirds of the country to the east of the Andes consist of generally flat, savannah-like plains and tropical regions, which are frequently laced by rivers, but not much else, and, in turn, form part of the headwaters of the Amazon region.

This relative isolation for much of the country not only encouraged the growth of self-sufficient communities but also facilitated the use of bribes and violent coercive measures against the few government authorities present in the area. These individuals generally stood alone and at high risk in attempting to confront the various criminal elements in the rural outback. That guerrilla groups generally dominated at least half of the countryside and that government officials were reluctant to challenge many of the illegal activities taking place within their respective zones, contributed to the provision of a natural safe haven which offered few or no risks to the traffickers in their drug manufacturing and transshipping operations. Equipment and precursor chemicals for processing cocaine were available through the various, albeit isolated, rural communities and numerous rivers traversing the region, which also served as the boundaries for Colombia's remote frontiers with Venezuela, Brazil, Peru and Ecuador.

A primary factor influencing the Colombian cartels' domination of the drug markets in the Americas has involved the use of often brutal and extensive violence as it suited their needs. A legacy of the prominence of homicides over the years inside Colombia has been the relatively low value placed on human life throughout much of society. To this end Colombians, in particular, have been quicker than most to resort to violence in resolving personal problems or confrontational and competitive business situations. This apparent inability to achieve a consensus on how to mediate disagreements through dialogue and compromise has served the traffickers well in their high-stakes, high-risk, narco-business operations. Violence and the threat of violence have been ruthlessly applied at will and without hesitation when dealing with Bolivian, Peruvian and American competitors, as well as within Colombia itself. An example is the late 1970s and early 1980s confrontation between Colombian and Cuban traffickers to determine who would control the Miami drug market. The supremely vicious Colombians literally wiped the more pliant Cubans off of Florida's narcotics map, shooting them down in the streets and on the highways throughout the Miami-Dade County area. In short, the ruthless application of violence to resolve any and all problems which might otherwise be resolved through astute negotiations became a key characteristic of the Colombian traffickers' modus operandi.

A final factor not generally recognized which also served the Colombians well in the establishment of their drug marketing systems was the presence of large numbers or well over half a million Colombian migrants living inside the United States. The natural emigration which took place over the years since the 1940s built up a large and diverse body of people, both legal and illegal, which facilitated the recruitment, organization, establishment, and functioning of a U.S.-based network of traffickers for the distribution and sale of drugs, principally cocaine. In short, the familial ties of this relatively close-knit group made it both difficult for American legal authorities to penetrate its operations and enabled it, in turn, to focus its proclivity to use violence on its competition, eliminating all who stood in its way. To this end the Colombian drug traffickers were able to quickly establish themselves and eliminate any competitors, such as the Cubans in Miami, as they secured their domination of the U.S. drug markets. The synergistic effect of all these factors has served to make the quashing of international drug trafficking within Colombia, as the primary base for production and transshipment of cocaine in the Americas, extremely difficult.

Further complicating matters inside Colombia have been the various insurgencies which have evolved over the years and subjected the country to an unremitting civil war, going on for a half century. One of the principal guerrilla groups in the field has been the FARC or Armed Revolutionary Forces of Colombia, which got its start in the late 1950s. Having determined that the nation's conservatives and liberals were practicing an exclusive monopoly in the form of a "National Front" to maintain themselves in power at the expense of all other political factions and groups and lacking any peaceful means to alter the situation, dissenters began to consider taking up arms. The advent of the Cuban Revolution in 1959 stimulated the process and guerrilla war commenced, with the FARC declaring that its objective was to force reforms or otherwise overthrow the government and the institute a Marxist-Leninist state.

Another group, the ELN or National Liberation Army also got its start around this time, and still another, the M-19, came on line, and like the FARC worked to overthrow the traditional order. Appealing to the poor and destitute of the outback, as well as idealistic students, the several groups slowly evolved, but never were able to increase their size to beyond more than a few thousand guerrilla fighters, who were generally dependent on lukewarm support from the Soviet Union and Cuba in the form of money, training and arms. With the early 1990s collapse of the Soviet Union and the failure of its Communist command-economy model and ever increasing socio-economic problems inside Cuba, the heretofore limited support for the insurgents in Colombia was now reduced to practically nothing. In conjunction with this situation was the new 1991 Colombian constitution, which guaranteed the rights and participation of all adults in the now very open, democratic, electoral process, which included any and all political factions and parties. During this period the M-19 had opted to become a political party and even assisted in the writing of the new constitution. With their traditional support mechanisms curtailed, the FARC and the ELN now turned to other sources to obtain money to keep their struggle going.

Traditionally the guerrillas had collected "war taxes" to sustain themselves by extorting rural farmers and cattle ranchers alike. In the early days the taxes were considered to be bearable and agro-industrial businesses of all types flourished. Nonetheless, as the FARC demanded that its guerrilla commanders increase their taxes towards the end of the 1980s, they ran head-on into the traffickers who had invested hundreds of millions of dollars in the ownership of over two million acres of some of the best farmlands in north-central Colombia and who now viewed themselves as an emergent entrepreneurial class on a par with Colombia's traditional landowning elites. The traffickers themselves had used violence in the form of some 130 paramilitary groups to force the small and medium-size peasant farmers, who in the main had received their lands as part of the government's agrarian reform program, to sell out or even abandon their holdings.

Now threatened with having to pay exorbitant guerrilla taxes in the Magdalena Medio Valley region and the army and the police unable to control the situation, the traffickers struck back. Using British and Israeli mercenaries to train them, the paramilitary groups were now converted into death squads, which unmercifully hunted down the FARC guerrillas, their sympathizers, and even campesino peasant organizations and unions lobbying for more land reform and higher wages. The defeat of the FARC in this part of Colombia enhanced the image of the traffickers in the eyes of the local population and, although also welcomed by the army and police, was an embarrassment to the Colombian government, which was being prodded by Washington to do more to put an end to the traffickers and their operations. The long-term result of this situation was the creation of paramilitary death squads which would ravage the Colombian countryside over the next decade and on into the twenty-first century. The FARC, in turn, now turned its efforts to exploiting the more lucrative drug trade which would provide it with a windfall of funds and enable it to increase in size several or more times.

While the ELN sought to finance itself by kidnapping and extorting the multinational British and Occidental petroleum companies along the Cano-Limon-Covenas pipeline in northern Colombia, the FARC, led by Manuel Marulanda Velez (alias *Tirofijo* or "Sure-Shot"), focused in the main on all levels of the coca-cocaine production and transportation systems within Colombia. By charging for each takeoff and landing by a drug carrying aircraft, the protection of the various cocaine-producing laboratories and clandestine airfields scattered throughout the eastern half of the country, and even the coca crops, the guerrillas levied a uniform 10 percent tax, called the *vacuna* ("vaccination"), on both the farmers and the traffickers alike.

As its finances increased, the FARC became so powerful that it assumed many of the functions of the state in the areas it dominated, imposing a draconian system of law, order, and discipline. In addition, the guerrillas defended the coca farmers against both the government and the traffickers, regulating the prices to be paid for coca leaves and the forms of payment. In exchange for this service, the coca farmers had to cultivate food crops for the guerrillas, as well as pay their own taxes on the coca leaves, paste or agua rica being produced. In one area along both the Colombian and Peruvian sides of the Putumayo River some two-thousand mom-pop paste laboratories functioned under the protection of the FARC. To enhance its earnings, the FARC sometimes even carried out its own coca cultivation in the Vichada, Vaupes, Guaviare, Caqueta, Putumayo, Meta and Magdalena Departments. The end result was that the FARC was now involved in a multi-million dollar enterprise. Offering to pay any new guerrilla recruit around $300 per month, or a wage which was equal to or greater than a policeman or a school teacher, the guerrillas increased their strength to well over 15,000 men and women by the end of the 1990s.

Initially, the cartels inside Colombia were made up of five, loosely organized groups, each with up to two-hundred smaller trafficking elements and subgroups focused on the Medellin, Cali, Leticia, Pereira, and Baranquilla areas. The groups not only collaborated among themselves but also cooperated, forming joint ventures in the refining of coca paste, cocaine base and HCl, insuring cocaine shipments, and working to thwart the government's anti-drug efforts. The remaining 30 percent of the drug trade not controlled by the principal cartels was generally spread out among hundreds of other independent, small scale producers, refiners and smugglers, which included in some cases elements of the insurgent-guerrilla organizations. When the costs of refining, transportation and wholesale commissions from distribution were totaled, the Colombian traffickers typically found themselves investing up to $2.4 million to successfully market a load of 660 pounds of cocaine, earning at the end of the process a profit of about $4.65 million.

Computer technology and modern communications systems with encryption devices and voice scramblers assisted the traffickers in protecting themselves and their operations from government interference, as well as coordinating the processing of precursor materials, construction and operation of laboratories, and the rental or purchase of boats, planes, helicopters and even mini-submarines to ship cocaine products from the generally remote laboratory complexes to their respective international market destinations. With strong markets in the United States, Europe, and other places in Latin America and Asia, the traffickers were garnering earnings of up to $6 billion per year, with roughly $1.5 billion returning to Colombia. With profits being so high and the propensity to use violence being so prevalent, the cartels often fought with each other over who would dominate the various local investment markets (drugstore chains for example) internal to Colombia. But it was the Medellin cartel that tried to throw its weight around, gangster-style.

The use of violence by the Medellin cartel contrasted significantly with the far more passive Cali cartel which in the main would try to bribe its way through problem areas, all the while avoiding violence so as not to attract attention to itself. Indicative of the Medellin Cartel's operations were the brutal assassinations of a popular, anti-drug advocating presidential candidate (Luis Carlos Galan), a minister of justice (Lara Bonilla) and a newspaper editor (Cano Laza) during the period 1985-89. This produced several short, but spectacular backlashes on the part of the government at the request of the economic elites who now felt themselves threatened. The national police and army arrested 535 traffickers and confiscated 989 buildings, 367 airplanes, 72 boats and 710 vehicles, striking a serious blow to the cartel's operations.

From 1989 to 1991 the Medellin cartel, under the leadership of Pablo Escobar, responded in reprisal for its losses, sponsoring more than 600 assassinations, including the 1989 sabotage bombing of a commercial airliner (107 deaths) and a car bombing of the national intelligence service headquarters (60 deaths). Within the city of Medellin, the infighting was so bad between the cartels themselves, the police, and the various criminal gangs that it was estimated that three-quarters of all males between the ages 15 and 25 years of age in major portions of the city were dead. Taking advantage of a presidential plea-bargaining decree, Escobar turned himself in to the national government, but continued to run his cartel operations out of his jail cell at the Envigado Prison. Assassinations by his cartel continued apace. Escobar eventually escaped from prison, but was tracked down in an extensive manhunt and killed in a shootout with the police. With Pablo Escobar put out of action, the government with Washington's backing then focused on the Cali cartel.

The more non-confrontational Cali cartel, led by brothers Gilberto and Miguel Rodriguez Orejuela, focused its financial assets on bribing government officials, members of congress and the judiciary to protect its interests. In the case of an individual who was intransigent and not cooperative, the bribe was coached in terms of "plata o plomo," which meant that the targeted individual could either take a money bribe or receive a lead bullet in the back of the head. One way or the other it was persuasive, since few people as individuals could stand up to the intimidating threats of the traffickers who also threatened the individual's family members. Politicians found that by getting elected, the various trafficking groups would approach them, offering tens of thousands of dollars in exchange for just doing nothing to inhibit the drug production operations. Corruption was so bad that one Colombian president, Ernesto Samper, even had his visa revoked by Washington because he allowed the various cartels to make contributions to his election campaign. With the Medellin cartel fragmented, U.S. and Colombian intelligence operations began to focus in earnest on the low key operations of the Cali cartel. Aided by the $2.2 billion Andean Initiative aid program of the Bush administration of the early 1990s, considerable progress was made and the Cali cartel found itself being slowly but surely decimated.

As had happened in Bolivia and Peru, SOUTHCOM became extensively involved in Colombia during the early 1990s. With some 1,300 aircraft and some 3,000 ship movements annually in support of smuggling and drug transshipment operations out of Colombia, it was obvious that the traffickers were trying to saturate the anti-drug defenses of the United States and Europe. Involved were some 1,500 persons who piloted the roughly one thousand privately owned aircraft and as many boats which were utilized to move the refined cocaine to its international destinations. In addition the traffickers also took advantage of the scores of thousands of cargo containers used by the international merchant marine fleets to further infiltrate illicit drugs into the world markets.

SOUTHCOM responded with aerial interdiction and intelligence tracking operations, using a combination of seven ground-based radars positioned in and around Colombia. Customs and Navy reconnaissance aircraft and offshore picket ships monitored narco-aircraft flying into Colombia from Bolivia, Peru, Ecuador and Brazil, as well as flights headed into Venezuela, Central America and across the Caribbean. In an area of southern Colombia known as *Tres Esquinas* ("the three corners" of Colombia, Bolivia and Peru, which come together in the vicinity of the town of Leticia), a Marine radar in 1992 identified 34 to 40 narco-flights per night en-route to some 200 airfields scattered throughout the Amazon flatlands or an area of around 400 square miles. In all, the radars were picking up 250 aerial tracks each day, of which between 50 and 75 were suspected trafficker aircraft. In addition, Army Green Berets trained up to nine battalions of UH-60 supported, anti-drug/counter-guerrilla troops, and Navy SEALs and Marines trained up a dozen or so Colombian riverine counter-drug forces using swift boats to interdict dozens of laboratories located along the some 26 rivers and their tributaries that plied the eastern half of the country, thereby complicating the traffickers' drug production operations.

While this was going on, the U.S. Departments of Justice and Treasury were simultaneously attacking trafficker banking and money laundering operations inside the United States with a multi-agency financial action task force. Over the period of about two years (1992-93) the DEA identified some 525 Cali cartel bank accounts in the U.S. and Colombia alone, involving around $70 million in drug profits. In addition, over 160 cartel-related traffickers and contacts in Costa Rica, United Kingdom, Canada, Spain, Italy, the Cayman Islands and the United States were apprehended. Panama and Venezuela were also noted as preferred countries for both money-laundering and transshipment operations. Nonetheless, despite dozens of interceptions in the air and on the sea, the cocaine continued to be transshipped at a rate of about 850 tons per year, with about 300 or more tons directed at the North American markets alone. A countervailing or inhibiting aspect for the anti-drug program was the "balloon effect," which meant that to the degree that the American and Colombian anti-drug efforts could harass and even close down the traffickers, the latter were merely shifting their operations into more remote regions or even over Colombia's national frontier to adjacent countries.

To deal with the traffickers Washington also brought into play various chemicals to attack first the coca bushes growing throughout southeastern Colombia and second the poppy plants, which supported the new and ever-growing heroin production industry. Introduced from Afghanistan and Burma, the gum-opium poppy production flourished on the hillsides and in the valleys of the wet, cold climates found at the 6,000-foot level of the Andes. With some 50,000 acres of heroin producing plants in play, the traffickers' were growing their product in 14 of Colombia's 25 departments, particularly Huila, Caldas, Cauca and Tolima, and producing about 30 tons of heroin each year, which earned several times more per pound than cocaine on the North American and European markets. Using herbicide spray planes during the 1990s, the DEA was able neutralize about a third of the heroin plants and about a fifth of the coca crops, using a coca plant-killing chemical called "Glifosate."

With the Medellin and Cali cartels severely suppressed, the drug production system fragmented in 1998 into approximately 43 smaller trafficking organizations or mini-cartels. Washington now took the initiative to implement "Plan Colombia," a $7.5 billion assistance plan, which would ultimately find itself dealing with both the drug traffickers and the insurgency forces. Bogota began extensive investigations into governmental corruption and links to the traffickers with its attorney general's office looking into suspected drug dealings on the part of 518 of the serving 1,066 town and city mayors. But it was the statistics that told a series of even harder truths: the first twenty years of the drug wars and related insurgencies and other criminal activities had caused some 500,000 deaths from homicide, 1.7 million displaced persons, 300,000 orphans and the migration of some 1.5 million Colombian citizens overseas.

The FARC, taking advantage of its quantum jump in finances with earnings from extortion, kidnappings and drug trafficking, earned over $500 million per year. By 1999 it had a size of somewhere around 17,000 men and women and an organizational structure of some 100 "fronts" of roughly 150 guerrillas each, which were responsible for as many zones of control throughout the country. While the size of the force leveled off, it was found that the promise of $300 per month, three meals a day, a weapon, and the self-esteem and excitement that came with being a guerrilla in the Colombian bandit-bandolero tradition continued to attract the young teenagers of the poor folk living in the rural outback.

While the Colombian army had some 127,000 military personnel, too many of them were simply ineffective against the guerrillas. Nonetheless, the FARC more than met its match in the highly trained and brutal, paramilitary United Self-Defense Forces of Colombia (AUC), which emanated out of the privately hired death squads of the 1980s. Led by Carlos Castano, the up to 16,000-man force, still supported by wealthy landowners, mercilessly tracked down FARC fronts, killing anyone who was suspected of being a guerrilla sympathizer. Unfortunately, other death squad victims included labor activists, human rights workers and journalists. As a result, the Colombia of the early twenty-first century appears to be a somewhat "balkanized" civil war with the northern part of the country contested by the guerrillas and the paramilitary forces, the central part of the country partially controlled by the government, and the southern part of the country controlled in the main by the FARC, but contested from time-to-time by the army and the AUC.

With the less and less popular FARC not able to recruit sufficient forces to overcome the government and the government unable to provide the resources to sustain a viable economy to the east of the Andes, a stalemate of sorts has ensued. Nonetheless, U.S.-trained and equipped army counter-guerrilla brigades, supported by some 72 helicopters, and accurate targeting by American and Colombian all-source intelligence assets have begun to take on and decisively defeat the insurgents in face-to-face encounters, front by front, on the Colombian battlefield. In addition, a system of village self-defense forces, involving over 100,000 males in the rural outback has begun to take hold, hamstringing the guerrillas more and more as time goes on. To this end during a one year period from 2004 into 2005 over five thousand guerrillas surrendered rather than fight to the death, while another some 600 died in combat. In the meantime the Colombian government offered to negotiate an end to the guerrilla war, offering amnesty to those who voluntarily switched sides and laid down their arms.

The herbicide spraying by the DEA did take its toll on the traffickers from 2002 onwards. In the Caqueta and Putumayo regions the coca farmers were operating at only 30 percent of their original capacity and, in general, coca growing dropped off well over 50 percent, with the total number of observable acres of coca under cultivation plunging from around 357,000 down to approximately 152,000. In addition, there was a 25 percent drop in heroin production and the acreage of gum opium poppies was down from around 16,150 to 12,100 acres. Nonetheless, under pressure from the DEA, SOUTHCOM, and a revitalized Colombian army, the traffickers began shifting their sources of coca supply back to Peru and even Bolivia. The situation in Peru during 2003 saw the acreages of illegal coca increase by 28 percent to a total of 90,400 acres or a production capability of some 200 tons of refined cocaine.

Even with its anti-drug successes, Washington estimates in 2004 were rating the Colombian traffickers with a capability to produce from all sources and ship 450 tons of cocaine and heroin, supplying 90 percent of the U.S. market. With Customs, DEA, the Coastguard and other agencies intercepting upwards of 200 tons of cocaine a year attempting to enter the U.S. market, there was still another some 200 tons that were actually getting through to support the around 3.6 million chronic cocaine users (out of a total of some 14 million illicit drug users). Even the remnants of the Cali cartel began to resuscitate their operations through 59 front companies, as part of the "new" Cartel's international business and financial network. The FARC, concerned that its financial sources were now more and more in jeopardy, began pushing farmers to expand their coca fields deeper into the Amazon basin, attempting to outpace aerial spraying, as well as forcing farmers in the coffee-growing regions to mix in coca bushes with their coffee plantings. In short, coffee and coca began to grow side by side in west-central Colombia (Caldas Department), while the AUC and the FARC fought it out for control of the coca fields.

* * *

Unfortunately, after more than a quarter century of fighting the drug wars, there appears to be no real end in sight. While the U.S. government has spent over $20 billion annually from the early 1980s on into the twenty-first century to quash the international drug trade by eradicating coca and fighting the traffickers at their sources in Bolivia, Peru, and Colombia, Washington's programs have bought little more than a great deal of frustration. There are several reasons for this. Most importantly Washington has attempted to apply a national security solution in the form of a militarized drug war to what is essentially a simple supply and demand or commercial situation. In short, strong international market demand has maintained the narcotrafficking business in cocaine as a viable enterprise in the face of the U.S. anti-drug policy. An integral part of the demand situation are the immense profits in the hundreds of millions and even billions of dollars that are made from trafficking in cocaine. A 1989 Senate Hearing 101-712 (19 April) depicted a typical distribution chain, which indicated that for *one pound* of refined cocaine the following prices were being charged:

At the farm.. $600

Export to Colombia $3,500

Import into Miami... $10,000

Wholesale in Detroit $20,000

Total retail from 1 gram units $125,000

The huge profits to be made at the market end of the production-transportation cycle are the driving forces behind the trafficking system and the make the risks of being captured, killed, shot down, or even drowned worthwhile, at least for some. Until the demand side of the drug phenomenon is adequately addressed and the associated high profits reduced significantly, narcotrafficking in Bolivia, Peru, Colombia, and today's Mexico will undoubtedly continue well into the future.

The severe inequality of income between the rural and urban populations in the Andean region, due to the mal-allocation of each country's productive structure and resources and the various governments' failures to provide essential services to all areas equally, have caused people to question the legitimacy of the state in many of the rural sectors. This is particularly true in all three of the Andean countries of Bolivia, Peru, and Colombia. Until such time as each government can effectively resolve the rural population's socioeconomic inequalities as conditions conducive to supporting insurgency and drug trafficking activities alike, it is likely that both the guerrillas' operations and the trafficking will continue indefinitely. The guerrillas and traffickers, while often antagonistic toward each other, do depend to some degree on each other in their often symbiotic and mutually supporting roles. While drug trafficking on the one hand provides an extensive rent resource in the form of extorted "war taxes" for the guerrillas, on the other hand the guerrillas do provide limited protection for certain trafficker and coca-poppy farming activities, all the while distracting to some degree the military and police forces away from the illegal drug production zones.

Washington's anti-drug policy currently finds itself only able to raise the risks somewhat for the traffickers inside Colombia, pushing the demand-driven narcotrafficking phenomenon around, but not stamping it out. Despite the capture of thousands of traffickers, the destruction of thousands of laboratories of all types, and the seizure of hundreds of tons of cocaine and other drugs anually, due to the self-generating nature of the demand-inspired drug business and its immense profits, the U.S. anti-drug policy finds itself producing inconclusive and less than decisive results.

While North American consumers typically spend around $20 billion a year on illicit drugs, the United States itself has become a major producer of illegal marijuana and by some accounts the biggest in the Western Hemisphere. Marijuana production in California, Hawaii, Kentucky and Tennessee has grown so much, that the country frequently exports marijuana into Canada. To this end drug trafficking has grown into a global problem, in which the United States plays no small a part. Perhaps the 1960s Pogo cartoon expresses the hypocrisy of the situation all too well: "We have met the enemy, and they are us!"

CHAPTER 5

TRACKING THE FALL OF A DICTATOR - PANAMA'S MANUEL NORIEGA

1972-89

Assignment in early 1972 to the country of Panama and the Army's 8th Special Forces Group based at Fort Gulick, Canal Zone, placed me in direct contact with one of the United States premier engineering projects of the twentieth century, the Panama Canal. Because of the nature of my work with the Research and Analysis (R&A) Section of the 9th Psychological Operations (PSYOPs) Battalion, I became intimately acquainted with certain aspects of Panamanian politics which would ultimately impact directly on the Canal and the U.S. national security interest in defending this key trans-isthmian waterway.

While my initial assignment to Panama would last less than two years, fate caused me to return on assignment for a couple of years in the mid-1970s and again for a couple more in the late-1980s. This enabled me to monitor quite closely Panama's political situation, which would ultimately require a formal invasion by the U.S. armed forces in 1989 to restore order and protect the Canal from an evil, power-mad military dictator of the Cold War era, General Manuel Noriega.

American interest in the area of Panama began in the 1840s as a result of the United States westward territorial expansion and the seizure of the northern half of Mexico, which included what would eventually become the state of California. With the right of way west of the Mississippi River for pioneers still being contested by dozens of hostile Indian tribes after the end of the war with Mexico, the desirability of developing an alternate route to its Pacific coast territories became a growing interest for Washington. In 1846 a right of transit agreement (the Mallarino-Bidlack Treaty) was worked out with the Republic of New

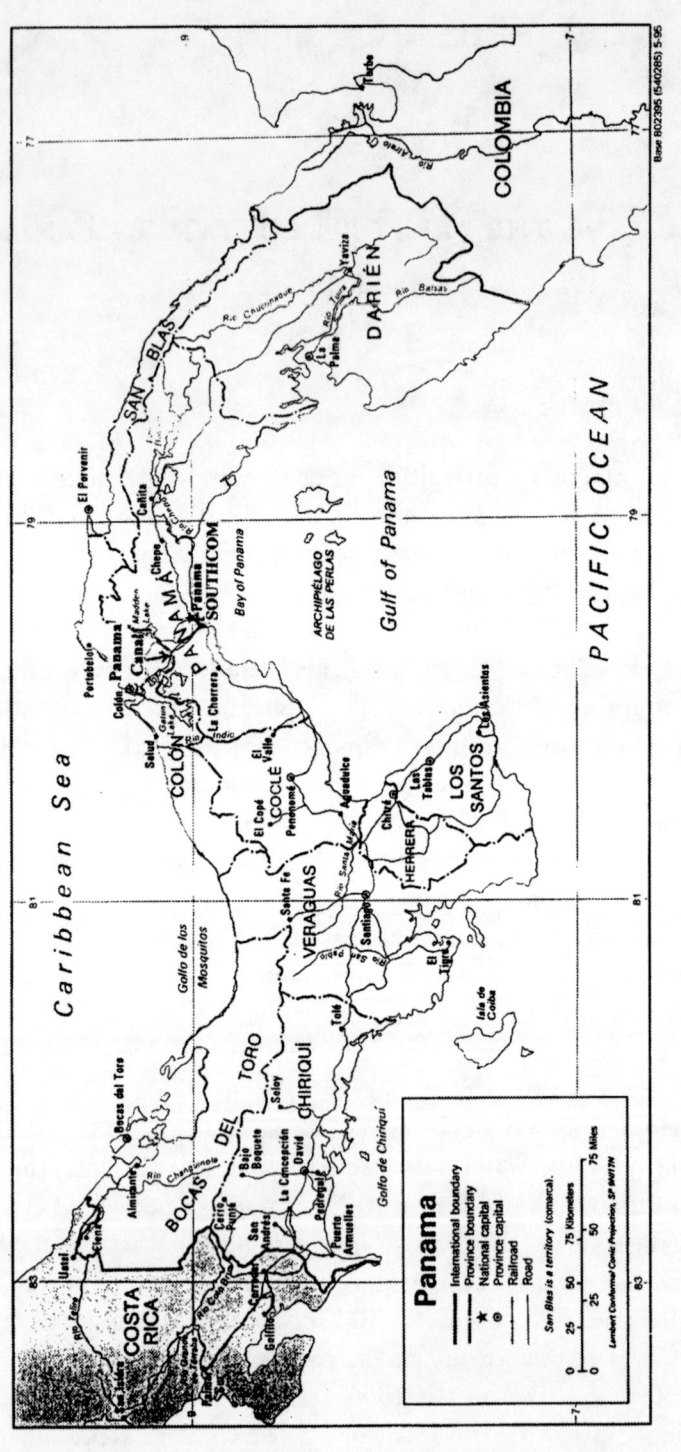

Granada, as the country of Colombia was then called, to guarantee U.S. citizens the right of transit and transshipment of merchandise, as well as secure access to any and all modes of transportation across its territory known as the Isthmus of Panama. Colombia further guaranteed the permanent neutrality of the Isthmus so that while the treaty was in effect the transit of goods and passengers between the Caribbean Sea and the Pacific Ocean would not be interrupted.

Shortly thereafter in 1849 gold was discovered in California and the famous "Gold Rush" was on. American citizens by the thousands came in steam- and sailboats to Panama's Caribbean port town of Chagre at the mouth of the Chagres River, fully intending to cross the isthmus as soon as possible. The crossing usually required a period of about a week and was only accomplished by canoeing up the river to a mid-point known as Las Cruces, with onward movement conducted via mule, horse or wagon to the country's Pacific coast Panama City. There, steamboats would pick up the weary travelers for the remainder of the voyage to California. While serving as an escort officer along the trans-isthmian route for the "Forty-Niners," an Army captain of note by the name of Ulysses S. Grant almost lost his life to malaria. But progress was the law and in time entrepreneurs such as Cornelius Vanderbilt saw the value and profits to be made from constructing a trans-isthmian railroad from the north coast town of Aspinwall (now Colon) to Panama City.

Once completed by 1855, the Panama Rail Road's relatively short train ride of several hours over some fifty miles of track quickly became the preferred way to go. Nonetheless, as train robbers began to harass the trains and their passengers over the years, Washington was forced to work out a security arrangement with the Colombian government. This permitted U.S. Marine sharpshooters to ride "shotgun" on the trains for a period of some decades, gunning down the *bandidos* as they were encountered along the route. A notable intervention took place in 1885 when the Marines successfully defended the railroad against a Colombian general, Rafael Aizpuru, who attempted an ineffectual revolt against his own government in order to make himself "President of Panama." Other interventions also took place from time to time and in 1901 Marines were landed in considerable force at both Colon and Panama City during the Colombian Civil War to protect the railroad from being disrupted by various insurgent bands. Nonetheless it was the advent of the Spanish-American War of 1898 during the time of "manifest destiny" and the rise of a new order of sea power that caused the United States to look to securing some form of a future trans-isthmian ship canal and control over its approaches to enhance nation's trade and national security interests.

The importance of a trans-isthmian canal somewhere in Central America had been dramatically demonstrated by the sixty-six day trip of the battleship U.S.S. Oregon, covering 15,000 miles from its Pacific Ocean station at San Francisco around South America's Cape Horn to take part in the naval battle of Santiago, Cuba, in the Caribbean Sea. As a result, a trans-isthmian canal constructed and controlled by the United States to effect a rapid transit of the Navy between the Atlantic and Pacific Oceans became a paramount objective of American foreign policy and a debate ensued as to where the new canal ought to be constructed: Nicaragua's San Juan River frontier with Costa Rica being one route and the now bankrupt French Panama Canal Company's abandoned effort being the other. Official investigations indicated that the Panama route was more likely to be the least expensive; at least $58 million cheaper than the Nicaraguan route. With this in mind and under the influence of William N. Cromwell, a part owner of the Panama Railroad and the bankrupt French Canal Company, the House of Representatives approved and President Teddy Roosevelt signed the bill in 1902 to purchase the rights from the ill-fated French company for constructing a canal through Panama. When the Colombian Senate refused in 1903 to approve a treaty with the U.S., authorizing Washington to proceed with the construction of the canal, Roosevelt took other action.

Coincidentally at this point in time, a handful of politicians in Panama City had been agitating for independence from Colombia and appointed Philippe Bunau-Varilla, a former chief engineer and investor in the all but defunct French canal company, as their representative for dealing with the United States. Bunau-Varilla, understanding Washington's interest in a Panama canal, in contact with Cromwell, and desperate to recoup his losses and even gain financially before the rights to his company's concession expired, offered his services to coordinate the separatist project for the Panamanians. The plot they hatched for their revolt in Panama envisioned Bunau-Varilla procuring funds for the insurrection from Washington; the U.S. then sending warships to prevent Colombia from landing troops to quash the revolt; and once successful, the new Panamanian revolutionary government having Bunau-Varilla arrange for the immediate conclusion of a canal treaty with Washington. In essence, this was essentially what happened.

Roosevelt justified blocking the access of Colombian troops to the railway system from Colon to Panama City by U.S. Marines in November 1903 on the grounds that the formers' passage and attempt to put down the Panamanian revolt would have precipitated civil war and disrupted the freedom of isthmian transit, which the U.S. was committed to protect under the Treaty of 1846. Intrigues aside, in the end Bunau Varilla and his associates earned $40 million for their efforts from Washington, Panama got its independence from Colombia, and the United States got its Panama Canal. The new country of Panama was about to become a strategic "bridge" from the Atlantic to the Pacific oceans for the transportation of goods from around the world, which would give it a special role in international economics forevermore. Nonetheless, the overwhelming presence of the Canal became the determining factor in Panama's modern history, economy, and politics.

The United States pledged itself to guarantee the independence of the new Panamanian state, and Panama granted the United States a ten-miles wide and roughly fifty-two miles long Canal Zone (about 550 square miles), as well as all the rights for construction and operation in perpetuity, "as if it were sovereign" over the zone and its adjacent waters. Other terms included giving Washington the right to take land outside the zone that was essential for the construction, maintenance, sanitation, and protection of the canal, as well as rights over sanitation and policing in the cities of Panama and Colon. The Constitution of Panama (Article 136) of 1904 even stated that the United States had the right to intervene in any part of the republic "to reestablish public peace and constitutional order in the event of their being disturbed."

The Canal Zone was now a protected territory of the United States and Panama received $10 million in gold up front and a commitment for additional annual payments of $250,000, beginning ten years thereafter. Construction began at once and after some engineering difficulties were solved and yellow fever was eradicated under a vigorous sanitation program, the Panama Canal was opened to traffic in August, 1914. Costing a total of $352 million to construct, including the cost of building military installations, as well as some five-thousand workers' lives lost in the main from malaria and construction accidents, the Canal acquired immense commercial and strategic importance for the U.S., involving both World Wars I and II, the Cold War, and remaining as such well into the twenty-first century. That the Canal Zone neatly bisected Panama into two distinct geographical entities, may not have seemed important to either Panama or the United States at the time, but, much like a burr under a saddle, it did tend to rub the political relationship between the two countries raw.

The U.S. exercised its police protection rights on numerous occasions, involving election disputes, demonstrations, and rent riots. Troops were sent into Panama City and Colon in 1918, 1921, and 1925, intervening to pacify the political situation and reestablish peaceful authority and control. At the request of the government of Panama, the U.S. supervised the national elections in 1906, 1908, 1912, and 1918. Other disorders in Panama's western Chiriqui Province in 1918 saw American forces landed, remaining there until 1920. If the political turbulence of the fledgling republic was not enough to create frictions, animosities developed over the dual pay scales maintained in the Canal Zone, which gave Americans working there much higher wages than their Panamanian counterparts. Finally in 1933, in an apparent about face as part of his "Good Neighbor" policy, president Franklin D. Roosevelt eliminated the intervention rights of the United States and increased the annuity received by Panama to $430,000. As a result, the relations between the two nations appeared to improve considerably.

Because of the strategic importance of the Panama Canal, early on it became an overriding consideration to create a Caribbean bulwark shielding the Atlantic approaches to the Canal. In the main this was because of the perceived potential threat from the European navies of the day, especially those of the British and German empires whose coal-fired battleships and cruisers required advanced, overseas bases and coaling stations to project imperial interests abroad. To this end the promotion of political, economic and social stability within the region became paramount for Washington so as to leave no excuse or opportunity for direct intervention on the part of the European powers.

As the Germans began to dicker for naval bases and coaling stations in the Dominican and Haitian Republics, President Theodore Roosevelt said: "The Monroe Doctrine is as strong as the United States Navy, and no stronger."

Out of this perception came the period of "speaking softly" (diplomatic coercion) and carrying a "big stick" (battleships and U.S. Marines), which meant that, in order to better protect the Panama Canal, Washington would militarily intervene in any Caribbean state whose commercial, political and social conditions could potentially lead to European meddling in the region to collect international debts and protect related private interests as an excuse to create naval bases. If it appeared that the ordinary process of elections would produce a government not regarded with favor by Washington, the Navy and Marine Corps took over the electoral process to ensure that a suitable government, adhering to American interests, was installed. Besides interventions into Cuba, the Dominican Republic, and Haiti, sometimes lasting decades, an important American focus during the early years of the century was initially on Nicaragua.

When Nicaragua's Liberal Party president and *caudillo*-style dictator, Jose Santos Zelaya became aware that the United States was going to build a trans-isthmian canal through Panama, he began to seek a canal deal with Washington's rival naval powers, Germany and Japan. In turn, to protect its canal construction project as a regional monopoly and citing Zelaya's cruel and graft-ridden administration, which had brought Nicaragua to the verge of bankruptcy, Washington responded in 1909 by encouraging Zelaya's Conservative opposition to rebel against him. When Zelaya ordered the execution of two American citizens who were caught attempting to dynamite a government vessel loaded with loyal troops, Washington broke relations and announced that it was supporting the rebels. Shortly thereafter some 2,000 Marines were landed to protect the opposition, forcing Zelaya to resign and turn over the government to the Conservatives and ultimately their new president, Adolfo Diaz, a former employee of an American company in Nicaragua. He, in turn, then allowed the U.S. to take over Nicaragua's collection of revenues to pay off New York banks to which his country was deeply indebted.

From 1912 to 1933, with the exception of a short period in the mid-1920s, a Marine occupation force oversaw the running of the country. More importantly, in 1914 the Diaz government in Managua signed up to a treaty with Washington (Bryan-Chamorro), granting the United States the sole rights to build a canal through Nicaragua. The project, of course, was never consummated, since the Washington had no intention of constructing another trans-isthmian canal which might otherwise compete with its cherished Panamanian route. In exchange Nicaragua received $3 million to be applied to the reduction of its foreign debt.

Strategic considerations also came into play because of the outbreak of World War II. Coming into direct conflict with American interests was Panama's Arnulfo Arias, an ardent and charismatic nationalist and populist leader who, as president of Panama, bitterly contested Washington's right to control the Canal. When Arias, an outspoken admirer of European dictators Hitler and Mussolini, refused to agree to Washington's desires that he bend Panama's neutrality laws in 1941 in order to permit the arming of Panamanian registered merchant ships, which were in the main American-owned, a coup was engineered with U.S. complicity to remove Arias from office. It was not the first nor the last time that Arias would be ousted from the Panamanian presidency. To this end any concern Washington might have felt for democracy in Panama was always overshadowed by the higher priority of preserving political stability and the security of the Canal. After the December 1941 Japanese attack on Pearl Harbor, Panama immediately declared war against the Axis powers and the U.S. acquired leases on more than a hundred sites for additional air and ground military bases throughout Panama to augment the defense of the Canal.

In 1955, in an effort to placate rising Panamanian nationalism and animosity towards the United States over the Canal issue, President Dwight D. Eisenhower raised the Canal's annuity to Panama to $1,930,000, and Congress eventually passed legislation providing for equal working conditions for Panamanian and American employees in the Canal Zone. In addition, the construction of a long-promised fixed bridge (the "Bridge of the Americas") across the Canal was finally accomplished in 1962, joining the severed territories of Panama (Previously, swing-bridges in the vicinity of the Canal's locking systems had accomplished this purpose).

Nonetheless, national sovereignty over the Canal remained a burning issue for most Panamanians. Riots had previously taken place to this end over the issue of flying the Panamanian flag inside the Canal Zone in 1959 and again in 1964, this time with considerable loss of life from four days of street fighting on both sides (twenty-four Panamanian civilians and four U.S. soldiers died). Exacerbating the issue was the fact that only one Zonian in five spoke Spanish and for the most part the Americans living in the Zone held the Panamanians in hardly-concealed contempt. Even Thomas Mann, who headed up President Lyndon Johnson's Latin American programs, symbolized American attitudes towards Panamanians with his comment: "I know my Latins. They understand only two things - a buck in the pocket and a kick in the ass!"

While the Johnson administration toyed with the idea of full Panamanian sovereignty over the Canal to preclude further frictions, Arnulfo Arias was once again elected president of Panama in 1968 by an overwhelming majority. Eleven days after his inauguration in October, he was again overthrown and replaced by a military-controlled junta. Of all of Panama's perennial hard-luck politicians, he appeared to be the unluckiest, having been removed from presidential office by coup not only in 1941, but also in 1951, as well as 1968 - and all with at least the acquiescence if not abetment on the part of the United States. The 1968 coup against Arias was one of several watershed events affecting Panama over the remainder of the century.

Colonel Omar Torrijos Herrera came to power as a result of the coup against Arnulfo Arias and it was within this setting that the 9th PSYOPs Battalion received a Joint Chiefs of Staff (JCS) directive via the U.S. Southern Command (SOUTHCOM), headquartered at Quarry Heights (Ancon Hill) adjacent to downtown Panama City, to develop a psychological operations study about Panama. The idea behind the study was that it might prove useful in the event of a conflict between the two countries. The R&A Section received the tasking within the 9th PSYOPs in early 1973 to do the research and develop the study. This meant that we would have to develop a comprehensive understanding of the political and socioeconomic factors in play which were working both for and against Panama. This would involve evaluating those persons and groups in positions of power who otherwise wielded considerable influence within the country. The research would take some months to complete, but it became the basis for my follow-on interest in Panamanian politics over the next several decades. There is an old saying that states: "There is never a dull moment in Latin American politics." And in respect to the struggle for power, wealth, and influence inside Panama, it was right on target!

Torrijos, originally the son of a poor rural schoolteacher, had reacted to President Arnulfo Arias's efforts to gain greater control of Panama's military institutions through the forced retirement or reassignment of senior National Guard (*Guardia Nacional*) military officers and replacing them with persons in whom he trusted by eliminating Arias himself. With the threat to the Guard eliminated, Torrijos now promoted himself as the champion of the underprivileged and as an adversary of the previously dominant economic elites or oligarchy. As the Guard consolidated its power after the coup and Torrijos emerged as the leading force within it, a significantly new role for the institution was forged. Very quickly it became the centerpiece in a renewed populist coalition that combined elements of Arias's old lower- and middle-class support, involving in the main students, professionals, rural workers, the leftist labor movement, and a new group of technocrats employed by the state. The traditional business elite, which for over a half century had dominated Panamanian politics, was excluded from the governing coalition and even the state itself, whose central element was now the National Guard.

Thus, the core of the Torrijos regime became the Guard, which served as the base for state power and an agent of social change. The glue binding this coalition together was solidified through the skillful use of moderate reforms, co-optive government patronage, and the enduring popular appeals for national sovereignty over the Canal Zone. The Guard was considerably more nationalistic than the traditional economic elites and deliberately maintained a cool relationship with the U.S. military, in spite of the training and the equipment that the United States had supplied over the years since World War II. Over time promotions and assignments within the institution were determined more by personal loyalty to Torrijos than any other factor.

With Omar Torrijos now a brigadier-general as well as president, the changes initiated by this charismatic, caudillo-style head of state involved a highly visible agrarian reform focused on collective farms and the distribution of public lands to small farmers, labor legislation favorable to collective bargaining, job security, enhanced social security benefits, the construction of public housing, and improved health and education throughout the country. His seemingly personal interest in and zeal for the various projects, along with highly publicized visits to all parts of Panama, capitalized on these reforms to build his popular image. It also provided him with direct feedback as to the concerns and interests of the Panamanian people as a whole. At the same time he also restructured the political system, banning the traditional political parties and creating a larger National Assembly of some 505 elected representatives, thereby giving additional power to rural and lower-class regions. In effect, this brought previously un-represented slum dwellers, peasants and workers into the political mainstream as a form of grass-roots democracy. A new constitution was promulgated in 1972, which officially designated the National Guard as the central core of the government.

Torrojos's approach to government was to be one of *pan o palo*, that is to say "bread or stick." Those who publicly supported the regime were given bread or a piece of the action in the form of patronage (money and jobs), and those who publicly opposed the regime were given the stick in the form of persecution and even exile. To this end an initial period of repression had followed the 1968 coup to power and was aimed at political opponents on both the far left and the right, discouraging early challenges to Torrijos's rule. In addition, during the early 1970s he began to build a populist political party to reflect the interests of the National Guard - the Democratic Revolutionary Party (*Partido Revolucionario Democratico* or PRD).

There was a positive economic impact to Torrijos's efforts. The economy based on industry and agribusiness improved and Panama became relatively self-sufficient in the production of basic foods and increased its exports of bananas, shrimp, sugar, tobacco, rice, cattle, and petroleum products from refineries processing Venezuelan-supplied oil. While new hydro-electric plants provided most of the country's energy needs, liberalized banking and tax laws attracted more than 134 international banks from all over the world to Panama City. With bank-secrecy laws being more advantageous than those of Switzerland's, Panama became a haven for money laundering and "narco-dollars," as well as a depository of stolen funds from various dictators around Latin America. In the Colon Free Zone more than eight-hundred companies conducted their international business dealings with earnings amounting to over $1 billion a year.

Many National Guard officers also prospered, usually by means of bribes paid them by large investors, bankers, and even drug traffickers. Local commanders hired out their soldiers in a "rent-a-soldier" program, whereby the commanders were paid monthly fees involving hundreds if not thousands of dollars in exchange for permitting National Guard soldiers to protect banks and other private enterprises both day and night. This trend towards self-serving corruption eventually caused the Guard's social-reform agenda to fall by the wayside as its top officers became increasingly more concerned with their own personal well-being at the expense of the nation.

As our PSYOP study progressed there was one other National Guard officer, besides Torrijos, who stood out starkly and this person proved to be very much a part of the dark side of the military dictatorship. Lieutenant-Colonel Manuel Antonio Noriega was part and parcel of this dark side of the government and was in charge of intelligence and security for not only the Guard, but also Torrijos himself. We characterized him as an "unsavory," if not sinister individual who served his master in a thug-like capacity, protecting the interests of the dictatorship. As the official "enforcer" of the state, Tony Noriega had originally endeared himself to Torrijos as a major, siding with the latter and helping him to quash an institutional counter-coup in the immediate aftermath of the overthrow of Arias. With his loyalty now proven, this sordid character now came to the fore on behalf of the "Maximum Leader" (*Jefe Maximo*), as Torrijos liked to be called and was frequently referred to by the local media.

Born a Creole, a mixture of black, Indian and Spanish blood, and orphaned at an early age, Noriega grew up "street-smart" in the poorer barrios of Panama City. But he was also intelligent enough to graduate near the top of his class in high school and, with the support of a half-brother, obtained a scholarship to Peru's Chorrillos Military Academy.

Returning to Panama in 1962 to join the National Guard, he was commissioned as an officer with the rank of lieutenant. Eight years later, at the age of 34 in 1970, he was promoted to lieutenant-colonel by General Torrijos and given the command of the G-2, the newly expanded intelligence branch of the National Guard.

If Torrijos ruled by dispensing "carrots," the new G-2, as head of all political police, intelligence and immigration, had the job of wielding the "sticks." Noriega's reputation for ruthlessness was quickly established and over time his involvement in drug trafficking, arms smuggling, money laundering, espionage, rigged elections, murder and much more were legendary. It became apparent to me in 1973 that, despite his already nefarious reputation as acknowledged by our intelligence and other sources, Noriega enjoyed an unusually close relationship with SOUTHCOM and was even highly esteemed by some members of its staff as a "reliable, good old boy" in whom one could confide and exchange information. By befriending the SOUTHCOM military and at the same time ruthlessly carrying out security-related repression of perceived opponents and other illegal activities, the National Guard's G-2 was playing both ends up the middle. For awhile he would get away with it, but over the long run it would be his downfall.

Early on in the Torrijos administration, Noriega also endeared himself to the CIA, which saw him as a useful informant in regard to Cuban activities. Once Torrijos was in power, Noriega traveled to Fidel Castro's Communist Cuba with some frequency. Of interest to the CIA's agents in Panama were his observations and feedback on his contacts with Castro himself and Cuba's ace insurgency operations coordinator for Latin America, Manuel Pineiro. As time went on delegations of athletes, students from the University of Panama, and labor unions also went to Cuba as "guests" of the Castro government, but only with the approval of Noriega's G-2 office.

This did not come as a surprise to SOUTHCOM, as the Torrijos family was well known for its overt sympathies on behalf of the Marxist-Leninist movement inside Panama. In 1963 two of Torrijos' first cousins, Edison and Nitido Diaz Herrera were reported as having gone to Pinar del Rio, Cuba, for indoctrination and training. Another relative of Marxist persuasion and member of the National Guard, was Lieutenant-Colonel Roberto Diaz Herrera, whose brother Efebro Diaz

Brigadier-General Manuel Noriega ran Panama as a dictatorship during the 1980s until he was overthrown in late-December 1989. (82nd Airborne Division Museum photo)

Herrera was appointed by Torrijos as Panama's ambassador to Cuba. Other Diaz Herrera brothers, Nitido Diaz Herrera and Edison Diaz Herrera served as Panama's Chief of Customs and Municipal Treasurer, respectively, for the regime. Still another member of Marxist persuasion from the family and actual brother of the dictator was Moises Torrijos Herrera, who became Panama's ambassador to Spain. Even the Maximum Leader, himself, made a trip to Cuba, accompanied by his Foreign Minister Juan Tack and the Rector of the University of Panama, Romulo Escobar Bethancourt. The big question for us by mid-1973 was where all this was headed? Were these die-hard revolutionaries or merely astute political opportunists, hoping to play Havana off against Washington?

Other noted activities of Manuel Noriega during his early years with the Guard first as a lieutenant and then as a captain were his drunken binges and rages, during which he would reportedly beat up and rape prostitutes. With his subordinate clearly out of hand, at one point in time Torrijos had to personally order him confined to his quarters for a month in order to calm him down. Nevertheless, the rapes continued and Torrijos had to frequently intervene on his behalf in order to protect him from his own rages.

Once the coup against Arias had taken place however, Noriega appeared to become more reliable and less and less an obvious embarrassment for the new regime in his highly influential and prestigious position as the G-2. To this end and into the early 1970s it was noted that he had overseen the imprisonment of some 1600 political dissidents, of whom some 70 had been murdered and another roughly 40 disappeared as part of a crackdown to further the consolidation of Torrijos's power. Some of Noriega's actions made him infamous almost overnight. Besides the persecutions, threats, arbitrary detentions and disappearances that took place, inside sources reported that detainees were often being tortured through blows from rubber hoses, electric shocks to vital body parts, and bamboo whips which flayed the skin off of one's back, buttocks, and legs. The degree of sadistic torture inflicted by the G-2 had a direct correlation to the victim's status in the political opposition. Sometimes there were situations verging on the bizarre.

A Roman Catholic priest, Padre Hector Gallegos, had been appointed by the Church in the summer of 1968 to the Parish of Santa Fe in Veraguas Province to the west of Panama City. With his parish badly impoverished, Gallegos worked at organizing agricultural cooperatives on behalf of the poor in the area. This brought him into competition and eventually a confrontational situation with the commercial interests of some local relatives of Omar Torrijos, who for many years had held an almost feudal control over the local population, which had only managed to eke out a living at a bare subsistence level. Padre Gallegos was now enabling his followers to break free from their condition of virtual servitude and being economically marginalized - and the small cabal of economic elites in the area did not like it! To deal with the situation in 1971, Manuel Noriega's G-2 office intervened on behalf of the Torrijos family and had Padre Gallegos arrested; he was never heard from again. Later reports indicated that he had been thrown out of a helicopter to his death while still alive. In brief, it was an object lesson for anyone who dared to oppose the Torrijos family's interests.

Over the next several years the dictatorship consolidated its control over Panama, while Omar Torrijos won over the majority of the masses with his reform efforts and charismatic personality and style. In the meantime the members of the traditional political parties, business associations, and the independent press chafed under the restrictions on civil liberties and denounced the growing corruption within the military regime. When the oil crisis of 1973 led to a serious economic decline, not only in Panama but other parts of Latin America as well, private investment, both domestic and foreign, began to fall off in the face of the weakening economy and the apparent inability of the government to achieve progress in terms of treaty negotiations with Washington. Extensive borrowing from international sources caused the public debt to soon grow out of proportion to Panama's ability to repay even the interest, rising to over 60 percent of total exports. As a result, by 1976 Torrijos began to reach out for an accommodation with the business elite and initiated a slow process of gradually reducing many of the earlier social and labor benefits. Justification for the change of position by the military regime was based on the announced need to maintain national unity during all future Panama Canal treaty negotiations.

Historical fate intervened on the side of Torrijos and Panamanian ambitions to gain national control of the Panama Canal. It came in the form of James Earl Carter, who very much sympathized with the Torrijos position that Panama should be in sovereign control of all its territory and not be saddled with a foreign enclave such as the U.S. Canal Zone in its midst. Elected president of the United States in November 1976 and, in an effort to correct the perceived injustice, Carter drove the issue forward. Building on earlier discussions and a framework for future negotiations concerning a new Panama Canal treaty in 1974 between Juan Tack and the Gerald Ford administration's Secretary of State Henry Kissinger, Carter and Torrijos worked together to develop a new treaty which would come to fruition in 1977.

The negotiations leading up to the new treaty led to a bitter and intense outpouring of both substantive and emotional issues. Some Americans wondered whether the Panamanians could even operate the Canal as well as defend it. Others saw dangers from the apparent influence of Communism inside Panama. And still others contended that the Canal was a symbol of American strength in Latin America and to turn it over Panama would not only be a national humiliation but also a betrayal of thousands of loyal citizens within the Canal Zone (often called "Zonies" or "Zonians"). These were portrayed as highly patriotic folks who had spent the better part of their lives working on behalf of Washington's interests since 1914 to insure that the Canal was always operational in support of world commerce and that conditions within the Canal Zone would always approximate those within the continental United States and duplicate the American way of life. Indeed, the Canal Zone, with its own police force, systems of courts, post offices, customs, ports, public schools, Boy and Girl Scouts, Rotary and Elks Clubs, as well as a plethora of other typically American activities such as football, basketball and little league baseball, caused it to become known as "little America."

In contention during the mid-1970s were national prides on both sides, as expressed in the graffiti painted on walls throughout Panama: "*Ni un paso atras! Yo no vendo mi patria*" ("Not one step back! I am not selling out my country!"). Veiled threats were bandied about by the Torrijos camp, indicating that Panamanians might attempt to rise up and close the Canal by force if the U.S. Senate failed to approve ratification. Panamanians were so confident of the success of their national imperative to gain control of the Canal that one of my USARSA classmates at the general staff course in the mid-1970s, National Guard Major Eduardo Herrera Hassan, confided to me one day that when his *uncle* Omar Torrijos Herrera finished his term of office *he* would then become the next *Maximo Jefe* of Panama, presumably running the country and the Canal. It was an interesting perspective and vision for the future, indicating that the Herrera family had ambitions leading toward the formation of a family political dynasty of some sort. Over time I came to the conclusion that Ed, although always formally correct and very polite when dealing with myself, was an ardent nationalist who deep down inside maintained an implacable hatred of the Americans and everything that their Canal Zone represented in terms of quashing Panamanian sovereignty.

Ironically, while the political effect in Panama of the Torrijos-Carter Panama Canal Treaty was to initiate a lengthy period of tranquility, defusing the hostility of nationalist sentiment regarding the Canal and the American presence in Panama, the end result of this watershed event was that Panama would gain full control and sovereignty over the Panama Canal and its affiliated Canal Zone, but only at the end of the century at midnight, 31 December 1999! This long period of transition leading up to the actual handover of the Canal had come about as a result of an astute Senate appraisal, which concluded it would not be seen as good form on the part of most Americans that Washington was going to turn the Panama Canal over to a dictatorship which was abusive of the human rights of its own citizens. This decision protected the short-term interest of the United States to continue its control over the Canal, while Panamanian politics became more ameliorated and the Torrijos dictatorship transitioned into some form of a democratic government. In reality, there were two treaties signed during the spring of 1978. One (the Neutrality Treaty) would make it legitimate for the United States to use military force against a foreign power that attempted to close the Canal or wrest it from Panamanian control and would be of an indefinite duration and the other (the Panama Canal Treaty) would deal with the return of the Canal and Zone to Panama over the remainder of the century.

Although Omar Torrijos became a national hero overnight as the man who had stood up to Washington and then gained victory when he signed the Panama Canal Treaties with President Carter, he was apparently stung by the public attacks on his dictatorship during the Senate hearings and treaty debates. To counter this negative image of himself and his regime, he verbally agreed to an opening of the Panamanian political spectrum with the establishment of political parties and an announcement that an eventual election of a civilian government would take place sometime in 1984.

Buoyed up with his diplomatic success over the issue of Canal sovereignty and with the economy having made a resurgence (6 percent growth) towards the end of the 1970s, Torrijos arrogantly began to support Cuba's anti-Yankeeism and the leftist guerrilla movements in Nicaragua, El Salvador, Guatemala and Honduras. During the Sandinista revolution's struggle against the Somoza dynasty, arms, munitions and other equipment were smuggled on behalf of the guerrillas from Panama, through Costa Rica and on into Nicaragua. By the early 1980s and the advent of President Ronald Reagan, an outspoken enemy of Communism, Torrijos now began to significantly tone down his support for the Central American revolutionaries. In addition to this, the ratification of the Canal treaties had pulled the rug out from under the militant left inside Panama, which now found it had lost the only cause that could have tilted the country in its favor.

The next watershed event in the drama of Panamanian politics was the July 1981 death of Omar Torrijos whose aircraft mysteriously crashed in the mountains of western Panama. His death and the power vacuum it created unleashed still more powerful and corrupted forces inside the National Guard; unlike any Panama had ever seen before. A junta of ambitious colonels from the Guard's top officers now ruled the country as part of a rotating-power deal. Included in the cabal of leaders was none other than Colonel Manuel Noriega who was scheduled to be the Guard's commander from mid-1983 to mid-1987. The political infighting was continuous and found Noriega exploiting his contacts within the Guard to outmaneuver the several other power contenders, including one of Torrijos' cousins, Colonel Roberto Diaz Herrera.

Eduardo Herrera Hassan, my former USARSA classmate and now a lieutenant colonel in the PDF, was also viewed by Noriega as a high threat to his fortunes. As a result, Ed found himself assigned outside of Panama for the remainder of the 1980s to a series of positions in various countries, which included that of military attache (Washington, D.C.) and even ambassador (to Israel). By the summer of 1983 the situation appeared to stabilize somewhat with the newly-promoted Brigadier-General Manuel Noriega taking his turn as the nation's top military commander, which now allowed him to solidify his control over the country under a renamed military institution: the Panama Defense Forces (PDF). As Torrijos had previously promised in 1978, open elections, involving a number of competing political parties, did take place in 1984.

Although not fully realized at that time, the 1984 elections proved to be the opening act in a series of events which would ultimately culminate in the 1989 U.S. invasion of Panama. To ensure that the PDF retained its control of the country, General Noriega manipulated the election results to guarantee victory for *his* presidential candidate, Nicolas Ardito Barletta. This was essential, since the military's own party (the PRD), even with full government backing, had received fewer votes than the party of Arnulfo Arias. Although international observers decried the election as "rigged," Washington accepted the results at face value. Nonetheless, when Barletta attempted to assert his authority by ordering investigations into the PDF's alleged use of torture-murder by death squads, Noriega arranged for the president's resignation. In his place Vice-President Eric Arturo del Valle, another Noriega figurehead, became the new president in the fall of 1985.

But things did not go well for the general as opposition in the form of Hugo Spadafora, a former Torrijos confident, publicly accused Noriega of using the PDF as an instrument of repression so as to maintain the military dictatorship. In addition, Panama's opposition press began to raise questions about the PDF's complicity in drug trafficking and money laundering. When Spadafora offered to testify to the DEA and show proof that Noriega was engaged in international drug trafficking, he was brutally murdered in September 1985; his headless body found in a U.S. mailbag. This murder produced an outrage in Panama, which resulted in anti-government rioting, and was also exacerbated by the fact that the international recession of the early 1980s had deflated the economy, causing general unemployment to reach a level of about 45 percent. Responding to the crisis, Noriega declared a ten-day "state of emergency," during which all constitutional guarantees were suspended.

Manuel Noriega ruled with an iron hand through his puppet president Arturo del Valle. An attempt by Diaz Herrera to overthrow the general while the latter was outside the country floundered and the general continued his rule. Giving confidence to Noriega was the support the CIA and the DEA were giving to him behind the scenes, always ignoring his unsavory reputation in favor of his seemingly solid record of cooperation with Washington in terms of providing intelligence information concerning Cuba, counter-drug operations, and support of U.S. policies concerning the Contras and Nicaragua.

The catalyst causing Washington to finally begin to turn against Noriega's regime in yet another watershed event occurred in January 1988 when two federal grand juries in Florida indicted the general on drug trafficking charges. In detail, the indictments stated that he had provided airstrips for drug smuggling, protected cocaine production laboratories located inside Panama, and had received some $350 million for his efforts. It was the first time that a foreign head of state had been formally accused by a U.S. federal court of narco-trafficking and forced the United States into open confrontation with the Panamanian dictator. This, in turn, provoked a dramatic shift in Washington's policy by making it impossible for the Reagan administration to be seen as friendly with a drug-trafficker.

The following February with Washington's encouragement Arturo del Valle attempted to fire Noriega, but found himself ousted instead by the Panamanian National Assembly, which then appointed Manuel Solis Palma, another Noriega lackey in his place. In response, Washington opened up a full-scale multi-media assault against the general, all the while searching for other forms of pressure to apply against the dictator in order to bring about his departure from the Panamanian political scene. Eventually various economic sanctions were brought into play, which materially worsened the lives of many Panamanians, but without any particular effect on Noriega himself. In March, all the monies the Reagan administration owed Panama from the operations of the Canal ($80 million annually) were placed in an escrow account by the new administration of President George H.W. Bush. The next month U.S. courts further froze some $40 million in Panamanian government assets in American banks and halted the operations of the national airline, Air Panama, inside the United States. In addition, the administration invoked emergency powers, banning all U.S. citizens and organizations from making payments in any form to the Noriega regime, as well as suspending Panama's preferential trade status, which had allowed up to 30 percent of its exports to enter the United States duty-free.

The judicial revelations about Noriega, in conjunction with earlier 1986 articles in the *New York Times* by correspondent Seymour Hersh, produced an outpouring of data and commentaries about the regime's illegal activities. The general's links to money laundering were exposed, as well as the fact that he was receiving a commission from the Colombian Medellin Cartel for the protected use of Panamanian territory for its operations. It was not that the Department of Justice (DOJ) did not know of the Panamanian military's ties with the drug traffickers. It did, going back into the early 1970s and identifying Noriega by name. In one case Moises Torrijos, Omar's brother, was indicted by the DOJ for smuggling drugs in Panamanian diplomatic pouches, but managed to escape U.S. capture through an insider's tip-off.

Furthering Noriega's trafficking operations was his control of the Panamanian Customs, Immigration and Passport Services, Civil Aeronautics and the control tower at Tocumen International Airport, the National Bank of Panama, and the Panamanian Attorney General's Office. Cemented by graft and corruption, and substantially funded by narcotics money, a full entourage of junior officers looked out for their own and the general's interests. One officer, Captain Luis Quiel, was simultaneously in charge of the PDF's anti-drug smuggling unit, all the while serving as a liaison to the Medellin Cartel. In addition, he was Noriega's personal representative to the DEA and thus in a position to alert the traffickers as to whatever information the U.S. agency had provided him. Quiel adroitly eliminated Medellin's competitors inside Panama by turning them over to the DEA. The result of this situation was that the DEA held the general in high esteem for assisting in Washington's counter-drug operations, all the while Medellin Cartel-controlled drugs continued to flow through Panama toward the United States.

While this was taking place and ostensibly aiding the Reagan administration's Contra operations against Sandinista controlled Nicaragua, Noriega was mixing cargoes of guns and drugs in Panamanian flights into Central America. The guns were dropped off in Costa Rica for Contra use and the planes involved then flew on into the United States with the drugs. In exchange for his efforts on behalf of the Medellin Cartel, Noriega received hundreds of millions of dollars. This included ignoring a cocaine processing plant that the Cartel had established in the Darien Province near the Colombian border. Other trafficking organizations in the Caribbean were also allowed by the general to use Panama for money laundering and safe haven for upwards of $1 million apiece. These activities went on and on with Noriega entering into full partnerships with many of the traffickers. In short, the general had made himself indispensable to both the CIA and the DEA and had remained on their respective pay rolls off and on for roughly two decades, receiving up to nearly $200,000 annually, all the while fostering his own private drug trafficking enterprise. In the end it was found that Manuel Noriega would support virtually anyone who would pay him; truly "a man for all occasions."

Encouraged by Washington's criticism and actions taken against the Noriega regime, as well as Colonel Roberto Diaz Herrera's accusations that the general and his cronies were involved in corruption, drug trafficking, the rigging of the 1984 elections, the murder of Dr. Hogo Spadafora, and even the planning of the crash that killed Omar Torrijos, there appeared after 1987 a resurgence of Panamanian nationalism against the general. Led in the main by the National Civic Crusade (*Cruzada Civilista Nacional*), which was made up of various business, labor, professional, and student groups, a series of anti-government demonstrations and strikes began to take place throughout 1988, jolting the economy and prompting a crisis of confidence that led to massive withdrawals from Panama's banks. The leaders of the Crusade advocated that Panamanians stop paying taxes and boycott any establishment doing business with the government, arguing that the dictator, also derided as *Cara de Pina* or "Pineapple Face" because of his badly pock-marked cheeks, was a drug trafficker, murderer and money launderer. With the absence of real public support for the de facto rule of Noriega (a public opinion survey indicated that 75 percent of the people wanted Noriega to relinquish power), pressure began to mount for new elections in 1989.

Shocked at the outpouring of protests against him, Noriega called for presidential elections on 7 May 1989. These were held as scheduled throughout the nation and witnessed by international observers, including former Presidents Jimmy Carter and Gerald Ford, as well as other high-ranking Latin American and European Community leaders. The general had entered into the elections as part of a strategy to convey the image of democratic governance in the eyes of the international community in order to provide legitimacy to the political status quo which he was attempting to maintain. One day after the balloting was complete, Jimmy Carter denounced the election as a fraud. At the same time the Catholic Church also announced that the opposition party, ADOC (Alliance of Democratic Civilian Opposition), led by Guillermo Endara, had won the election by a margin of three to one over Noriega's candidate, Carlos Duque. This would appear to have resolved the issue of legitimate rule, but it did not.

In spite of the evidence of Endara's victory, on May 10th, the Electoral Tribunal, whose members had been appointed by Noriega, declared Duque the winner. That same day the government's infamous "dignity battalions," gangs made up of thugs and other loyal riffraff from around Panama City, physically assaulted the ADOC leaders with Doberman attack dogs, brutally beating up Endara and two of his other party friends and leaders, Billy Ford and Ricardo Arias Calderon. With the bloody encounter dramatized on videotapes played by the international television media, Noriega found his election strategy backfiring against him. Over the ensuing months Washington began a drumbeat of media pressure, insisting that the general relinquish power to the legitimate winners of the May election. If Noriega did not realize it at the time, the fraudulent election of May 1989 had begun the countdown to his ultimate ouster from Panama.

Following the fraudulent May elections, President Bush began to take a series of actions to prepare for a more formal confrontation with the general. One of these was to send 19,000 additional soldiers to Panama as reinforcements for the ten thousand U.S. soldiers, airman, sailors and Marines already on station. The president then ordered the evacuation of American citizens from Panamanian soil, declaring that even without the old Canal Zone structure in play Washington would enforce its treaty rights to move its forces freely between its bases in Panama. In my case, having elected to retire from the Army after twenty-five years service In the summer of 1989, I and my wife Patricia and two sons, William and Stewart, also formed part of the evacuation process. Flying out of Panama in a C-141 Starlifter transport jet in late June from Howard Air Force Base, located on the west side of the Canal in the vicinity of Panama City, to Charleston, South Carolina, was not the actual end of my involvement with Panama.

Although I had completed my work with the Army Security Assistance Agency for Latin America and SOUTHCOM's Directorate of Political-Military Affairs (J-5), several months later I was back in Panama, doing graduate studies with the University of Oklahoma at Albrook Air Force Station, located a few hundred yards to the north of SOUTHCOM's Quarry Heights headquarters. This enabled me to keep in touch with key intelligence personnel and reasonably well informed as to what was happening in Panamanian politics.

During this time the Bush administration had also galvanized the Organization of American States in Washington into action to approve a resolution condemning the election abuses in Panama and to begin formulating courses of action which would lead to a transfer of power to legitimate authority through democratic means. One of these proposals was that a provisional government take over in Panama in September to begin the process towards holding new elections. This initiative was rejected outright by Noriega.

When Washington then announced that it would not accept *any* candidate proposed by Noriega or his government to serve as the administrator of the Panama Canal, the general responded by claiming that the United States was trying to stop the process of the transfer of the Canal to Panamanian control. Albeit gaining full control of the Canal was of paramount importance to Panamanians, Noriega's ploy to manipulate the situation in an effort to pit local nationalistic fervor against the United States failed. Washington, through its SOUTH-COM headquarters, then suggested that the PDF take care of the situation internally.

On the morning of 3 October 1989 one Major Moises Giroldi, chief of security and commander of the PDF's 4th Infantry Company at the PDF's main headquarters (called *La Comandancia*) in Panama City, led a coup attempt to force Noriega into retirement. Having captured the general and now holding him isolated at gunpoint in a room, the major negotiated with his commander, explaining that the regime with all of its corruption and evil doings was tarnishing the image of the PDF's officer corps; thus it would be necessary for Noriega to withdraw from the institution in order to reform it. The major had taken on the task of confronting Noriega because the two were, according to U.S. intelligence sources, actually quite close, the general having been godfather to one of Giroldi's children. Still, Noriega was accustomed to turning seeming adversity into political success in the dog-eat-dog situations involving Panamanian politics. As such, he apologetically asked the major to reconsider the demand that he step down as the commander of the PDF and instead allow him to personally make all the necessary reforms so as to please the PDF officer corps. It was a subtle ploy.

Major Giroldi first pondered the general's offer and then finally accepted the idea. Suggesting that they cement the agreement that would enable him to remain on as the commander of the PDF in order to implement the reforms, Noriega now asked the major to recognize him with a symbol of his authority as the PDF's commanding general by handing over to him his pistol. This having been done, and without the slightest hesitation, the general promptly turned and faced the major, shooting him dead between the eyes at point-blank range! This abruptly ended the coup and the *Maximum Jefe* returned to power, his style. To make sure that he remained in power, Noriega initiated a harsh crackdown with a systematic purge of the PDF to ensure that no one else would be likely to revolt against him in the near future.

It had become apparent to George Bush in mid-1989 that more drastic action might have to be taken against the Noriega regime, so the "decks were cleared" of anyone who could possibly become an impediment in making the key decisions to deal in a militant manner with the dictator, his Panamanian cronies, and the PDF. Beginning in the summer and on into the early fall of 1989, General Fred Woerner, one of the Army's foremost Latin American specialists and the commander of SOUTHCOM, was suddenly retired and replaced by General Maxwell R. Thurman, an Army officer who had never served in Latin America and therefore had no special psychological or sentimental ties to the region and its people. In addition, the commander of U.S. Army South, a component service of SOUTHCOM located at Fort Clayton and adjacent to the Panama Canal's Miraflores Locks, was transferred out of the area to a new assignment in Washington, D.C. Some weeks later Army South's chief of staff was relieved and retired from active duty.

Brigadier-General Marc Cisneros, SOUTHCOM's J-3 or Director of Operations (who had led Wallace Nutting's SOUTHCOM security assistance study team in Honduras during the early 1980s) was then promoted to the rank of Major General and appointed by Thurman to command Army South. It was obvious that Thurman, who sometimes had been referred to as "Mad Max" by those working for him, was to be the "hatchet man" for any future operations that President Bush and his new JCS Chairman, General Colin Powell, might be inclined to initiate. If it required chopping off heads in Panama without any qualms, Thurman was just the man to do the job.

Despite all possible inducements from the Bush administration to leave Panama and open the political spectrum to fair elections, Manuel Noriega at this point in time undoubtedly calculated his chances of successfully surviving in exile as being very unattractive. At that moment he still enjoyed inside Panama the protection and security that the PDF offered, especially in the face of the fact that he had recently double-crossed the Medellin Cartel's operations inside Panama in order to placate DEA interests and was now on the drug lords' own hit list. In terms of other trafficking interests, once out of power, he would no longer be particularly useful to his former patrons and would even constitute a security risk to the their illicit operations. To avoid this situation, Noriega, like so many other former dictators in Latin America, opted to stay in power as long as possible so as to maximize his chances of survival. Because he knew Panama and its politics better than any other place in the world, the general felt that he was safer within the confines of his own digs, especially if he could remain in power. Still in all, it was an arrogant decision which would prove very costly to his fortunes.

On 16 December a Marine lieutenant and some of his buddies had just completed eating a meal at one of Panama City's seafront restaurants and were returning to their base at nearby Quarry Heights, when they were accosted by a guard as they passed by the PDF's main headquarters downtown. The guard, apparently having been drinking heavily and in a foul mood, aggressively demanded to see the Marine's driver's license. Feeling insulted and not seeing that this was appropriate behavior in terms of respect for an officer of the United States Marine Corps, the lieutenant sped away in his car. A few seconds later a burst of AK-47 assault rifle fire slammed into the vehicle from the rear, killing the lieutenant. While this incident was bad enough as it was, just some hours earlier a Navy officer and his wife had been arbitrarily detained and roughly searched by the guards at the same headquarters. Distraught and humiliated, with his wife having been apparently threatened with sexual abuse, the officer had filed a formal report of complaint at the SOUTHCOM headquarters. The reports of these two incidents arrived almost simultaneously at the White House Situation Room just one day before General Noriega was quoted as having declared that Panama was now in "a state of war with the United States," and that he was, in fact, the "maximum leader" and president of his country. This effectively ended any last illusions of the possibility of constitutional government inside Panama while Noriega was in power.

During the afternoon of the day the Marine lieutenant was killed, I was enjoying some leisurely time off from my studies by visiting the old Spanish-colonial port town of Porto Bello. Almost four-hundred years old, the town and its picturesque ruins overlooking a bay by the same name was one of Panama's historical, Caribbean-coastal treasures and an interesting tourist delight. The monsoon-like rainy season had come to an end and gentle, dry Caribbean breezes now wafted through the rows of cinder block houses and their tin roofs that constituted home for most of the eight-hundred or so inhabitants. As I was walking along one of the town's dirt tracks which served as a street and enjoying the late-afternoon sunshine, a little old lady suddenly burst out of her house, hollering in desperate Spanish: "Colonel! Colonel! Get away quick! You can't stay here - they are killing Americans!"

While one can sometimes sense a good situation or even a bad situation cropping up, my experiences in Vietnam had made me acutely aware of the "bad." In short, and to use an old Army-airborne vernacular, the "shit had hit the fan" somewhere in Panama. Not certain of what was transpiring on the Pacific side of the isthmus, I hurriedly revved up my run-down, 1956 Ford pickup truck, which my Citadel classmate Bill Brunner, the Director of Safety for the Panama Canal, had so generously loaned me, and headed back towards Diablo Heights where Bill lived and I was bunking-up during my studies in Panama. The trans-isthmian trip by the main highway normally took about an hour and a half - I made it in forty-five minutes!

Knowing that there were two PDF check points along the highway, guarded by soldiers and police armed with automatic rifles, I pressed the gas peddle to the floor, figuring that, if they were going to shoot me, they would have to hit a moving target. My pucker factor was sky high as I approached the first check point, expecting to see agitated guards and menacing rifles. But no, there was nothing, not a sole around! It appeared that the PDF had pulled all its forces off the trans-isthmian highway; a first time as far as I could remember in my fifteen-years association with Panama. This was unusual and indicated that something was definitely up. At the second check point in the vicinity of the Madden Dam access road, likewise there was no one around. The PDF was obviously regrouping in preparation for something else. Sighing a sense of relief, but with perspiration running down my face, I cut off the main highway to make the run through the National Rain Forest Preserve, past the Panama Canal's Miraflores Locks, Fort Clayton, Albrook Air Force Station, and on into Diablo Heights where Bill and a mix of other Americans and Panamanians lived side by side.

The several intelligence reports about the incidents of the 15th and 16th of December arrived at the White House situation room almost simultaneously, indicating that something very wrong was taking place in Panama. Interpreting these reports as evidence that Manuel Noriega and his PDF were now out of control and acting in an unstable manner in terms of threatening the integrity of Washington's treaty interests in operating and protecting the Panama Canal, the democratic future of Panama, and of more immediate importance the lives of the American military and Panama Canal Commission workers and their family members, George Bush turned to Colin Powell and directed that he execute "Operation   ."

It was not a moment too late, for intelligence reports had also indicated that one of Noriega's options in the event of an invasion included a plan to take Americans hostage and then withdraw into the mountains in order to further negotiate a "solution." This was not necessarily idle speculation as in one case the PDF maintained a ten-man infantry detachment located in a two-story wooden building directly across the street and only ten yards away from the main entrance to the Diablo Heights Elementary School. If given the order, in a matter of seconds the detachment could have moved across the street and entered the school at will, taking hostage the some two-hundred children and their teachers. It was a dicey situation from any standpoint. With the "buck in the pocket" policy towards the dictator having failed, Washington was now forced to implement its preferred policy alternative: "a kick in the ass!"

Roughly 72 hours after Bush ordered the invasion to commence on 17 December and beginning around 1:00 a.m. on 20 December, Army Rangers and paratroopers from the 82nd Airborne Division rained down over the Omar Torrijos International Airport. On the initial approach at a height of 500 feet, the paratroopers' lead C-141 aircraft began taking heavy tracer fire and hits from the brush around the airport's runways. The seconds ticked by and the lead paratrooper, festooned with hand grenades and heavily laden with his assault rifle, ammunition, and parachute, stood in an open exit door, bracing himself against its sides in the familiar, half-crouch position, which the lead jumper assumes in this situation. As the plane's jump-lights flashed from red to green (the "Go!" signal), the soldier collapsed dead on the exit ramp with a PDF rifle bullet drilled squarely through his forehead.

A deft kick from the aircraft's alert jumpmaster cleared the door of the fallen soldier and the following fifty-five man "stick" of paratroopers proceeded to hurtle themselves into the night air and the battle below. In one airborne infantry platoon, a 42-year old sergeant first class was noted as having jumped with his 19-year old, private first class son! Ordinarily this was not supposed to happen during a war, but an exception had been made for this special "family-bonded tradition." Nevertheless, the airborne assault on the airport was just one facet of an operation involving simultaneous attacks against some twenty-six distinct locations and targets, for the most part in and around the Panama City and Colon areas, as well as certain key points out to the west.

While the PDF did have some combat-ready units among its up to 15,000 men scattered around the country, most of its military and police forces were not well equipped or even trained for battle action. Accordingly, it had occurred to Colin Powell that here was an opportunity to quickly overwhelm and decapitate the PDF as a military institution, destroying it forever as a threat to Panamanians and decent, civilized life. To make sure the operation would go according to plan, General Powell had tasked Lieutenant-General Carl Stiner and his XVIII Airborne Corps battle-command staff with the mission of coordinating and running Just Cause for General Thurman. To accomplish the mission as fast and efficiently as possible, Stiner completely reconfigured the older Army South plan, which had advocated a slow, ponderous build-up of forces and then a piecemeal attack implementation at selected points, into one which would eliminate Noriega and the PDF with an overwhelming, simultaneous attack against every major PDF unit and affiliated installation, destroying Noriega's military capability in one fell swoop. In its conception and execution, it was a strategy right out of the Army War College's text book on how to conduct offensive operations. By the end of the first six hours or around 7:00 a.m. of the day of the attack, the PDF had ceased to exist as a viable military force.

The PDF main headquarters, located little more than a mile away from Quarry Heights, found itself under bombardment from the onset of the operation. One Army infantry company, mounted in M-113 armored personnel carriers and moving to attack the headquarters, was working its way towards its attack position through a maze of buildings in the vicinity of the *Comandancia* when it began taking heavy casualties from PDF snipers. Turning to his artillery forward observer the company commander directed that the snipers be "suppressed." A few seconds later all the buildings in the area received dozens of volleys of pre-planned, 105mm high explosive shells, complements of an 18-gun artillery battalion dedicated to carry out exactly this type of mission. Fires created by the shelling raced through the poor, working-class neighborhoods surrounding the Comandancia, destroying most of the buildings, but also eliminating the threat of the deadly snipers.

Unfortunately for the U.S. forces involved in this attack, Noriega was not at his headquarters and was able to initially avoid the onslaught, spending the next couple of weeks eluding pursuing U.S. forces on foot before finally being captured on 3 January at the Papal Nuncio's quarters inside the Vatican Embassy where he had sought refuge. But the tables had turned for the general and even the Catholic Church's Pope at the Vatican in Rome had come out against the dictator, labeling him a common criminal and therefore ineligible for political asylum. From the Vatican Embassy in Panama City, the now deposed despot surrendered and was transported to nearby Howard Air Force Base, formally arrested by the DEA, and then flown to the United States to stand trial on drug-trafficking and money-laundering charges - Manuel Noriega, the dictator, had fallen!

The invasion of Panama, as a last watershed event, destroyed a tyrannical government and reinstated the authorities chosen by the people in
the frustrated election of May 1989. It also represented a new beginning
for that country and an opportunity to right most of the wrongs of the
preceding twenty-two years. A poll taken in Panama in early January
1990 found that 92 percent of Panamanian adults approved the Bush
administration's actions in sending troops to overthrow the Noriega
regime and inside the United States some three-quarters of all Americans also felt that the invasion had protected Washington's interests in
the region. But the invasion had not come without a cost. Twenty-three
U.S. servicemen were killed and scores more were wounded during the
combat that took place. Several thousand Panamanians were also killed
and injured; about half of them being civilians. The Army's 7th Infantry
Division, which conducted a series of thorough mopping up operations
throughout the country, recovered well over 33,000 weapons captured
or turned in, which had been at the disposal of the PDF.

Arriving in Florida courtesy of the Air Force, Manuel Noriega was
eventually tried and convicted in U.S. federal courts in 1992 on eight
counts of racketeering, conspiracy, distribution of drugs and money
laundering, receiving a sentence of forty years in prison (reduced in
May 1999 to 30 years). Inside Panama it was eventually found during
financial audits that the former dictator had misappropriated around $1
billion via overdrafts on the National Bank. Further investigation by the
Justice and Treasury Departments revealed that Noriega had some $772
million in drug, contraband, and gunrunning profits stored in various
bank accounts in Europe and the Western Hemisphere. This was in addition to the well over a million dollars he had been able to bamboozle
the CIA and DEA out of in exchange for information of nebulous value
about Cuba and drug trafficking inside Panama. Nonetheless, it was his
own arrogance and blatant greed that eventually did him in.

In 1993 the new government of President Guillermo Endara charged
and convicted Noriega in absentia for the 1985 murder of Hugo Spadafora, illicit enrichment and other human rights violations, requesting
that Washington extradite the former dictator to Panama to stand trial
upon completion of his thirty-year sentence. In short, the former *jefe*

maximo would apparently never see the light of day outside of a prison cell, since the Endara government intended to tack on 70 years in prison to those already being undergone in the United States. Historically speaking, Noriega was not the first dictator in the Caribbean to receive "a kick in the ass," as Batista, Trujillo, and the Somozas before him had all gone that same route into oblivion. Albeit the freeing of Panama from the hands of Manuel Noriega and his claque of corrupt officers was a deed well done, Washington now faced the challenge of reconstructing a war-torn nation, providing security, and rebuilding a functioning democratic system, almost from the ground up.

As the PDF was decapitated and its military/police institution eliminated as an element to be contended with in Panamanian society, law and order broke down almost from the onset of Operation Just Cause. Not much thought had been given by General Thurman to post-war security inside Panama and looting and pillaging was rampant. In the vacuum of law and order, Panamanian businessmen and store owners found themselves trying to protect their holdings alone against a wave of violent crime that descended upon Panama City and other outlying urban areas. Simply put, the U.S. military police (MPs) should have been deployed in force, but were not, and it would take some years before Panamanians would get over this miscue on the part of the SOUTH-COM headquarters. But Washington did go to work to reestablish an effective police force and government, rebuild the economy, and prevent the resumption of drug-trafficking and money laundering activities; all with the idea that this would protect the Panama Canal.

With Panama's military or defense forces having been formally abolished through early-1990s legislative action, a new police force and successor to the PDF for security was created and designated as the "Panama Public Force" or *Fuerza Publica*. Commanding the new Public Force (PF) was none other than Colonel Eduardo Herrera Hassan, the ardent, anti-American nationalist of earlier days at USARSA. Ironically, Washington had tapped into Herrera because of his animosity towards Manuel Noriega and his efforts to obtain U.S. assistance in opposing and eventually overthrowing the dictator. But Herrera was unhappy in his new role. His PF officers and men wore disheveled, if not sloppy-looking fatigue uniforms, were armed with .38 caliber revolvers, and were roundly ridiculed and often ignored by the population at large, who as often as not outgunned the PF with their own privately acquired Uzi submachine guns and AK-47 assault rifles (the PF had great difficulty dealing with the crime wave that racked the country in the early 1990s).

Indeed, the Public Force was subordinated to civilian control under the Ministry of Government and Justice and a budgetary oversight of the institution was maintained by the Panamanian Office of the Comptroller General and the Legislative Assembly. This was a far cry from the "good old days" of the '70s and '80s, when the spit and polish PDF wore crisply starched uniforms, shinny brass buckles and badges of rank, rocked garrison hats, and sported gloss-shined shoes. Gone were the days when the PDF's *Machos del Monte* ("jungle fighters") track team would perennially win the annual, 50-mile trans-isthmian, long distance race against competing Army, Navy, Air Force and Marine Corps teams, further bolstering its arrogant and domineering attitudes towards Americans in general. Not able to withstand what he perceived as the humiliation and indignity of having to command such a desultory force and his pride thoroughly deflated, Ed Herrera conducted a late-1990 coup attempt against the Endara government.

Only the quick intervention by U.S. military forces saved the democratically elected regime from being overthrown. Herrera, not particularly enamored by American concepts of civilian control of the military and democracy, now found himself serving a sentence of several years in prison within his own country. Had the colonel been more astute in reading Panama's political tea leaves, he might have been able to parlay his PF command into a legitimate election bid for the presidency, realizing his expressed dream of one day running Panama, as his uncle Omar Torrijos had once done. Respected Panamanian columnist, Roberto Eisenmann, commented on this and other situations facing Panama in the early 1990s: "We got rid of a dictator, but not his habits."

Despite other coup attempts of one sort or another, riots, and a precipitous drop in public support (down from 70 percent in early 1990 to around 10 percent by 1994), due to high unemployment rates of 40 to 50 percent, Guillermo Endara, the country's first post-invasion president, managed to complete his term in office. With Noriega's "gag orders" censoring and even suppressing the media having been removed, it was evident that Panama's society was now enjoying a high degree of media freedom, as indicated by the constant criticism and vilification of Endara that actually took place throughout his administration. Despite the government's lack of credibility, ineptness, and a climate of frustration and confusion, the May 1994 elections proved to be some of the cleanest, fairest and freest in Panama's history. In many respects Panama appeared to be evolving into another Costa Rica. Nonetheless, in a surprise turn of events, the PRD, a party closely associated with the Noriega regime was returned to power in the form of Ernesto Perez Balladares, a former campaign manager of the deposed 1989 regime. Simply put, the PRD had capitalized on the feelings of frustration among Panama's citizens to win the presidency.

By 1997 Perez Balladares found himself being roundly criticized for having appointed Manuel Noriega's former Foreign Minister, Jorge Ritter, as his Minister for Canal Affairs and chairman of the new 11-member Inter-Oceanic Regional Authority, which was to oversee the final transition of the Panama Canal into Panamanian hands. Nonetheless, at this time the country had almost a 90 percent adult literacy rate and 80 percent of the nation had access to health services and potable water. Nonetheless, as the end of the century came on and Panamanians looked forward to gaining full control of the Canal, the people remained cynical about politics in general, seeing parties and elections as a means of gaining jobs and favors from cronies, rather than seeing government as an effective way to resolve the problems of the nation as a whole. Unfortunately, this had played out over the years in the form of contraband and the embezzlement and misappropriation of public funds. In short it was still "a deal for my friends and the law for my enemies," like so many of the other "banana republics" in Latin America. Despite the unsavory history of the Noriega era, problems with drug trafficking continued apace, further reinforcing the public's generally negative view of the government.

By the late 1990s Colombian drug cartel cocaine and heroin continued to transit Panama towards the United States and Europe. Not helping matters in this regard were the some 200 small landing strips in the San Blas Islands along the country's Caribbean coast and the still very much remote regions of the Darien, which fronts on Colombia's northwestern border. The situation became so bad along the Darien frontier towards the turn of the century that PF policemen found themselves completely outgunned (.38 caliber pistols against American-, Belgian-, and Russian-made assault rifles and machine guns) and became afraid to deal with the drug traffickers and the variety of heavily armed guerrilla (ELN and FARC) and paramilitary (AUC) forces who used Panama as a safe haven from pursuing Colombian army forces. The situation remained as such until the PF intercepted a Nicaraguan sourced shipment of some 2,000 AK-47 assault rifles and associated ammunition, which then enabled them to increase their firepower and establish some form of law and order along the border. In addition, money laundering continued unabated inside Panama through the purchase of hotels, condominiums, office complexes and shopping centers, as well as through the Colon Free Zone with its now over two-thousand businesses and affiliated containerized shipping ports and terminals.

But the real dog-fight in Panamanian politics revolved around who would win the 1998 election and oversee the final transition of the Canal into the hands of the Panamanian government. The grand prize for the winner would be the treasure trove of prime real estate that included family housing, hospitals, schools, port facilities, ware houses, airports, clubs, and golf courses. In short, whoever won the election would take full control of the some 8,500 houses and buildings that constituted part of the $10 billion value that the former Canal Zone was said to be worth.

On 1 September 1999, Mireya Moscoso, Panama's first woman president, was inaugurated, ousting the PRD from power. Ironically, she represented her late-husband's (Dr. Arnulfo Arias) highly nationalistic Panamenista Party. The daughter of a schoolteacher in rural Panama, she had become involved in local politics and had met her future husband at a relatively young age, marrying him when she was 23 years old and he 67. When Arias passed away in 1988, she took up the mantle of leadership of the Panamenista party, easily winning the election ten years later and insuring that the memory of the former president and her late husband would carry over into the next century. If the test of a true democratic governance is that opposing political parties can replace each other cyclically in a peaceful manner as part of an open electoral process, then Panama was well on its way to a passing grade.

The early years of the twenty-first century find Panama as the guardian of the Panama Canal, providing an efficient and secure operation for the passing of roughly 70 percent of United States sea-borne trade. Every day some 35 ships, each paying up to about $55,000 per passage, provide the Panama Canal Authority (ACP) with a daily income of around $1.5 million, of which about half goes to the maintenance, operations and overhead of running the Canal. With ship transit and support revenues totaling upwards of a billion dollars a year and ACP contributions (profits) and taxes paid to the state equaling at least $500 million annually, the government will undoubtedly do everything it can to maintain its position as the "bridge of the world," insuring that the golden goose that the Canal represents to the nation continues to lay its annual eggs. Fostering this interest has been the container-transport industry and the parallel cruise ship industry, which now docks some two-hundred passenger ships with over a quarter of a million tourists annually at the Colon and Panama City ends of the Panama Canal. To add icing on the cake, in late 2003 Panama celebrated its 100th anniversary as an independent country with Colin Powell, then the United States Secretary of State, in attendance.

But time marches on and as destiny might have it in another ironical twist in Panamanian history, the 2004 national elections found Martin Torrijos, a son of the late Omar Torrijos, winning the presidency as the head of the PRD, the party his father had founded some twenty-five years earlier. Nonetheless, when all was said and done, it was Teddy Roosevelt's great vision and actions to bring about the trans-isthmian canal that gave Panama its true destiny and future value to world commerce; an importance all out of proportion to its actual size.

CONCLUSION

From the inception of the twentieth century to the present, the United States has attempted to influence the politics of Latin America. In the main this has always been based on Washington's perception of its national security interests in the region. During the first part of the century the policy was to protect the approaches to the Panama Canal from potential European naval threats through outright military occupations of a half dozen countries around the Caribbean. During the middle part of the century, Washington's frequent embrace of blatant dictatorships over more liberal governments during World War II and the Cold War period represented a calculated judgment that authoritarian regimes would be more predictably anti-Nazi or anti-Communist than any other form of rule. This appeared to work in the short run, but then backfired as time went on, when Communist revolutionaries and other nationalists, feeding upon the political exclusion, economic marginalization, and quashed aspirations of their peoples suffering under the heel of brutal dictatorships, attempted to shape their own destinies by militant means.

John Kennedy's Alliance for Progress and Jimmy Carter's human rights advocacy were both attempts to turn around Washington's earlier Cold War errors in judgment through the promotion of democratic and socioeconomic reforms. These approaches ultimately became the basis for the successful counter-insurgency efforts in El Salvador and Honduras during the 1980s. In short, it had became obvious over time that one not only needed to know what they were against but also to know what they were *for* in order to deal successfully with the Communist revolutionary wars that America was facing in the region.

The military operations conducted by Washington from 1965 through the end of 1989 were generally successful in confronting the Castro Communist threat to Latin America and promoting American foreign policy interests throughout the region. In the Dominican Republic the 82nd Airborne Division bottled up the militant Constitutionalists and other revolutionaries, thereby creating the conditions necessary to achieve open, democratic national elections in 1966; thus politically stabilizing that country into the next century. In Guatemala, deeply entrenched and countervailing racist attitudes and values within that country's military significantly undermined the 1972 8th Special Forces Group's long-term goal of implementing counterinsurgency through a human rights-based approach to win the hearts and minds of the indigenous, Indian population. This reflected the naïve faith on the part of Washington and its U.S. Embassy personnel in Guatemala City that American values could be readily transferred and assimilated in a dominant Ladino culture which for centuries had held habits, beliefs and customs which were antithetical to democracy, human rights and justice. Although the insurgency would eventually lay down its arms in the mid-1990s, Guatemala remains even today an unjust and racist culture. Albeit well-intentioned, we Green Berets were in over our heads in terms of promoting lasting political and socio-economic reforms.

During the decade of the 1980s, Washington's campaigns in Central America were successfully conducted via a blend of security assistance advising, logistical support, military training, and from time to time joint and combined military exercises designed to intimidate Sandinista-controlled Nicaragua. To this end the CIA weighed in with its harassing, surrogate-guerrilla Contra operations inside Nicaragua. The sum effect of all these activities not only intimidated the Sandinistas but also stressed their government's rule economically and financially to the degree that its continuation was rejected in an open, democratic national election in 1990. Nonetheless, the countries of El Salvador and Honduras were each expected to carry their own weight in waging their respective counterinsurgency wars. Fortunately, reform-minded militaries in both countries eventually saw correctly the advantage of democratically-based government and socio-economic reform as the best means of taking the "just cause" of an insurgency out of the hands of its perpetrators. Over time the militaries of both countries withdrew from politics and went back to their barracks, enabling civilian rule to prevail. Even in Panama, the clever, thug-like dictator of the day, Manuel Noriega, could only pull the proverbial "wool" over Washington's eyes for a while before he was found out (blatant narco-trafficking and political and human rights violations) and eventually overthrown.

Washington hoped that by giving power to the people through the promotion of democracy, democratic reforms should make it possible for everyday common citizens to determine their destinies, pursue their interests, increase their share of benefits, and thus reduce societal inequalities. All this was to be accomplished with justice, equity, and fairness. Unfortunately since the end of the Cold War, often seemingly reformist groups have taken office by demanding open elections, only to rule as despotic politicians themselves. These situations continue to be conducive to blatant corruption, undermining the basic trust of their local populations and representing more than a mere pilfering of the public treasury. In short, they also mean that political leaders all too frequently continue to pursue personal gain at the expense of their constituents' collective benefits, placing their own individual interests above the needs of their constituencies, and, in many countries plagued by inequity and poverty, making private deals favoring friends and cronies instead of fulfilling their public pledges. To this end *corruption* represents a fundamental violation of the public trust and is the greatest threat to democracy in the region. Its all-pervasive presence in so many countries in Latin America underscores the helplessness of citizens to deal with it to the degree that no matter how they vote, they still have little control over corrupt public officials inundating government offices at large. Disenchantment can lead to frustration, which in turn can lead to a volatile situation, provided that the right leadership is there to funnel the desires for change into militant action.

Even though the structure of democracy appears to have taken root throughout most of Latin America, the above leads one to the conclusion that in the end it is very difficult for one country to *make* another country democratic. Democracy can be cultivated where the desire for it exists, but it must come from a people's heart and soul if it is to have meaning and survive. All too frequently undermining democracy is the fact that as the twenty-first century wears on Latin Americans of the last generation have experienced little or no improvement in their per capita income and that abject poverty, ranging at more than 40 percent remains a serious problem for many countries (Bolivia, Honduras and Nicaragua have annual per capita incomes of less than $1,000). Inequity has increased, as the "rich get richer and the poor get poorer." For this reason polls indicate that over half of the region's peoples have taken on a cynical view of democratic government, claiming that they would support an authoritarian or any other similarly-styled government, provided that it could resolve the endemic economic problems of the day. Democracies do generally outperform dictatorships in regard to social programs, but not so much with regard to economic growth, employment and poverty reduction.

Ironically, despite Washington's roughly half-century-long embargo of Cuba, the local dictator's numerous political setbacks throughout the Americas, and a stagnant, if not crippling economy, Fidel Castro and his anachronistic, heavy-handed, caudillo-style dictatorship have managed to survive, outliving ten U.S. presidents. That he was able to maintain himself in power for so long in the face of his great hegemonic adversary just ninety miles to the north was due in large measure to the grudging esteem that many Cubans still held for him personally as the one person in Cuban history who had given their island its *sovereignty*. Over the years since the advent of his revolution in 1959, those who hated Castro and represented a source of serious political opposition to the regime were allowed to emigrate abroad; thus lessening the possibility of a counter-revolution. This tended to strengthen the pro-Castro revolutionary consensus within the island and the defense of the revolution now became synonymous with the defense of national sovereignty. Indeed, this evoked a deep wellspring of national sentiment going back to the time of the revered nineteenth-century revolutionary hero, Jose Marti. To this end, when under pressure from Washington to liberalize his system, Castro could always invoke among his still millions of followers the notion of the struggle for self-determination and sovereignty. Washington's castigation and embargo of the dictator and his abysmally authoritarian system, designed to humble and otherwise weaken the regime, instead tended to strengthen local popular resolve and further release deep stirrings of historic nationalism against "Yankee imperialism." For this reason Castro was able to defy the United States and survive well into the twenty-first century, albeit no longer as a security threat to the Americas.

Another phenomenon which has continuously plagued U.S. foreign policy has been the only moderately successful War on Drugs. While scores of billions of dollars have been lavished by Washington on the region since the late-1970s, and in particular Colombia, Peru and Bolivia to combat the drug traffickers on their own ground, it has become apparent that this threat to American society will not go away until the *demand* side of the supply-demand equation is properly addressed. Billion dollar profits for the narco-traffickers continue to drive the system forward and make the frequently lethal risks involved from cartel infighting and anti-drug interdiction operations worthwhile. Even the taking down of Panama's Manuel Noriega in 1989 only represented an insubstantial setback to trafficker operations in the Americas. When the large cartels in Colombia were throttled during the 1990s, their surviving members merely fragmented into dozens, if not hundreds of smaller, but still highly effective drug operatives, producing and selling their illicit products worldwide. Already over thirty years old, the War on Drugs may eventually make a run of a century or longer, or at least until international demand of the cocaine-heroin vice diminishes or becomes outmoded and no longer considered in fashion by the consuming public.

The end of the Cold War did not mean that the United States and its military would no longer have to confront challenges and threats. As the number one hegemonic great power in the world, America has been looked to in order to help resolve problems world-wide. As such, it found itself involved in two Persian Gulf wars against Iraq (1992 and 2003-06), a failed humanitarian mission in the horn of Africa's Somalia (1992-93), the Balkans (1992-94), Haiti (1994-95), Afghanistan (2001-06), and an international war on terrorism (2001 to the present). Albeit keenly interested in spreading its values and concepts of human rights, basic freedoms for all, participatory democracy, and transparent government to facilitate its influence throughout the world, Washington's military occupations of Somalia, Haiti, Irak, and Afghanistan revealed that imposing American values by force, no matter how well-intentioned, were often counter-productive or simply had no staying power. This was especially true in the face of countervailing, deep-seated, authoritarian-based values of the societies involved, going back in some cases centuries. While this may have appeared to be something new in terms of a lesson learned for the current American generation, it is merely a reflection of Washington's own experience in Latin America throughout most of the last century.

The painfully traumatic events of September 11, 2001, pitched America into an extended global war against terrorism and, because it appeared on the surface to be a clash of civilizations (Islamic versus Western), there was once again a messianic desire to spread American social and political values worldwide so as to inoculate the United States against further attacks from abroad. Unfortunately, democracy is not a commodity that can be exported or simply shipped from one country to another. It is usually a slowly evolving internal process, with roots necessarily going back hundreds of years, which only gradually emanate from a concern for the preservation of human rights, justice and basic freedoms. In the long-run America's strongest suite remains its soft power or socio-economic and political norms and values which are often attractive to and even shared by some, but not all, nations. When these norms and values coincide only then can they be used to mobilize international coalitions to assist in addressing mutual threats and challenges to America's national interests and security.

I N D E X

About The Author

Sewall ("Stu") Menzel was born in Chicago, Illinois, in 1942 and shortly thereafter moved to the city's northern suburb of Winnetka on the shores of Lake Michigan. After graduating from Winnetka's New Trier Township High School in 1960, he went on to attend The Citadel, The Military College of South Carolina, from which he received a B.A. in history and a commission in 1964 as an officer in the U.S. Army. The next twenty-five years found him campaigning and serving in Latin America with the 82nd Airborne Division, the 8th Special Forces Group, the U.S. Southern Command, the U.S. Department of State, and the Defense Intelligence Agency (DIA). A graduate of the Army's Command and General Staff and War Colleges, he retired from active service in 1989 and went on to complete his Ph.D. in international relations with the University of Miami (Coral Gables) in preparation for teaching at the university level. During the 1990s and on into the twenty-first century, he served with the faculties of the Departments of Political Science at Florida Atlantic and Florida International Universities, teaching in the fields of U.S. foreign and national security policy, Latin American politics, and American military history. He currently lives with his wife and two sons in Pembroke Pines, Florida. Other books by the author include:

Battle Captain: Cold War Campaigning with the U.S. Army in Vietnam, Cambodia and Laos 1967 - 1971

Cocaine Quagmire: Implementing the U.S. Anti-Drug Policy in the North Andes - Colombia

Printed in the United States
96811LV00002B/164/A

9 781425 935535